Studies in Continental Thought

John Sallis, general editor

Kierkegaard's Instant

Kierkegaard's Instant

ON BEGINNINGS

DAVID J. KANGAS

Indiana University Press
Bloomington & Indianapolis

This book is a publication of

Indiana University Press
601 North Morton Street
Bloomington, IN 47404-3797 USA

http://iupress.indiana.edu

Telephone orders   800-842-6796
Fax orders   812-855-7931
Orders by e-mail   iuporder@indiana.edu

The paper used in this publication meets the minimum requirements of
American National Standard for Information Sciences—Permanence of
Paper for Printed Library Materials, ANSI Z39.48-1984.

MANUFACTURED IN THE UNITED STATES OF AMERICA

Library of Congress Cataloging-in-Publication Data

Kangas, David J.
  Kierkegaard's instant : on beginnings / David J. Kangas.
    p. cm. — (Studies in continental thought)
  Includes bibliographical references and index.
  ISBN-13: 978-0-253-34859-3 (cloth)
  ISBN-10: 0-253-34859-5 (cloth)
  1. Kierkegaard, Søren, 1813-1855. I. Title.
  B4377.K36 2007
  198'.9—dc22
                                        2006033236

1 2 3 4 5 12 11 10 09 08 07

An unconditional *Yes* certainly, but not a naive one:
a *Yes* older than naive spontaneity.

Levinas

Whoever searches into the essences and actions of
creation rather than its groanings and expectations
is without doubt a fool and a blind man.

Luther

CONTENTS

PREFACE

In what follows I read certain of Kierkegaard's early, mostly pseudonymous texts written between 1841 and 1844. I treat the texts each in its own terms, refraining, in particular, from organizing this book around the "stages of existence," as often is done. To organize a book on Kierkegaard around stages is already to decide on the most decisive issues of interpretation. The stages, whose interpretive prestige is formidable, guarantee a teleological reading of the problematic of existence. Although stages do appear and function importantly in many of Kierkegaard's texts, the more basic, and logically prior, concern of the texts is existence, not stages. The various stages—the aesthetic, the ethical, and the religious—reflect diverse self-understandings of an already existing subject; they lay out a diverse set of *responses* to a prior situation. But what of that prior situation? What of existence itself? What is necessary is to clarify the problematic of existence as such. Not to do this is uncritically to import a whole ontology in which stages gain their meaning. Moreover, it is to fail to ask a basic question: why just those stages? What I argue is that Kierkegaard's problematic of existence involves a break from the horizon of ontology; moreover, that existence, as the *event* of coming-into-existence, falls always prior to the narrative and teleological ordering of the stages. The stages exist to set the problematic of existence into relief; they do not exist to fill out the fundamental ontology of the subject.

The problematic of existence can be clarified, however, only by seeking the point at which Kierkegaard's thinking both appropriates and undoes the egological conception of subjectivity articulated within the texts of German idealism (Kant, Fichte, early Schelling, Hegel). These idealist texts, fascinated by the thetic power of the subject to posit and realize itself—indeed to function as the very ground of the real—give extraordinary new life to one of the more ancient obsessions of the West: the obsession with origins, with absolute beginnings. Hegel's *Science of Logic* represents this obsession in an especially exemplary way. Hegel's decisive, defining gesture is to interpret the event of beginning, the radical origin, in the terms of self-consciousness: namely, in terms of its re-presentability, or being-for-consciousness. He interprets reality on the foundation of self-consciousness, in a fundamentally teleological manner, in terms of a movement of *self-realization* and *self-coincidence*; he maintains nothing more essentially than the recuperability of the absolute beginning, the foundation.

Most basically at issue in Kierkegaard's texts, I argue, is a beginning, a coming-into-existence, that falls essentially prior to any beginning that could be represented, posited, or recollected by a subject: a beginning prior to all beginning, prior to the total horizon of presence—hence, an "anarchic" beginning that will always already have begun. This is what is meant by "Kierkegaard's Instant." The problem is one of thinking a beginning that cannot be translated as a first principle or ground, a beginning that neither serves as a foundation nor can be posited. Self-consciousness, we learn from these texts, arrives always *too soon* or *too late* to the instant in which existence is given; it cannot be made to coincide with itself. Vis-à-vis this infinite beginning, existence shows itself as absolute departure, without foundation or goal.

My readings show that this beginning virtually consumes Kierkegaard's early texts. Not only this, it defines the terms of what is, rightly, taken as Kierkegaard's primary concern: the religious. Often performed as much as explicitly announced, the "infinite beginning" appears wherever the texts become paradoxical, aporetic, or tautological. Kierkegaard's texts have not been read closely enough. The hard passages have been avoided, perhaps because one will already know that their meaning is to be found in the theory of the stages. No use pausing over aporias when the end is in sight—yet within Kierkegaard's texts the pause is the most significant gesture, for that is where speech turns to silence.

ACKNOWLEDGMENTS

I wish to thank all my colleagues in the department of religion at FSU for their longstanding support. Especially I want to thank Martin Kavka, whose proximity has been invaluable to my thinking; Aline Kalbian, for her generosity and hospitality; and Shannon Burkes, for blazing the way. I am grateful also to my seminar students, who intrepidly walked with me down the highways and byways, mostly byways, of idealist and Kierkegaardian texts.

I have received important scholarly support over the years from the Søren Kierkegaard Research Centre in Copenhagen, for which I thank Niels-Jørgen Cappelørn and Jon Stewart, and from the Howard V. and Edna H. Hong Kierkegaard Library at St. Olaf College in Northfield, Minnesota, for which I thank Gordon Marino and Cynthia Lund. Thanks are owed as well to Ed Mooney, whose early support meant a lot, and Vanessa Rumble, whose comments substantially improved the book. To John Sallis I am especially grateful for publishing this work. My thanks for their professionalism and buoyancy to the editorial staff at Indiana University Press, Dee Mortensen, Elisabeth Marsh, and Miki Bird, and to copy editor Carol Kennedy.

Finally I am grateful to my parents, Nick and Sandy, and to my family: Inese, Olaf, and Sevrin Radzins, for whose very existence I am grateful—*Liels Paldies!*

NOTE ON SOURCES

All references to Kierkegaard's works in English are to the Princeton University Press edition of *Kierkegaard's Writings,* edited by Howard V. and Edna W. Hong. Abbreviations to these texts, which will follow quotations in parenthesis and include page numbers, follow the nomenclature below.

CA   *The Concept of Anxiety.* Trans. Reidar Thomte and Albert A. Anderson. Princeton University Press, 1980.

CI   *The Concept of Irony.* Trans. Howard V. Hong and Edna H. Hong. Princeton University Press, 1989.

EO   *Either/Or.* 2 vols. Trans. Howard V. Hong and Edna H. Hong. Princeton University Press, 1987.

FTR   *Fear and Trembling* and *Repetition.* Trans. Howard V. Hong and Edna H. Hong. Princeton University Press, 1983.

PF/JC   *Philosophical Fragments* and *Johannes Climacus.* Trans. Howard V. Hong and Edna H. Hong. Princeton University Press, 1985.

JP   *Søren Kierkegaard's Journals and Papers.* Ed. and trans. Howard V. Hong and Edna H. Hong, assisted by Gregor Malantschuk. Indiana University Press, 1967–1978. The numbers listed in these references are to entries rather than pages.

In addition, I will refer to the forthcoming Danish critical edition of *Søren Kierkegaards Skrifter,* published by the Søren Kierkegaard Research Centre in Copenhagen, Denmark, abbreviated as *SKS.* References will refer to volume and page number. As not all of Kierkegaard's journals have yet appeared in this edition, I will sometimes refer to *Søren Kierkegaards Papirer,* edited by P. A. Heiberg, V. Kuhr, and E. Torsting (Copenhagen: Gyldendal, 1909–48). The abbreviation is *Pap.*

I also refer in the notes to the following original language editions:

Johann Gottlieb Fichte's Sämmtliche Werke. 8 vols. Ed. I. H. Fichte. Berlin: Veit und Comp, 1845–46. Abbreviated as *Fichte.*

George Wilhelm Friedrich Hegel, Sämtliche Werke, Jubiläumsausgabe in 20 Bänden. Ed. Hermann Glockner. Stuttgart: Friedrich Frommann, 1928–41. Abbreviated as *Hegel.*

Schellings Werke. 6 vols. to date. Ed. Manfred Schröter. Munich: Beck, 1958–. Abbreviated as *Schelling.*

Kierkegaard's Instant

Introduction:
Ungrounding Subjectivity

❧

A new approach to Kierkegaard," Paul Ricoeur wrote in 1963, "must also be a new approach to German idealism."[1] To read Kierkegaard must always also be to read the texts of idealism. In this book I place Kierkegaard's thought in relation to certain idealist texts that are particularly important for clarifying the meaning of his thought: Hegel's *Lectures on the History of Philosophy* and *Phenomenology of Spirit*, J. G. Fichte's *Vocation of Man*, and Friedrich Schelling's *Philosophical Investigations into the Essence of Human Freedom*. These are all texts Kierkegaard knew well. To read these texts seriously alongside Kierkegaard is to see the inadequacy of interpreting him merely as an external critic of idealism. For one thing, the idealist texts themselves constantly overflow their own terms and so can always be read non-idealistically;[2] for another, Kierkegaard's critique of idealism is conditioned wholly by an appropriation. One could even say the appropriation *is* the critique: simply put, Kierkegaard appropriates the entire content of idealism under the proviso of a reversal. If one likes, he deconstructs idealism by reading its texts *backward*, namely for what they occlude. At stake is the question of the beginning.

THE ABSOLUTE BEGINNING IN IDEALISM:
SUBJECTIVITY THOUGHT AS GROUND

One cannot treat the movement "from Kant to Hegel" as if it were monolithic or systematizable. So many gaps, reversals, false starts, undoings, and redoings occur. Even so, a certain trajectory is discernable: the effort to regard self-consciousness, ever more radically, as what constitutes the condition for any and all consciousness. The conditions of self-consciousness show themselves as the very conditions of being. It begins somewhat modestly in Kant: "The a priori conditions for a possible experience as such are at the same time conditions for the possibility of objects of experience."[3] Self-consciousness is the condition for any possible consciousness of an object. The objectivity of the object is secured through the synthetic work of the subject. Fichte first realized the radical implications of Kant's transcendental analysis, specifically Kant's notion of apperception, by setting forth "intellectual intuition" as the "first, absolutely unconditioned principle" of all knowledge.[4] The primordial intuition consciousness has of itself, its pure presence to itself, is that light in which any and all knowledge, any and all phenomena, acquire sense and intelligibility. Such intuition, being completely an intuition of itself and not of anything other, is not a passivity, since nothing is given, but a pure activity. To intuit oneself is to posit oneself (*sich selbst setzen*), to put oneself in being. The egological subject thus accomplishes an auto-genesis. As Fichte remarks in his 1800 *Vocation of Man:* "I am thoroughly my own creation."[5] This could not be a clearer statement of the egological understanding of the subject: the subject emerges unconditionally from out of itself, beginning absolutely with and from itself, just as the God of prior onto-theology. Schelling's *System of Transcendental Idealism* (1800) expanded Fichte's viewpoint to include not only the emergence of self-consciousness from the side of subjectivity, as self-positing, but also from the side of objectivity, or nature. Nevertheless, this early Schelling wholly reaffirmed Fichte's egological interpretation of the subject as constituted by intellectual intuition: "The *self* is such an intuition, since it is *through the self's own knowledge of itself* that that *very self* (the object) first comes into being. For since the self (as object) is nothing else but the very *knowledge of itself,* it arises simply out of the fact *that* it knows of itself; the *self itself* is thus a knowing that simultaneously produces itself (as object)."[6]

It is Hegel, however, who truly radicalizes idealism's egological interpretation by grasping and expressing the truth of being, "not only as Substance, but equally as Subject."[7] The being of beings, the absolute, is in truth subject, which means that "it is in truth actual only in so far as it is the movement of positing itself, or is the mediation of its self-othering with itself."[8] What is real is what posits itself, what arrives at itself, what finally coincides with itself. Thus for Hegel too, as in Fichte, there is nothing given that self-consciousness cannot take up and re-comprehend, in principle, in terms of its own work of constitution or positing; nothing of the real would, in these terms, remain foreign to self-consciousness. As Hegel put it: "Reason is the certainty of consciousness that it is all reality; thus does idealism express its concept."[9] Idealism thus articulates the metaphysical idea of *immanence,* wherein self-consciousness constitutes the being of beings.

The decisive question of immanence is the question of the beginning. Hegel clarifies this in the introductory section of his *Science of Logic,* titled "With What Must the Science Begin?"[10] It is an extraordinary meditation on the problem of beginning in philosophy, full of paradoxes. In that section Hegel is clear about the apparently paradoxical structure of all beginning: "It must be admitted that it is an important consideration—which will be found in more detail in the logic itself—that the advance [of thought] is a *retreat into the ground,* to what is *primary* and *true,* on which depends and, in fact, from which originates, that with which the beginning is made. Thus consciousness on its onward path from the immediacy with which it began is led back to absolute knowledge as its innermost *truth.* This last, the ground, is then also that from which the first proceeds, that which at first appeared as an immediacy."[11] Philosophy is a movement outward toward what is innermost, a movement forward toward what is always prior: the principle or ground.

In the preface to his *Phenomenology of Spirit* Hegel had already affirmed the paradoxical thesis that the absolute, what would otherwise be affirmed as already accomplished, is a *result:* "Of the absolute it must be said that it is essentially a *result,* that only in the *end* is it what it truly is; and that precisely this consists its nature, viz. to be actual, subject, the spontaneous becoming of itself."[12] The origin becomes real as origin, the beginning as beginning, only in terms of what it will have brought about. Arché is telos anticipated; telos is arché unfolded. In this circular or archeo-teleological movement thought need not, and ought not, to found itself on the basis of some hypothetical or arbitrary content. Any content that would be merely posulated by a subject as its first principle, for example, would be merely one-sided and unjustified. Hence Hegel strongly criticizes any purely formal first principle, or presupposition. Schelling's intellectual intuition is dismissed as a "shot from a pistol"; so too are Jacobi's faith, Fichte's intellectual intuition, and even Descartes' *ego cogito.* Although Hegel affirms the general thrust of transcendental idealism, namely, that it is an important and essential step of modernity that the subjective aspect of knowledge be given full weight—to the point where subjectivity or inwardness becomes the very principle of philosophy—it is a mistake, he thinks, to separate subjectivity from its total context: its standing in being as a whole. Hegel demands that subjectivity be understood starting from and on the basis of a thoroughgoing wholism. *The Science of Logic* thus sets forth its point of beginning—not immediately as subjectivity—but as pure being, the being of beings. Philosophy begins in being as such; the principle of philosophy is pure being.

If Hegel thinks the beginning in terms of being as such, however, he still thinks being as immanentizable or recollectable, that is, on the horizon of presence, or in terms of "absolute knowing" (*absolutes Wissen*). Absolute knowing is for Hegel the principle of philosophy. In a double sense: that *in which* philosophy unfolds its determinate content, where "principle" signifies the source or ground of intelligibility; and that *toward which* the system of philosophy, as the presentation of absolute knowing, strives— where principle now signifies an anticipative insight into the culmination of philosophy, that is, its end or consummation. Absolute knowing, as the principle of philosophy, is at the same time the beginning and end of philosophy.[13]

To raise the question of Kierkegaard and idealism is to question his relation to this egology become archeo-teleology. The basic thrust of the early texts I analyze is to reopen the question of transcendence by means of the question of beginning. Kierkegaard does not assert transcendence in terms of a *given* reality that somehow remains outside the scope of self-consciousness or over against it. He shares with idealism the notion that what appears as "given" is in fact what is constituted. Where he differs though, and where he presents the question of transcendence in a new way, is in the idea that the work of constitution or positing itself has an essentially *prior*, irrecuperable condition. Kierkegaard refuses to grasp the movement of positing as a radical origin, ground, or "absolute beginning." The question of transcendence emerges in terms of a certain anteriority, vis-à-vis a beginning that *cannot* be identified with self-positing, a beginning that is not a ground, but rather an un-ground (or *Af-grund* in Danish).

What transcends self-consciousness is not what stands over against it, but what falls prior to it. Through paradox after paradox Kierkegaard's early texts exhibit a movement toward the radically anterior, the irrecuperable, the unrecollectable. They return thinking to an "infinite beginning," which he names "the instant" (*Øieblikket*),[14] in which temporality itself begins. The instant is the name for a beginning that cannot be interiorized, appropriated, recollected, represented, or possessed. It is not a work of self-consciousness, not mediation, but rather the event through which self-consciousness is first enabled. The instant is the gift or *birth* of presence. An instant cannot claim to be. Of itself it is nothing, it is nowhere; it neither is nor is not. And yet everything changes in the instant. An instant enters into experience, or becomes present, either essentially too soon or too late. Anytime one says "and before I knew it," or, "and then suddenly," one will have felt the *residual effects* ("traces") of the instant.

Vis-à-vis the instant, Kierkegaard's early texts show themselves capable of thinking reality otherwise than according to a logic of presence. A "metaphysics of birth" deconstructs a metaphysics of the subject-as-ground. Therefore I cannot agree with Heidegger's assessment of Kierkegaard's philosophical importance:

By way of Hegelian metaphysics, Kierkegaard remains everywhere philo-sophically entangled, on the one hand in a dogmatic Aristoteleanism that is completely on par with medieval scholasticism, and on the other in the subjectivity of German idealism. No discerning mind would deny the stimuli produced by Kierkegaard's thought that prompted us to give renewed attention to the 'existential.' But about the decisive question—the essential nature of Being—Kierkegaard has nothing whatever to say.[15]

Kierkegaard never problematizes, in other words, the way the question of being is posed; he never questions the core logic of subjectivity found within idealism: that a subject is what posits itself, represents itself to itself, pursues its authentic being through its projects. Like all the idealists Kierkegaard thinks true reality in terms of its becoming present for a subject; his criticism of idealism remains trapped within its problematic.[16] This book as a whole offers a counterargument.[17] The radicality of Kierkegaard's early texts turns on articulating the distinction between the temporal instant, which allows or grants presence, and the present itself. In idealist terms, the present is in fact a re-presenting, a positing. If Kierkegaard's instant cannot be re-presented, this is because it serves as the condition for re-presentation. Very often, however, Kierkegaard's early texts perform rather than explicitly thematize the distinction between the instant and the present, the real and its re-presentation. The instant appears nonetheless everywhere: above all, wherever Kierkegaard's texts become explicitly aporetic or paradoxical. In a certain sense, this book moves from one aporia to the next. So many aporetic passages in Kierkegaard's authorship have rarely if ever been the object of an explicit and sustained analysis. An example, from *Fear and Trembling:* "but the one who will work gives birth to his own father" (*FTR* 27; *SKS* 4:123). Giving birth to one's own father: this is not a twisted metaphor, but an aporia demanded by the very nature—the very "logic"—of the problem Kierkegaard is formulating—that of temporality, the birth of presence. In this inversion, the origin can be written only as an effect, the effect as the origin.

The movement of Kierkegaard's texts is to bring the idealist configuration to the point where it runs aground upon that which it is unable to contain or interiorize. It is, I show, temporality—what Kant, inaugurating the idealist interpretation, called precisely the form of *inner* sense—that remains outer. With temporality or temporalization, the event of coming-into-existence, one encounters a negation that overflows the integrating, mediating work of self-consciousness. The instant is not a work of self-consciousness; nor is it merely an abstraction, as most of the tradition, including Hegel, thought. Rather it is the preeminently real event through which self-consciousness is opened up, or first of all born, again and again.

Nothing is more concrete than the instant, but for that very reason the philosophical tradition, to the extent it has ceded priority to what the instant allows—namely, the present—has obscured or even missed it. Thus Kierkegaard's texts bring critical attention to the instant of beginning, remaining always prior to presence as its condition, and the beginning as posited or re-presented for thought.

It is a question, then, of reading Kierkegaard's early texts through their most aporetic moments. Aporias serve an analogous role in Kierkegaard's thought to that which the concept (*der Begriff*) serves in Hegel: they organize the discourse. If Kierkegaard's texts appear often distant from philosophy, this is because they possess a rigor and coherence that derives from his attention to the aporetic. Since for idealism the horizon of presence constitutes the in-which of philosophical thinking—indeed of consciousness itself—then what falls always prior to or after presence, the instant, cannot be named except through some kind of rupture. Kierkegaard's texts return again and again to the instant by way of clarification of certain phenomena associated with a tearing of consciousness away from meaningful presence: phenomena such as boredom, melancholy, anxiety, despair. Kierkegaard reads these phenomena in a way that is philosophically radical, as disclosing a reality suppressed within idealism.

THE RELIGIOUS AND THE "STAGES OF EXISTENCE"

Undoubtedly the motive of Kierkegaard's critique of idealism, which reaffirms transcendence, is not only philosophical but religious. Faith (*Troen*), an "absolute relation to the absolute," emerges in explicit contrast to absolute knowing as the consummate act of a self. But what does faith signify and how does it relate to the critique of idealism? One gathers that Heidegger's critique of Kierkegaard derives from the judgment that his thought, precisely insofar as it is religious, remains onto-theological. Is this the case? Without a doubt to exist is for Kierkegaard to exist "before God" (*for Gud*); God is the *before whom* of existence itself. Yet by itself this leaves unclarified how Kierkegaard conceives God more precisely and whether or not—and here is the onto-theological question par excellence—God fulfills the role of a unifying, *grounding ground* in his thought.[18] This book shows the decisive role an abyssal ground, or *Afgrund,* plays in the early work. What thinking means in these texts undergoes inversion: from the metaphysical or onto-theological effort to secure or legitimate the ground—whether that ground is thought transcendentally as in Kant and Fichte or archeo-teleologically as in Hegel—to the clarification of phenomena associated with a loss of grounding (irony, boredom, anxiety, etc.). Such phenomena contain the disclosure of nonbeing or nothing, of that which cannot be drawn into determination and presence; they refer to an occlusion or withdrawal of the ground. If Hegel could regard thinking as a retreat to the ground, a recollection, Kierkegaard's texts turn thinking toward a ground that will always already have withdrawn. To exist will mean to face what ungrounds: the indeterminate, nonbeing, an irrecollectable past, an unanticipatable future. The religious, far from being opposed to this turn toward the *Afgrund,* receives its meaning only through it.

In fact, none of the "stages" of existence—the aesthetic, the ethical, the religious—can be understood apart from the sense of the groundless and the phenomena that disclose it. An unfortunate constant of Kierkegaard interpretation, however, has been to regard the "theory of the stages" as, in effect, a system of existence opposed to idealism and Hegelianism.[19] Yet there is a certain irony in locating Kierkegaard's resistance to idealism in his theory of the stages, for the stages, it may be pointed out, inevitably take on an entirely Hegelian form: they are supposed to trace a teleological movement from immediacy (the aesthetic) through mediation (the ethical) to a mediated immediacy (the religious, a "later immediacy").[20] Moreover, they are typically regarded as what a subject *necessarily* has to progress through if it is to realize the truth of its being. Only the religious subject is an authentic subject. The religious is thus supposed to constitute both the arché and the telos of human existence.

Yet as long as one interprets the religious archeo-teleologically—or more simply, as long as the notion of self-realization provides the guiding interpretive horizon of Kierkegaard's thinking on subjectivity—it will be impossible to grasp his critical distance from Hegel. Stages, in fact, are an essentially Hegelian idea deriving from his transformation of ontological categories. A category is for Hegel not a modality of a being in its beingness (as in Aristotle), but rather a *moment,* a stage, in the self-exposition of a subject. A subject is no longer an underlying *hypokeimenon,* but a self-mediating drive toward the realization of its being; and its ontological predicates are nothing other than the various stages of this movement of realization. In aiming to realize its telos, the subject unfolds what lies in it—its original principle—and this unfolding takes place across a temporality; it *constitutes* a temporality. Fundamental to Hegel was the image of a plant unfolding from its seed to the fruit.[21] This image works just as well for teleological readings of the stages.

Any teleological reading of Kierkegaard will inevitably think the stages as the diverse moments of a single whole, in terms of the unity of self-consciousness. In this sense, a teleological reading will presuppose a *continuous temporality* defined by the movement of self-consciousness in coming to itself. Each stage would acquire its proper truth and meaning only in being sublated by a "higher" stage, that is, one better expressing the implicit principle. The self would come to itself and find itself grounded in the same moment. But this is pure Hegel. It matters not at all, in terms of the metaphysical problematic, that Kierkegaard's subject would be "the individual" and Hegel's would be, supposedly, world-historical spirit to the exclusion of the individual.[22]

Nevertheless, one has to look beyond the apparent teleology of the stages.[23] If the religious acquires a priority in Kierkegaard's texts—and no doubt it does—this is not because the subject realizes therein the implicit telos of its existence. On the contrary, it is because the subject finally discovers the representational or egological status of every telos. A telos is something inevitably posited or mediated by consciousness; it has the ontological status of a representation. Yet the religious is the name for the referral of the subject to, and its holding itself open for, the infinite beginning, the instant of coming-into-existence, which it can neither posit nor recollect. It coincides with the subject's impossibility to take itself as origin, ground, absolute beginning (as still happens in both the aesthetic and the ethical). This is exactly why the texts (especially *Fear and Trembling* and *Repetition*) link the religious to the "impossible," to "the ordeal," and refuse to regard it as the *outcome* of a process for which the subject constitutes the origin. If one insists upon teleology, then one could say that the telos of human existence, the point at which it becomes religious, is the abandonment of every telos. The abandonment of every telos is the *absolute* telos. One possesses only in agreeing not to possess.

Religious existence has abandoned an understanding of reality that allows it to nourish itself on what grounds. It holds itself open to an ungrounding ground or abyssal ground; it holds itself open for nonbeing. This is why at every decisive point Kierkegaard's texts invoke not transcendent *being*, but *nothing*. The decisive meaning of Socrates in *The Concept of Irony*, for example, whereby he must be regarded as a "divine missionary," is that he grasped the absolute "in the form of nothing" or even simply *as* nothing.[24] Socrates relates to the absolute as absolvent from being, to the absolute as ab-solute. Then again in the final chapter of *The Concept of Anxiety*, where it is a question of articulating the relation between faith and anxiety—anxiety being a relation to the nothing of possibility—Kierkegaard's author presents faith as an "absolute sinking" into the abyss (*Afgrund*) of possibility.[25] Faith is a sinking into nonbeing, to what absolves itself from being, a relation to what cannot be gathered into presence, to what cannot be posited, to what cannot become a *project* of the subject. Faith is existence without or beyond "why." The *Afgrund*, or abyssal ground, plays an essential role, then, in the articulation of the religious. Indeed, each stage may be regarded as a certain response to the groundless, a certain effort to arrive at a self-understanding in face of the *Afgrund*. Thus: the aesthetic emerges as an effort to defer the disclosure of the groundless and so preserve the structure of representational consciousness; the ethical emerges as the embrace of the groundless *in order that* the subject may discover itself as ground, or posit itself; and finally the religious emerges as the letting go of the demand for grounding.

KIERKEGAARD AND THE
ECKHARTIAN TRADITION

What finally carries the critical force of Kierkegaard's texts vis-à-vis idealism, then, is the religious. Religion, not scientific cognition (absolute knowing), is the "absolute relation to the absolute." The religious names those moments in Kierkegaard's texts, always marked by aporiae, where thinking takes the instant in all rigor according to its difference from the present and the re-presentable—the moments where it is necessary to think otherwise than in terms of being and on the horizon of presence. It is the problematization of self-positing or self-realizing consciousness; it indicates a logic at odds with archeo-teleo-logic. What is involved is not a logic of positing but of *letting-go* or releasing. As I interpret it, the religious or critical dimension of the early texts emerges as a repetition of two great themes of the Eckhartian tradition: the sustained critique of presence in the name of the granting or birth of presence—which amounts to privileging the *event* of coming-into-existence (Eckhart's *Gottesgeburt*) over being—and the discovery of "releasement," or *Gelassenheit*, as the subjectivity of the subject.

I say the Eckhartian *tradition* rather than Eckhart himself because it cannot be ascertained definitively that Kierkegaard read Eckhart himself—indeed, the texts may not even have been available to him.[26] He did, however, read texts whose metaphysical horizon is entirely derived from the thought of Meister Eckhart: the *Theologia Germanica*,[27] *Die Nachfolgung des armen Leben Jesu Christi* (pseudo-Tauler), Johann Arndt's *Von warhem Christentum*, Jacob Boehme's *Der Weg zur Christo*,[28] as well as other pietists such as Gerhard Teersteegen.[29] In addition, Eckhart is adequately represented in a number of secondary works Kierkegaard read, including both Franz von Baader's *Vorlesungen über die Speculative Dogmatik* and *Fermenta Cognitionis*—in which both Eckhart and Boehme figure prominently.[30] He also in all likelihood was acquainted with the dissertation of his teacher (and nemesis) Hans Lassen Martensen, *Meister Eckhart: A Study in Speculative Theology*, a study that contains an extensive section of quotations from Eckhart's sermons.[31] Most important for establishing the Boehme connection, in particular, is Kierkegaard's reading of Schelling's *Philosophical Investigations into the Essence of Human Freedom and Related Matters*.[32]

Kierkegaard had read Schelling's treatise sometime probably in 1843 (before writing *Repetition, Fear and Trembling,* and *The Concept of Anxiety*).[33] Though Schelling himself never mentions Boehme, Kierkegaard wrote in his notes—apparently on the basis of his own reading—that Schelling was essentially paraphrasing Boehme. The Boehme connection is strongest, I will show (following the hint of Jean Wahl), in *The Concept of Anxiety.*

Beginning with Eckhart himself, *Gelassenheit* (along with the related theme of *abegescheidenheit*) becomes the characteristic theme and incessant preoccupation of this tradition. *Gelassenheit* expresses the idea that the self must become dispossessed of itself, its *Eigen-wille* (will to possession of itself), and make itself nothing. To "become nothing," to "sink" into nothing—a theme first articulated by Eckhart,[34] and one Kierkegaard explicitly picks up also in his edifying works of the period,[35]—signifies the self's letting go its conception of itself as originally capable of securing its being. A "released" self does not attempt to secure itself in relation to some ultimate ground (for that is what a ground *does,* it secures), but rather holds itself open to the groundless, ungrounding ground: what Eckhart names the "Godhead" (*Gottheit*) and Boehme names the "Unground" (*Ungrund*).[36] Releasement is the one and only condition in this tradition through which the self may avoid thinking God according to being, in terms of its own representations, and relate to God as the ab-solute, to God *as God.* It is out of a released sense that Eckhart could pray his famous prayer: "So therefore let us pray to God that we may be free of God."[37] Through its letting go its need for grounds, through *un-learning* the onto-theological will toward foundations, the self finds itself precisely liberated toward its temporality and finitude. This movement, *into* time and into finitude, becomes essential to Kierkegaard's notion of "faith."

In viewing Kierkegaardian faith as a repetition of Eckhartian *Gelassenheit,* however, I intend to highlight more a genealogical link than a historical one. Though Kierkegaard's reading of texts deriving from Eckhart is demonstrable, my referencing that tradition functions primarily as a template, almost a grammar, for reading Kierkegaard's notion of the religious. The center-point of all of these "Eckhartian" texts—which I argue is decisive for understanding the religious in Kierkegaard—is the letting go of self-will and the critique of the onto-theological metaphysics that allows the self to think itself as *something* rather than *nothing,* as grounded rather than ungrounded. The religious is always for Kierkegaard a sinking into nothing, a letting of nonbeing "be." And this finally is why Kierkegaard's thought, at its most fundamental point, involves a critique of the dialectical interpretation of nonbeing. For the self to let itself sink into nothing, to become nothing—the praxis of faith—is to relate to itself vis-à-vis an absolute surprise, an instant of beginning in which "thought is bewildered, language is confused." Bewilderment and lucidity, joy and suffering, become identical. As soon as one sees the religious in Kierkegaard as a repetition of the Eckhartian tradition of releasement, then, there is no longer any reason to set the religious over against the deconstructive critique of transcendental subjectivity and representation: they belong to each other.

ONE

The Infinite Beginning (The Concept of Irony)

K ierkegaard's dissertation, *The Concept of Irony with Continual Reference to Socrates* (1841), treats the figure of Socrates under the idea that he constitutes the origin of the concept of irony. The clarification of the "historical-actual, phenomenological existence" (*CI* 9; *SKS* 1:71) of Socrates—what Kierkegaard will call his "standpoint"—is the clarification of irony according to its "eminent" sense. Yet why, we may ask, does irony become a problematic? And why does the clarification of irony take place at precisely the beginning of Kierkegaard's authorship? Finally, why Socrates?

The Concept of Irony meditates upon the beginning of philosophy as a conceptual work of making visible the ground of things. Socrates is essential to this beginning insofar as he stands, in more than a historical sense, at the origin of speculative thinking in the West. Kierkegaard's text treats him under a double heading: both as the historical point of departure for speculative thought and, more phenomenologically, as a sign for the radical beginning, that is, the original possibility, of philosophy. The question at the center of the text is this: Is philosophy capable of an absolute beginning? Is it capable of grasping the real in terms of its originary principle or ground? Or is philosophy originally a seeking of grounds at all? As will be evident, the beginning of Hegel's *Science of Logic* haunts *The Concept of Irony.*

Yet *The Concept of Irony* offers not one, but rather *two* accounts of Socrates as the beginning of philosophy.[1] The most prominent one is that of Hegel, who, in his *Lectures on the History of Philosophy,* understands Socrates' position as a radically new, indeed *absolute,* departure point for thinking. He names this absolute beginning the turn toward "interiority" (*Innerlichkeit*), but understands interiority as the power to gather phenomena, through recollective thinking, around originary principles. What governs Hegel's interpretation of Socrates, and hence of the beginning of philosophy, we shall see, is the logic of double negation. To turn inward means for Hegel that thought absolves itself from finite determinations in order to face "the absolute," that is, being as such and as a whole in its distinction from every particular being. The absolute, though it initially looks like "nothing" due to its lack of determination, is nevertheless for Hegel the milieu of incipient determination. This is to say that, for Hegel, Socrates' beginning is to grasp nonbeing, the absolute, as a *principle* (an origin to which thought may coincide).

We shall see that Kierkegaard shares Hegel's notion that the birth of interiority constitutes the beginning of philosophy. Where he differs—and this will be the fundamental difference effective in all the later works—is in the interpretation of nonbeing, what he will call "infinite absolute negativity." To turn inward is for Kierkegaard, as for Hegel, initially to turn toward what is neither this nor that, the ground or principle. Yet Kierkegaard thinks he discovers in the standpoint of Socrates a relation to the absolute as what cannot be converted into a ground or principle. The absolute emerges as a groundless ground or ungrounding ground. Kierkegaard sets forth nonbeing in this way, then, not merely as lack or what is on the way toward being (the Hegelian reading of nonbeing), but rather as what falls *between* the dialectically constructed opposition of being and nonbeing. He opposes the Socratic beginning, to which thought cannot coincide, to the Hegelian beginning. This "between" is the space of existence and the space of irony. Socrates' whole life is between—he is *atopos,* without place, or perhaps a placeless place.

Kierkegaard also opposes the Socratic beginning to the Platonic beginning. In Kierkegaard's mind Plato and Hegel are linked as unripened to ripened fruit. He regards Hegel the way Hegel regarded himself: namely, as the consummating moment of a teleological development in thought. Specifically, Kierkegaard links Plato and Hegel under the idea that both think phenomena require an ideal ground; or rather, that what is real of reality is an eidetic structure. Plato and Hegel are both "metaphysical" thinkers—or in Kierkegaard's language "speculative" thinkers—in that thinking becomes the elaboration of what ideally explains phenomena. But what of phenomena that don't seem resolvable in terms of some eidos? What about irony in its "eminent" sense? These will be the questions. Yet what makes Plato "unripe" vis-à-vis Hegel, according to Kierkegaard (a view Hegel shares), is that his thought bears traces of an excess, something irreducible to dialectical thinking. For Plato philosophy begins in wonder, the astonishment that there is being at all. The shock of being stands in excess to the thinking that seeks to discover grounds. For Hegel this is a defect. For Kierkegaard, it is a circumstance Plato did not succeed in grasping. Ultimately, it is a circumstance Plato positively represses.

Kierkegaard appreciates the excess of wonder in Plato, yet in the end Kierkegaard seeks to uphold the Socratic version of excess against both Plato and Hegel: namely, that the absolute neither is nor is not, that it is beyond being and nonbeing. The excess in Plato appears in the form of the dialogical and especially mythological presentation of this thought. Kierkegaard's reading of Plato, which is extensive, thus makes the mythical the primary point of analysis. He understands the mythical in Plato as no mere addendum to conceptual discourse, but rather as an essential moment of it.

The main object of this chapter, then, is to clarify Kierkegaard's account of the Socratic beginning in its contrast to both the Hegelian-dialectical and the Platonic-mythical beginning. The "infinite beginning" of Socrates, phenomenalized in irony (though we shall have to problematize the notion of phenomenon here), refers to a beginning to which thought cannot coincide. It "is" a beginning that will always already have taken place, a beginning that can be recollected only as what breaks open the closed immanence of recollection. In a sense, Socratic thinking can never depart, never make any determinate beginning, but must remain always *at* a beginning whose contours cannot be grasped. It is this "infinite beginning," remaining in excess to any principial interpretation, that Kierkegaard opposes to the absolute beginning of Hegel and that plays a decisive role in the pseudonymous authorship. The infinite beginning of Socrates is the placeless place of existence itself.

THE STRUCTURE OF
THE CONCEPT OF IRONY

The Concept of Irony is a large and unwieldy book with an elaborate structure. Nevertheless there is a primary break between two parts: part one is entitled "The Standpoint of Socrates Conceived as Irony," whereas part two is entitled "The Concept of Irony." The former, whose main concern is to legitimate the irreducibility of the Socratic standpoint to its philosophical appropriation within the texts of Plato and Hegel is, arguably, the more original and more important.[2] Part two operates with a "concept" in the more strictly Hegelian sense.[3]

Depending largely upon Hegel, part two offers a critique of romantic irony and takes positions that Kierkegaard later regretted.[4] Specifically, part two ends with a gesture of closure: irony, developed as "infinite absolute negativity," turns into a "mastered moment" (*CI* 324; *SKS* 1:352). In a perfectly Hegelian sentence Kierkegaard concludes: "As soon as irony is controlled, it makes a movement opposite to that in which uncontrolled irony declares its life. Irony limits, finitizes, and circumscribes and thereby yields truth, actuality, content" (*CI* 326; *SKS* 1:355). One has to attend closely to this moment of closure, however. The irony that is mastered in the conclusion, that "uncontrolled" irony, is not Socratic irony—which remains as non-negatable—but romantic irony. Romantic irony is irony "after Fichte." It is a shape of irony that presupposes the Fichtean understanding, an essentially modern formation, of the *subject* as a force of negation. With Socrates one is not yet dealing with a subject in the strict sense, but merely with the "lightest and weakest indication of subjectivity" (*CI* 6; *SKS* 1:65). The Socratic "standpoint" constitutes an opening in which a subject in the strict sense (as a self-positing freedom) first becomes possible. Socrates fills out what is prior to the subject. His position cannot be identified with Hegelian or romantic subjectivity.

Kierkegaard's reading of Socrates in part one, however, follows Hegel's interpretation in his *Lectures on the History of Philosophy* so closely that many commentators have regarded *The Concept of Irony* as a Hegelian book —either as a barometer of Kierkegaard's early commitment to Hegel, later abandoned, or as a kind of elaborate Hegelian parody.[5] It is neither. The decisive interpretive question for the book was framed by Lee Cappell in this way: "The puzzling thing about Kierkegaard's conception of Socrates is how it is possible to be so thoroughly dependent upon Hegel's conception of Socrates in all its significant detail, and yet add up to such a wholly different totality."[6] What is puzzling is that the picture of Socrates that emerges in Kierkegaard's reading is both Hegelian and non-Hegelian. As we shall see, however, this ambiguity is anything but adventitious. It will be continually necessary to grasp the double-sided nature of Kierkegaard's conception of existence: it will be just as dialectical as non-dialectical, just as centered upon principles and grounds as turned against them. Socrates' standpoint will not in any *direct sense* oppose the Hegelian concept. Rather, it will signify ambiguously both the essential condition of the concept, opening its possibility, and the essential limit of the concept, bringing about its closure or delimiting its range. The subject as self-positing both is born and dies in the Socratic standpoint. The negation it embodies both liberates and binds.

To proceed, then, I will consider first Hegel's reading of Socrates in his *Lectures on the History of Philosophy,* followed by Kierkegaard's critique and revision; then I will consider the critique of Plato.

HEGEL'S READING OF SOCRATES: EGOLOGICAL SUBJECTIVITY

In *The Concept of Irony* Socrates becomes the site of a conflict of interpretations. Although many voices are brought to bear (including Xenophon, Plato, and Aristophanes), the *primary,* governing conflict in the text is with

Hegel. Even Kierkegaard's reading of Plato, I already indicated, links him in a continuous way with Hegel's thought. The crux of Hegelian metaphysics is to frame a certain relation between essence and manifestation, inner and outer—and to frame it in such a way that a phenomenology of the absolute would be possible, even to the point of absolute knowledge. Hegel pushes philosophy from the love of wisdom to wisdom itself. Although the problem of essence and manifestation is also crucially determinative of Plato's thought, Hegel's post-Kantian location brings the position of the subject into far greater focus. Subjectivity itself becomes the knot in which essence and manifestation are tied, the very locus of a phenomenology of the absolute and of absolute knowing. Subjectivity is *in itself* an absolute relation to the absolute, something that it becomes *for itself* in absolute knowledge.

Kierkegaard's reading of Socrates, though dependent upon Hegel in many respects, aims to displace the whole network of Hegelian concepts: subjectivity, the relation of essence and manifestation, and absolute knowledge. The decisive issue concerns the place of negation in the movement of manifestation: Hegel's whole aim will be to validate a phenomenology of the absolute, whereas Kierkegaard's is to think the absolute only under the form of its withdrawal.

What is most powerful about Hegel's reading of Socrates is that it is informed by an approach to the history of philosophy in its total course. Hegel conceives the history of philosophy for the first time as a unified problematic, as "the history of thought finding itself" (*Sich-selbst-Finden des Gedankens),*[7] or as the self-unfolding of self-knowing thought, absolute knowledge.[8] In Hegel's narrative, more specifically, Socrates' standpoint constitutes the phenomenological presentation of absolute knowing according to an *anticipatory* shape. To be precise: Socrates constitutes the moment in which subjectivity grasps itself explicitly according to its interiority. Turning inward, it comes to understand itself as the radical origin of meaning. Thus Hegel can say—and this is a point Kierkegaard will emphasize—that Socrates is the founder of morality in the strict sense, that is, in the sense that all values are shown to be conditioned on a consciousness of them. Hegel writes: "We now see Socrates bringing forward the opinion, that . . . everyone has to look after his own morality, and thus he looked after his through consciousness and reflection regarding himself."[9] The Socratic move toward interiority is not, for Hegel, merely one moment among others. Rather, it is a "fundamental turning point" (*Hauptwendepunkt*) in the history of thought finding itself.[10] With Socratic interiority, philosophy, and not merely morality, begins according to its inner essence even if, in a historical or contingent sense, it had already begun.[11] Socrates founds an egological interpretation of being (one that finds all reality validated through the subject's consciousness of it). That is the main significance of Socrates for Hegel. Hegel writes:

> Thus Socrates' principle is that the human being has to find from himself both the end and principle of his actions, the end of the world, being in-and-for-itself; and that he must attain to truth through himself. [Socrates' principle] is the return into itself of consciousness (*Rückkehr des Bewustseins in sich*), which is counter-determined as the coming out from itself of particular subjectivity. Precisely herein is implied that the contingency of consciousness and of events, its arbitrariness and particularity, is banished, and that the human has this outside, the in-and-for-itself, within. Here objectivity means the being in-and-for-itself of universality, not outward objectivity. Thus, truth is posited as mediated, as a product, as posited through thought.[12]

Socratic interiority, consequently, is dialectically constituted: the turning inward is simultaneously a turning outward, introversion is extroversion, and vice versa. In turning inward *away from* immediately given being (e.g., given values), Socrates turns simultaneously outward from particularity, contingency, and arbitrariness, and inward toward "being in and for itself." He turns, one may say, from beings to being. Being as such, in and for itself, however, is not an object; it has no "exteriority." For this reason it is purely "inner." Moreover, what is initially regarded as inner, that is, the contingent states of consciousness available to empirical reflection, shows itself as something "outer," that is, not of the essence of consciousness. Thus Socratic consciousness involves a reversal in the very meaning of interiority: the interior is being in and for itself, being as universal, whereas the exterior is particularity.

Hegel puts the point in his own terms: "true being is mediated through thought" (*durch das Denken vermittelt*); or again, "consciousness creates and has to create out of itself what is true."[13] In other words, self-consciousness conditions all phenomena; it counts as a radical origin of reality and normativity. In terms of this movement Socrates demands that every given —in particular, the contingently fashioned customs and mores that constitute the *Sittlichkeit* of the Athenians—be validated by its origin in the subject's reflection. Whatever of the given cannot be shown to be validated through self-consciousness must be judged an illegitimate possession.

Socrates' "principle," then, coincides with an egological interpretation of being in which the being of a being is that wherein it is mediated through self-consciousness.[14] Subjectivity constitutes the normative ground of reality. Hegel recognizes here the foundation of his own dialectic and phenomenology. As the very principle of the real (the validating instance), Socratic interiority constitutes the ground upon which to establish absolute knowledge. However, for Hegel Socratic interiority only *anticipates* absolute knowledge. In one sense, it is *already* absolute knowing; in another sense, however, it is radically deficient. Thus Hegel makes an interpretive gesture that will prove to be totally emblematic of his handling of subjectivity: he interprets Socratic interiority as a *mere* beginning. That is, he regards the beginning as something essentially *untrue* (non-actual, incomplete, abstract). Hegel writes: "[The Good] is a principle, concrete within itself, which, however, is not yet manifested in its development, and in this abstract attitude we find what is wanting in the Socratic standpoint, of which nothing that is affirmative can, beyond this, be adduced."[15]

Socrates' entire orientation, then, is deficient because he never proceeds beyond the beginning of philosophy, which is the absolvent movement toward being in and for itself. He does not grasp the absolute as self-determining, as development, and so he fails to grasp the task of thinking as "system," that is, that of recollecting the given in terms of its immanent, teleological genesis. Socrates turns inward toward being in its distinction from beings; he makes ontological difference resonate; but he fails to grasp the absolute concretely as a self-mediating, *self-determining* whole. The thought of ontological difference has to be redeemed, according to Hegel, in terms of a dialectical and teleological interweaving of being and beings—otherwise, he argues, it is the mere promissory note of philosophy.

The fundamental deficiency of Socrates, Hegel summarizes, is to have lacked a system,[16] and in these terms his wisdom was rightly said to be a form of *ignorance*. But one has to attend closely to Hegel's understanding of the ignorance of Socrates: it is not a real non-knowing, but rather a *represented* ignorance. Hegel writes: "Thus Socrates taught those with whom he associated to know that they knew nothing; indeed, what is more, he himself said that he knew nothing, and therefore taught nothing. It may actually be said that Socrates knew nothing, for he did not reach the systematic construction of a philosophy."[17] Socrates actually knew nothing only in Hegel's terms of a systematic construction of philosophy. Yet, according to Hegel, Socrates' whole position aims, implicitly, at such a construction. Hence, the contradiction in the Socratic point of view: it proclaims a knowledge that it refuses to develop; it remains fixated upon an abstract right of questioning.

It is from this understanding of the Socratic standpoint that Hegel treats the *irony* of Socrates. If the fundamental element of Socratic consciousness is mediation, the identity of inner and outer, truth as indicated, then irony —which posits a difference between the inner and the outer—can function only as a contingently adopted *manner of conversing*. Hegel regards Socratic irony as a means toward the work of drawing forth the universal content of consciousness, the good, as a simple determinate whole, a concrete universal, from the contingent diversity of external opinions. Socrates makes a *show* of irony: "This is the celebrated Socratic irony, which in his case is a particular mode of carrying on intercourse between one person and another, and is thus only a subjective form of dialectic, for real dialectic deals with the reasons for things (*Gründe der Sache*)."[18] Socratic irony and Socratic dialectic fail to grasp, in the end, the ontological meaning of the turn inward.

Kierkegaard's reading of Socrates, to which we now turn, aims at a reversal of Hegel. As we shall see he reads Socrates according to another logic entirely: namely, one that regards the beginning outside of a dialectical economy of essence and manifestation. The infinite beginning of Socrates is precisely the end-goal of thinking—not, as in Hegel, insofar as the end always coincides with and completes the beginning, but insofar as it will be a beginning that thinking will never yet have begun. Thinking comes to the edge of an abyss.

KIERKEGAARD'S INVERTED READING: ANARCHIC SUBJECTIVITY

In the appendix to part one of *The Concept of Irony*, titled "Hegel's View of Socrates," Kierkegaard explicitly criticizes the latter's interpretation in his *Lectures on the History of Philosophy*. It is no mere appendix, but a summary of the total, anti-Hegelian trajectory of the book. As already indicated, Kierkegaard's reading leans heavily upon Hegel. In particular, he appropriates Hegel's idea that the primary significance of Socrates is to have introduced interiority, and in this way to have inaugurated an essential beginning in philosophy: "Socrates' significance in the world-historical development," Kierkegaard writes, "is to be the infinite beginning that contains within itself a multiplicity of beginnings" (*CI* 216–17; *SKS* 1:261). For Hegel this would mean Socrates' standpoint constitutes an essential shape of spirit presupposed in every authentic philosophy. The systems that follow from Socrates (e.g., Plato's or Hegel's) complete his position. For Kierkegaard, on the other hand, an unmediatable gap opens between the infinite beginning of Socrates and every effort to determine that beginning according to a dialectical logic. The concept of irony developed in the text fixes that gap categorically.

In broad terms, Kierkegaard's reversal of Hegel consists in reading what, to Hegel, appears as a mere lack of determination—that is, Socrates' ignorance—as the consummation of a movement of thought. Hegel's lack is Kierkegaard's consummation, and vice versa. Thus, the ignorance and irony of Socrates count, for Kierkegaard, not as a moment in a larger dialectic of ontological determination, but rather as the perfection of a standpoint that cannot be thought within the horizon of ontology. Socratic ignorance/irony bring negation into a positive, non-sublatable "presence." As will become quickly evident, the entire horizon of thinking has changed between Hegel's and Kierkegaard's reading: Kierkegaard more or less systematically reads lack as positive excess. He launches his critique of Hegel in the following passage:

> It is essentially here that the difficulty with Hegel's conception of Socrates lies, namely, the attempt is constantly made to show how Socrates has conceived the good. But what is even worse, so it seems to me, is that the direction of the current (*Strømningens Direction*) in Socrates' life is not faithfully maintained. The movement in Socrates is to come to the good (*at komme til det Gode*). His significance for the development of the world is to arrive at this (not at one point to have arrived at this). Now this does not mean that he arrived at this towards the end of his life, as it were, but that his life was constantly to come to this and to cause others to do the same. In this respect he also arrived at the true, i.e. the true in and for itself, the beautiful [etc.] . . . and in general at being in-and-for-itself as being-in-and-for-itself for thought. He came to this and he constantly came to this (*CI* 235, slightly altered; *SKS* 1:277).

The first criticism, then, is that despite Socrates' protestations of ignorance concerning the good, Hegel's interpretation has him aiming continually at positive conception. Hegel understands Socratic ignorance as the condition for a more universal conception of the good. For Kierkegaard, however, this is to run roughshod over the "historical-actual, phenomenological" evidence concerning Socrates (i.e., the presentation of him in the works of Xenophon, Plato, and Aristophanes).[19]

More fundamentally, Kierkegaard charges that Hegel does not remain faithful to the "direction of the current" of Socrates' life. What is necessary is a reversal of polarities: even if all the details remain the same, everything will be subjected to a different flow.

As we have seen, both Hegel and Kierkegaard grasp Socratic interiority in terms of a turn toward "being in and for itself." For both, the turn inward, which grasps being in its distinction from beings (or the Good in its distinction from particular goods), is presupposed in all philosophical cognition. Philosophy aims at the absolute as its sole object. But what is meant by the absolute? That is where the difference emerges. To put it simply, for Hegel the absolute constitutes the totality of ontological determinations (the "system" of the real); for Kierkegaard, the absolute must be thought as *ab-solute*, that is, as what absolves itself of all determinations. The Hegelian absolute is indeed identical to nothing insofar as it is the mere incipience of determination. The absolute as nothing is the *abstract absolute*, the unarticulated absolute, which Socrates indeed grasped. But according to Kierke-gaard—and here is where the reversal of current applies—Socrates' position is not a mere failure of articulation, but rather the consummation of a thinking of the absolute as ab-solute.

For Hegel, thinking moves dialectically from indetermination to deter-mination, from nonbeing to being, from arché to telos. For Kierkegaard, thinking takes shape rather as a stripping away of determinations. Socrates, he says, lets the absolute "work itself out (*via negationis*) of the determina-tions of being in which it had been hitherto" (*CI* 236, altered; *SKS* 1:277). He carries through the movement in which the absolute manifests itself as ab-solute, that is, absolvent from determinations of being. The absolute is indeterminate (absolutely without determinations). This is to think the ab-solute as, in a sense, beyond or outside of being. It is to think the absolute as what does not enter into the dialectical interplay between being and non-being. In this sense, for Kierkegaard's Socrates, the absolute can only be grasped "in the form of nothing" (*CI* 236; *SKS* 1:277). "Nothing" here does not mean nonbeing as the dialectical opposite of being, but rather what neither is nor is not. The absolute, approachable only *via negationis* under the form of nothing, falls "between" being and nonbeing.

The difference between Hegel and Kierkegaard can thus be summa-rized this way: for Hegel, the absolvent turn toward being in and for itself constitutes a "mere" beginning in thinking. The beginning must be re-deemed and legitimated in terms of a positive development—ultimately, in terms of the development of a knowledge of the absolute through its de-terminations. For Kierkegaard, by contrast, the turn toward a thinking of the absolute in its distinction from beings is precisely the endpoint, the goal of thinking. The Socratic movement is the incessant rearticulation of the difference between being in and for itself and beings. It aims to make onto-logical difference visible. Its thought is the thought of ontological differ-ence—which is to say, the thought of transcendence rather than totality.

Yet why, we may ask, does Kierkegaard break from Hegel at precisely this point? What guides his thinking beyond the horizon of ontology to-ward an ab-solute that remains without determination, and so an absolute that is nothing? What allows him to grasp nothing, not as lack, nor as the anticipation of some later pleromatic presence, but as an evacuation of de-terminations? It seems clear that Kierkegaard was inspired by the move-ment of apophasis or *via negationis* found in negative theology. This sup-position is strengthened by the fact that Kierkegaard places the emphasis, something ignored in Hegel, upon Socrates' role as a divine emissary. He writes:

> By way of the absolute, reality became nothing, but in turn the absolute was nothing. But in order to be able to hold him fast at this point, in order never

to forget that the content of his life was to make this movement [of stripping the absolute of determinations] at every moment, we must recollect his significance as a divine missionary. Although Socrates himself places much weight on his divine mission, Hegel has ignored this (*CI* 236; *SKS* 1:277).

Hegel ignores the religious meaning of Socrates, that is, the way he maintains the good beyond being. To reverse the poles of interpretation is thus also to reinscribe the Socratic position within the religious. But here religion itself is reinscribed within a context of negation. To relate to the divine as the absolute is to abandon positive determinations. Once the absolute is grasped as ab-solute, positive determinations appear as essentially and fatally relative. Socrates' whole effort of thinking was, ever anew, *to arrive* at this sense of the relativity of all ontological predicates. His *irony* consisted in the dialectical work of destroying predicates in terms of their ultimacy by showing their internal contradictions. The divine of Socrates remains unsayable.

THE GROUND THAT UNGROUNDS

The absolute can be thought also as "the ground" (*Grunden*) and as "the Idea." Thus, thinking the absolute as ab-solute, Socrates relates to "the Idea," the "ground (*Grunden*) underlying all things, the eternal, the divine" (*CI* 169; *SKS* 1:217), as a mere "limit" or "boundary." Kierkegaard continues: "[Socrates] knew that [the Idea] was, but he did not know what it was. He was conscious of it and yet not conscious of it, since the only thing that he could predicate of it was that he knew nothing about it. But this is to say no more than we have previously expressed in the words: Socrates had the Idea as a limit (*Grænse*)" (*CI* 169; *SKS* 1:217–18). But is this not a contradiction? Wouldn't Hegel point out that knowledge of the fact *that* the absolute is, without being able to say *what* it is, already sets thinking within the horizon of being? Doesn't Kierkegaard confirm here Hegel's assessment that Socrates remains an abstract thinker in the sense that his thinking of the absolute as ground begs for completion? Finally, doesn't the description of Socrates' thinking remain within the framework of thinking reality in terms of a ground and in light of the Idea? Has there been any movement away from the horizon of ontology?

Undoubtedly the notions of ground and Idea are repeated. The decisive questions, however, will be whether the ground, for example, still exercises the function of grounding. In what sense does the ab-solute of Socrates accomplish grounding? Actually, the way Kierkegaard reads Socrates, the ground effects an ungrounding, a rupture in the texture of knowledge. This can be seen by considering how Kierkegaard treats the theme of "recollection" (*Erindringen*)—the movement of knowledge par excellence.[20] Socrates, he says, *recollects* the Idea, and to this extent it would appear that he brings the Idea to presence, to consciousness. Recollecting it, he would know *that it is*. This means he knows also *what* it is: it is what cannot be known. In recollection he would apprehend the *being* of the absolute as such. But no, Kierkegaard reverses this thematic too. Rather than concentrating upon bringing the absolute to presence in light of the Idea, he emphasizes the way in which the Idea has *always already* withdrawn for recollection. To recollect the ab-solute as nothing means neither to know, nor to know that one does not know; it means to fall into bewilderment. Thus, referring to the problem as to whether the virtues can be taught, that is, recollected, Kierkegaard writes: "It would be Platonic to fortify existence by the upbuilding thought that man is not driven empty-handed out into the world, by calling to mind his abundant equipment through recollection. It is Socratic to disparage all actuality and to direct man to a recollection that continually retreats further and further back toward a past that itself retreats as far back in time as that noble family's origin that no one could remember" (*CI* 60; *SKS* 1:120). The Platonic notion of recollection, which stands here opposed to that of Socrates, would stress the power for recollection to bring the Idea to presence. It grasps the Idea through its grounding relation to the phenomena and remains confident that thinking is capable of attaining to the ground.

Kierkegaard's Socrates, by contrast, refers recollection toward precisely what "nobody can remember," that is, toward the non-recollectable. Recollection is always, paradoxically, of the immemorial. The ground cannot be brought to presence—not even indirectly as what is present under the mode of its absence. The consciousness of an absence of ground is not the real presence of the ground in that consciousness. Rather, recollection is the movement whereby the origin looses any determination it might have had (or is represented as having). This subversive understanding of recollection appears in Kierkegaard's reading of the *Protagoras* dialogue, concerning the question of whether virtue is one or many. Kierkegaard summarizes his interpretation of the overall result of Socrates' arguments: "But what I must particularly point out is that this unity of virtue [i.e., the Idea] becomes so abstract, so egotistically closed in upon itself, that it only becomes the rock upon which individual virtues, like well-freighted sailing vessels, run aground and are smashed to pieces" (*CI* 58; *SKS* 1:119). The unity of the virtues, that is, their principle, or that in which they find their ground, is so closed in upon itself that it ceases to function *as* a ground. The ground turns positively against what it is supposed to ground and hence the idea becomes explicitly that which prevents grounding, that upon which reasons run aground. Recollection thus signifies precisely the foundering of notions.

To maintain the Idea in this way, as a self-consuming, withdrawing, and ungrounding ground, is entirely different than the Platonic or Hegelian notion of the Idea. Here the Idea is, according to its very structure, what one is always *about to* possess, but what never *is* possessed. The Idea neither is nor is not possessed. And if it neither is nor is not possessed, this is only because it neither is nor is not. To relate to the Idea as the Idea, then, is for thinking to grasp its irreducible "betweenness"—that is, that one can neither leave off a thinking of the ground nor accomplish it.[21] In fact, one can begin to gauge the significant departure from the metaphysical tradition, at least as represented by a certain Plato and a certain Hegel, from this point. The Idea does not coincide with presence. This is to suggest a primordial gap between essence and manifestation, thought and being; it is to suggest a difference that does not fall under a grounding identity. To stand and remain in this gap is for Kierkegaard the "essence" of the Socratic standpoint, a position that "is as difficult to hold fast as the point between thawing and freezing" (*CI* 78; *SKS* 1:136). Yet Socrates maintains himself entirely in this "in-between," in this vanishing moment. He relates to the absolute as what neither is nor is not.

What falls ever between being and nonbeing and cannot be integrated into their dialectic—and thus, following Hegel, into "logic"—Kierkegaard names "infinite absolute negativity." I shall discuss this momentarily. What I wish to underscore at this point, however, is that the thought of ontological difference is central to the Kierkegaardian project. Knowledge, exposition, ground-laying is the opposite of the Socratic movement. The flow of Socrates' life is rather toward stripping away knowledge and ungrounding grounds. He makes the question concerning the good resonate; and that is the whole point, the goal or terminus, of the Socratic movement. The question receives a radical priority over any expository discourse aiming at knowledge. And in maintaining the priority of the question—or rather, in all strictness, by maintaining the priority of the original possibility of questioning—Socrates maintains a relation to the excess implied in any new beginning. Remaining faithful to this excess is the condition for remaining faithful to Socrates' "historical-actual, phenomenological existence."

IRONY AS EXISTENTIAL POSTURE: SOCRATIC DETACHMENT

As a standpoint, or existential posture, Socrates' position is that of irony. What characterizes irony as a posture is its essential disinterestedness, or lack of seriousness. To note Socrates' ironic detachment, of course, is a commonplace in the interpretation of his standpoint. What marks Kierkegaard's reading as radical, and what distinguishes it specifically from Hegel's, is to frame Socratic disinterestedness explicitly in terms of its "meta-physical" meaning. For Hegel Socrates' ironic posture is mere posturing; it is tantamount to a method. This implies Socrates retains intentional control over the irony. Hegel keeps the egological meaning of Socratic subjectivity at the forefront.

For Kierkegaard, Socratic detachment stems from a living sense of the absolutely unmasterable, the absolutely non-recollectable. For his Socrates, what is essential about reality, what the philosophical tradition after Socrates names *eidos,* or ground, remains in withdrawal. This withdrawal of the recollectable heart of phenomena is what obsesses Socrates and makes him indifferent to all the discourses that speak of what is (i.e., ethical, social, political discourses). His disinterestedness stands exactly coextensive with his sense of the absolute as withdrawn from predicates of being. What is, what stands revealed as present, is absolutely uninteresting in relation to the always previous event of withdrawal. Socrates gets taken into this movement entirely, swept away by it, into the "infinite Oceanus" of the negative. According to the sixth Latin thesis, "Socrates not only used irony but was so dedicated to it that he himself succumbed to it" (*CI* 6; *SKS* 1:65). He succumbs: he does not, in the end, master his own irony; it masters him.

An essential defect of Hegel's reading of Socrates, for Kierkegaard, is precisely to have missed how the Socratic standpoint is impossible to maintain. Irony is nothing other than a passage to the limit. It is an experience, to be sure, even an "enjoyment" (*Nydelse*). And indeed Socrates sustains this position to the very end. He relates even to the event of his own death as simply another determination of what is objectively present, something akin to any other event: "he becomes alien to the whole world to which he belongs. . . . What bears him up is the negativity that still has engendered no positivity. This explains why even life and death lose their absolute validity for him (*CI* 196; *SKS* 1:243). Everything capable of being thought as determinate loses its interest in the face of the impossibility to recollect the origin or principle of what is.

In the vacuum of ultimate foundations, the sophists, with whom Socrates is often misidentified, *pluralize* and *finitize* the question of the ground through "reflection" (*Reflexionen*): "But in Sophistry, reflection is awakened; it shakes the foundations of everything, and it is then that Sophistry lulls it to sleep again with grounds (*ved Grunde*). By means of *raisonnements,* this hungry monster [i.e., groundlessness] is satisfied (*CI* 205; *SKS* 1:250). In contrast to this approach, which Kierkegaard links to casuistry and calculative thinking—ultimately to self-interest—Kierkegaard's Socrates maintains the thought of groundlessness in a radical way. The sophists, too, emerge only once "the foundations of everything have been shaken" (*CI* 205; *SKS* 1:250). Yet what distinguishes the sophists from Socrates, according to Kierkegaard, is this: The sophists seize the instant where the foundations of everything have been shaken as an opportunity to proliferate grounds, whereas Socrates maintains the thought of an ungrounding ground that "was turned not only against the Sophists; it was turned against the whole established order" (*CI* 213–14; *SKS* 1:258).

Now, to a certain extent Socrates was self-conscious about his own inability to control irony. As Kierkegaard puts it: "Therefore we can say of [Socrates'] irony that it is earnestness about nothing—insofar as it is not earnestness about something. It continually conceives of nothing in contrast to something, and in order to free itself of earnestness about anything [including nothing], it grasps the nothing. But it does not become earnestness about nothing, either, except insofar as it is not earnestness about anything" (*CI* 270; *SKS* 1:307). Socrates exercises his subjectivity by reflexively grasping the content of his own position, that is, its sense of the nothing at the heart of all phenomena. He achieves a certain consistency in becoming neither serious nor not serious about his own standpoint. He escapes the objection that he is, after all, becoming serious about his irony. The movement of thinking is for him an "infinitely light *playing* with nothing" (my emphasis).[22]

Nevertheless Socrates succumbs to his own irony. He remains blind to it at one decisive point: he fails to see, or at any rate cannot control, how history will regard him. History will inevitably grasp his standpoint as a "turning point." He will inevitably be read as offering a *new ground* for the constitution of phenomena: self-consciousness. The whole problem of his standpoint will be interpreted, as Kierkegaard undertakes at the beginning of part two Of *The Concept of Irony*, in terms of its "world historical validity."

In short, the irony of Socratic irony is that it will meet its negation. Of course, this is exactly what Hegel said: in the end, after the fact, Socratic irony points to the way subjectivity constitutes an ideal origin, a principle, for all phenomena. And yet, beyond or prior to this movement of double negation, Kierkegaard will want to point to a certain remainder. Even after being negated, Socratic negation still "haunts" and "teases" (*spøger*) the tradition with the memory of the immemorial. That is to say, careful reading of the sources, as *The Concept of Irony* attempts, will still be able to discover in the standpoint of Socrates the negation against which any principle, even subjectivity, runs aground.

This is where the whole question of irony has to be treated from a more radical side. It becomes necessary to ask concerning the withdrawal of the ground—the event that elicits Socrates' irony as a standpoint—as a "metaphysical" problematic. The withdrawal of the ground constitutes an "ironic" movement that, originally, has nothing to do with a subjective stance. At issue is the irony of being itself, so to say. This problem, which Kierkegaard treats under the heading of "infinite absolute negativity," is fundamental to *The Concept of Irony.* At stake for Kierkegaard is to think *both* what allows something like a subject in the first instance and what prevents it from thinking of itself (or reality) according to grounds. Or again, at stake is thinking what both enables and destitutes subjectivity, what kills it *and* makes it alive.

INFINITE ABSOLUTE NEGATIVITY

In the Hegelian conceptual milieu in which *The Concept of Irony* operates, the problem of negation or difference relates closely to the problem of manifestation. Difference or negation is the condition in which there can be appearing at all. Something must become other to itself in order to *appear.* This is a general condition for any phenomenon. The motif of "infinite absolute negativity" appears in Hegel in terms of the conditions for a phenomenology of the absolute. In order for the absolute to manifest itself, to become conscious of itself, it must negate itself infinitely and absolutely: it must stand beyond or outside itself. In Hegel, however, infinite absolute negativity always refers, dialectically, to the *self*-differing of the absolute. Difference is something posited.

Kierkegaard, though, borrowed the term "infinite absolute negativity" from Hegel. In fact he lifts the term, not from Hegel's reading of Socrates in *Lectures on the History of Philosophy,* but from his *Aesthetics.* Hegel writes:

> [T]he dialectical moment of the Idea [is] that transition point which I call the "infinite absolute negativity," the activity of the Idea in its negation of itself as infinite and universal, in order to pass itself into finiteness and particularity, and with no less truth once more in order to annul this negation, and in so doing to establish again the universal and infinite within the finite and particular.[23]

Infinite absolute negativity thus signifies, for Hegel, a transition point, or dialectical moment, whereby the absolute makes itself relative (particular, contingent), and so negates itself as the absolute; then again it signifies that same transition point thought from the other side, namely, as the movement of the particular negating itself as particular and discovering itself in the absolute. Infinite absolute negativity, in short, is the dialectically conceived *between* of being and beings, the absolute and the relative, the universal and the particular, and so on. It is the condition both of the appearing of the absolute, for appearing always takes place in space and time (contingently, particularly), and of the conceptual grasping of the absolute (which, be it noted, coincides with the absolute's conceptual grasping of itself).

From a Hegelian perspective, then, the theme of infinite absolute negativity reopens, from a different angle, the question of the emergence of interiority and hence the question of the beginning of the philosophical concept. One could say it is the "objective" condition for subjectivity in general. Subjectivity, in its consciousness of itself as distinct from the totality of what is, in itself has the character of an infinite negation. Subjectivity is an infinite negating of being. And yet, as the above passage makes clear, the "negation" that constitutes subjectivity maintains a dialectical relation to being and is ontologically subordinated to the work of manifesting being in objectivity. This becomes the primary theme of Hegel's *Phenomenology of Spirit:* the path of self-negation, the "highway of despair," is in reality a movement toward absolute knowledge.[24] What guides the whole course of Hegelian phenomenology is the idea that the absolute remains identical to itself amidst its negation of itself. Appearing gives rise to an intelligibility. Thus the truth of finite subjectivity is found, for Hegel, in the work of bringing being into its full manifestness: the labor of knowledge. As appearing, however, the absolute is not given as a whole, but only through contradictory phenomena. It is the work of thinking, according to Hegel, to surpass the dialecticity of being as appearing by integrating its contradictions into a concrete whole—something achieved only in a definitive sense in the concept (*Begriff*). Yet, as soon as there is appearing, subjectivity, there is the possibility of the concept and of a beginning with the concept.

It is quite different with Kierkegaard. For him, infinite absolute negativity, a term that he appropriates from Hegel, will refer to what originally accounts for such differing at all—in other words, it will refer to a radical origin or beginning that cannot be made to coincide with a dialectically conceived origin (a principle). Infinite absolute negativity, to be specific, will refer to a difference that cannot be thought as *posited*—consequently, to a difference that is more than the condition for something to manifest itself in objectivity. If for Hegel infinite absolute negativity names the condition for a phenomenology of the absolute, and ultimately for absolute knowledge, for Kierkegaard it will name the condition in which a phenomenology of the absolute becomes precisely impossible. In each case, however, the knot is tied within, or as, finite subjectivity. Thus ultimately at stake is the question as to whether the motif of subjectivity is exhausted in the role of bringing essential being to manifestation. For Kierkegaard subjectivity has to live itself as an excess to such a role.

Now irony links to the question of infinite absolute negativity insofar as it names precisely the difference between an essence and its phenomenon: "Already we have a quality that permeates all irony—namely, that the *phenomenon is not the essence but the opposite* of the essence" (*CI* 247; *SKS* 1:286). As a phenomenon irony indicates a gap between what appears to be and what really is, between the essence (the said) and the phenomenon (the saying). It is difference phenomenalized. This opens an essential ambiguity concerning irony: it is both a phenomenon and the condition of a phenomenon. Without the emergence of distance between essence and itself, essence could not appear; and yet irony is itself the appearing of this distance. However, Kierkegaard makes an essential distinction between irony as a mere trope and essential or "eminent" irony. "The ironic figure of speech," Kierkegaard writes, "cancels itself . . . inasmuch as the one who is speaking assumes that his hearers understand him, and thus, through a negation of the immediate phenomenon, the essence becomes identical with the phenomenon" (*CI* 248; *SKS* 1:286–87). Although a momentary break between essence and phenomenon opens up in the ironic trope, introducing a negation into the phenomenon, in irony as a trope this negation is itself negatable. An ironic comment, though indirect, can easily be understood. As a figure of speech, then, irony does not in any way break the basic structure of intelligibility or manifestation. It preserves itself within an interplay in which "the essence is and is only insofar as it is in appearance, or that appearance is the truth of the essence, essence is the truth of appearance (*CI* 212; *SKS* 1:256).

What Kierkegaard discovers operative in Socrates, however, is a "total irony," which is "irony [that] turns against all existence" (*CI* 257; *SKS* 1:295). Total or pure irony would thus point to an originary *and non-negatable gap,* an originary splitting, between essence and phenomenon, beyond their recuperable identity. Kierkegaard formulates the basic structure of total irony in this way: "[Total irony] negates the phenomenal, not in order to posit by means of this negation, but negates the phenomenal altogether. It runs back instead of going out; it is not in the phenomenon but seeks to deceive with the phenomenon; the phenomenon exists not to disclose the essence but to conceal it" (*CI* 212; *SKS* 1:256). At work in total irony is a negation that cannot be negated. Essence does not come forth into the phenomenon, but withdraws back into itself, leaving the phenomenon empty of essence.[25]

Infinite absolute negativity, as Kierkegaard understands it, thus refers to this *withdrawal of essence.* What is crucial, however, is that the movement of withdrawal is not merely the condition for essence to appear in a milieu of difference; rather, the withdrawal of essence is itself a positive phenomenon. Essence dis-appears; a void becomes "manifest." Or rather, essence appears only as what has *already* withdrawn, as what has absented itself in a moment no longer recuperable; it appears in the mode of an irreducible enigma. This withdrawal, nevertheless, does not annihilate the phenomena completely: "Now, essence is surely the negation of appearance, but it is not the absolute negation, since thereby essence itself would actually have disappeared" (*CI* 212; *SKS* 1:256). As a withdrawal of essence that positively marks itself in a phenomenon, irony is structurally involved in every phenomenon that is enigmatic: the *non*-appearance of what is indicated is precisely what appears. At issue is a "trace" phenomenon.

As the very figure of total irony Socrates himself becomes the topos for an exploration of the phenomenalization of difference. His replies, his whole "historical-actual, phenomenological existence," are enigmatic. He incarnates the withdrawal of essence; he manifests the condition of all manifestation. He is himself the presence, under the form of an irreducible enigma, of infinite absolute negativity.

Kierkegaard illustrates infinite absolute negativity both as a phenomenon and as the condition of a phenomenon in the following figure:

> There is a work that represents Napoleon's grave. Two tall trees shade the grave. There is nothing else to see in the work, and the immediate observer sees nothing else. Between the two trees there is an empty space; as the eye follows the outline, suddenly Napolean himself emerges from this nothing, and now it is impossible to have him disappear again. . . . So also with Socrates' rejoinders. One hears his words in the same way one sees the trees; his words mean what they say just as the trees are the trees. There is not one single syllable that gives a hint of any other interpretation, just as there is not one single line that suggests Napoleon, and yet this empty space, this nothing, is what hides that which is most important (*CI* 19, slightly altered; *SKS* 1:80–81).[26]

How could infinite absolute negativity, the condition of every phenomenon in the Hegelian milieu, itself appear? How does (what is as good as) "nothing" appear? Generally to appear signifies at least to become determinate, to become *something*. Yet Kierkegaard points to a modality of manifestation in which nothing is given, *positively given,* to representational or objective thinking. The face of Napoleon appears and thus becomes a phenomenon. Moreover, once it appears it becomes an object constituted by determinate predicates. Nevertheless, what most strikes Kierkegaard is the anxious reverberation of the phenomenon: the enigmatic quality of the face, which suddenly leaps from nothing into presence, causes the eye to be anxious.

The "immediate observer" (*den umiddelbare Iagttager*) sees only what is given, what is present. Such an observer does not see phenomena *as phenomena*. Consequently, he does not see the nothing from which phenomena emerge. Indeed, nothing cannot be seen otherwise than on condition of an irreparable break with immediacy. Once Napoleon's face has emerged, suddenly, from its submersion in immediate being, there is no going back. Nothing cannot be made to disappear; it persists and produces anxiety.

Translated more broadly: once the phenomenality of phenomena has been caught sight of, as precisely within the entire Hegelian problematic, this will imply the persistence of negation as a positive phenomenon, or rather quasi-phenomenon, at the heart of the given. Hegel, the point will be, will have the face of Napoleon reclaimed by being. He will aim to link phenomena continuously back to their ground: to be able to see phenomena in their ground and as the expression of their ground. The phenomena will make the ground available. But Kierkegaard's "image" shows something else: one cannot simultaneously see the phenomenon and its ground—one sees either Napoleon's face or nothing. There is an aporia here: the ground is the ground only once the phenomenon emerges; but once the phenomenon emerges, it occludes the ground.

It is not a coincidence that Kierkegaard formulates this aporia in terms of temporality. Napoleon appears "suddenly." As later texts show, the sudden (*det Pludselige*) is another name for what Kierkegaard calls "the instant" (*Øieblikket*), which itself translates what Plato called *to exaiphnes*.[27] The sudden is the instant of transition, the difference, which falls between being and nonbeing. The sudden translates ontological difference *as* temporal diachrony (the gap between one present and another). The suddenness of coming to appearance would thus signify the way in which one present arises from the next in an indeterminate, unanticipated, and *unanticipatable* way. Coming to appearance is, thus, the emergence of what eludes anticipative foresight from out of an empty space between presences (in the above image, the empty space between the trees).

From this angle it becomes possible to see the depth of Kierkegaard's revision of the Hegelian motif of infinite absolute negativity. To become manifest is, for Kierkegaard, to obey a discontinuous or sudden temporality. Kierkegaard translates difference, as the condition for phenomenalization, into the temporality of a rupture or surprise. And the point of this would be to suggest that the movement of phenomenalization ultimately exceeds something's becoming objectively present. Phenomena are not ordained toward their becoming conceptually graspable via their ground (which here occludes itself). Or, perhaps more precisely: the phenomena that pertain to subjectivity, that "manifest" the subjectivity of the subject—phenomena such as total irony, anxiety, melancholy, and the like—do not have their telos in absolute knowledge. What this would say, then, is that subjectivity is to be gauged according to a phenomenality that respects the sudden character of appearing—and that means, in terms of an origin that does not itself appear.

In fact, as we shall see in further chapters, the decisive phenomena for Kierkegaard will be those that obey a discontinuous, sudden temporality. The discontinuities of time (i.e., temporal diachrony) will refer either to an origin that has always already withdrawn, and that therefore is irrecuperable, or to one that withholds itself within a future that cannot be anticipated. In either case, the gap between essence and phenomenon (irony) remains open. Subjectivity is itself what remains "open"—that is, not determinable as a definite moment in the "history of thought finding itself." Subjectivity "is" that uncloseable gap between essence and phenomenon: simultaneously the condition for an appearing and itself something that appears. Yet subjectivity appears only vis-à-vis the withdrawal of its ground. This will suggest a void at the heart of the subject whose further meaning will have to be determined.

I turn now to Kierkegaard's critique of the Platonic beginning.

THE PLATONIC BEGINNING: CRITIQUE OF PLATONIC MYTHOS

Kierkegaard's critique of Plato constitutes the largest single section in *The Concept of Irony.* As with Hegel, this critique centers upon the interpretation of Socrates. What is at stake in this critique is again the question of the beginning of philosophy as a discourse of concepts. Kierkegaard's principal critique is the following: Plato does not merely present Socrates' standpoint, he in fact inaugurates an "entirely new beginning" (*CI* 107; *SKS* 1:160) under the name of Socrates, a beginning whose core operation, appearances to the contrary, constitutes the *erasure* of Socrates' standpoint (i.e., infinite absolute negativity). On Kierkegaard's reading, Plato inaugurates "speculative thought," philosophy as metaphysics. This is why he may be regarded as the "unripe fruit of speculation," a fruit that reaches its maturity with Hegel. In Kierkegaard's mind, Plato and Hegel are linked along a continuous line of development and, he argues, in each case the Socratic standpoint—subjectivity in general—is suppressed. In fact, the suppression of the standpoint of subjectivity *is* the beginning of the concept speculatively thought. That is the essence of his critique.

Kierkegaard's critique of Plato consists in separating out or absolving Socrates from his inscription within Plato's dialogues. This means "separating what time and intimacy had apparently made inseparable" (*CI* 96; *SKS* 1:150)—an admittedly painful prospect.

As Kierkegaard understands it, though, Plato's erasure of the standpoint of Socrates is no merely negative move. Plato erases Socrates by reproducing him and poetically creating him; he forgets him in a profound way, by remembering him otherwise. The beginning that Plato inaugurates is conditioned by the standpoint of Socrates, yet in each moment, he argues, it misconstrues the nature of the relation. At bottom, we shall see—something that was also the case with Hegel—the charge is that Plato misconstrues negation.

The Infinite Beginning | 33

Kierkegaard recalls the fact that Plato came to philosophy, under the impact of the Socratic dialectic, from *poetry;* and, "in particular, a very creative poetic temperament is scarcely qualified to grasp [irony] *sensu eminentiori*" (*CI* 124; *SKS* 1:177). Plato the poet founds philosophy as metaphysics.[28] Moreover, he does so through an essential and far-reaching misapprehension of Socratic negation. The infinite absolute negativity of the Socratic standpoint, as indicated above, is to have the Idea merely as limit, to recollect it only *as* the non-recollectable. The Idea ungrounds. Recollecting the Idea signifies the destruction of grounds. As Kierkegaard reads Socrates, though, this destructive move is not a prelude to some groundlaying. On the contrary, Socrates consummates this relation to the Idea and goes no further because "he has no deeper speculative need." He enjoys the negative relation to the Idea in irony. For a "speculative individual" such as Plato, however, the destruction of all given grounds could be both liberating and immensely seductive: "But insofar as the speculating individual feels liberated and an abundance spreads out before his observing eyes, he may readily believe that he also owes all this to irony and his gratitude may wish to owe everything to it" (*CI* 123; *SKS* 1:175). Plato's rich poetic disposition, in short, led him to regard the infinite absolute negativity of the standpoint of Socrates as the *promise* of an infinite, pleromatic wealth of content (*CI* 118; *SKS* 1:170).

According to Kierkegaard Plato allows the interests of *knowledge*—which is to say, of intuition, vision, presence—to supervene upon the purely "negative dialectic" of Socrates. Plato submits the Idea to the exigencies of vision: the in-and-for-itself in the strictest sense is *the seen,* what can be rendered present before the mind's eye. The crucial index of this "entirely new (Platonic) beginning," in which "all things are new," may be found in the significance of the *mythical* in Plato: "[T]he mythical presentation . . . lets the negative be seen" (*CI* 106–107; *SKS* 1:159–60). In the *Symposium,* for example, Kierkegaard argues that the mythical element is not that Diotima appeals to a myth in order to present the nature of eros; rather, it is "in setting forth the beautiful as the object of eros" (*CI* 107; *SKS* 1:160). "The mythical clearly consists in this," Kierkegaard writes, "that beauty in and for itself shall be seen (*skal skues*)" (*CI* 107; *SKS* 1:160).

The presence of the mythical is the "indication of a more copious speculation" (*CI* 96; *SKS* 1:150). A *mythos* is the first speculative word in terms of content; as to form, the "mythical presentation" (*mythiske Fremstilling*) becomes the very grammar of the speculative insofar as, at bottom, it responds to the demand for vision. The mythical, consequently, is that Plato makes the beautiful the intuitable *object* of eros, even if this must finally be thought as a purely objectless object, a pure in-and-for-itself. In a certain way this is not merely an example of the speculative gesture, but the speculative gesture itself insofar as the beautiful is par excellence the visible.

Thus Kierkegaard understands the mythical and mythical presentation as always already operative under the speculative demand for intuitive insight (*Anskuelsen*). Moreover—and this is the crucial point—according to Kierkegaard the mythical and mythical presentation constitute an *essential* and not merely contingent moment of Plato's thought. Kierkegaard goes against the grain of much interpretation, then and now, by arguing that for Plato myth is neither a bow to religious tradition nor a mere sensible accommodation to those incapable of abstract thinking.[29] Rather, it is the very relation to the Idea: "in these dialogues [the mythical] is not so much Plato's free composition, tractable and obedient to him, as it is instead something that overwhelms him and is to be considered not so much a secondary account for younger or less gifted listeners as a presentiment of something higher" (*CI* 98; *SKS* 1:152).

For Plato the Idea is par excellence *the seeable,* what offers itself to intuitive apprehension. A mythos is the immediate form of its visibility: "But if we ask what the mythical is basically, one may presumably reply that it is the idea in a state of alienation, the idea's externality—i.e., its immediate temporality and spatiality as such" (*CI* 101; *SKS* 1:154).[30] The mythos manifests the Idea for sensibility, "under the determinations of space and time, the latter understood wholly ideally" (ibid.). The accent therefore is not so much upon the sensuous form of the myth as its subordination to spatiality and temporality as such. This becomes especially apparent in that, more exactly thought, the mythical is the product, not of dialectic or reflective thought, but of the imagination: "The dialectical clears the terrain of everything irrelevant and then attempts to clamber up to the idea, but since this fails, the imagination reacts. Weary of the dialectical work, the imagination begins to dream, and from this comes the mythical" (*CI* 101; *SKS* 1:154). The mythical is an altogether spontaneous and original production of the imagination in its "enthusiastic" effort to present to itself the unpresentable, to bring the Idea before intuitive apprehension. It coincides with an ecstasis of consciousness beyond its merely reflective faculties, and therefore the mythos always stands in excess to reflective control.

Kierkegaard's image is precise: the imagination *dreams.* Ideal content is apprehended under an estranged form. Myth must be decoded by reflective thought in order to elicit its ideal content. Thus, as Kierkegaard understands the function of myth in Plato, the element of estrangement—the passivity of consciousness where it finds itself overwhelmed by unpresentable content—constitutes the condition in which "a more" (*et Mere*) slips into and under the purview of consciousness. In myth consciousness receives more than it could have given itself through dialectical exertion—but *not* more than it can assimilate within itself, that is, bring under the subsequent control of reflection. The sleep of the mythical, in which the imagination dreams, is the negation necessary for a new day of insight. Thus in Plato every mythos is already a logos in an analogous way as, in Hegel, the element of *Vorstellung* is already *Begriff.* The grammar of double negation dominates this understanding of myth. And again, this is why Kierkegaard is able to regard Plato as the mere "unripe fruit" of speculation to Hegel's ripe fruit.

In Hegel the concept (*der Begriff*) constitutes the *Aufhebung* of the representational, drawing out its ideal content and assimilating it within itself, as logos, without remainder. For Plato, as Kierkegaard reads him, the movement of *Aufhebung* is implied, but not consummated: "The fruit of speculation, however, never fully ripens in Plato because the dialectical movement is never fully accomplished" (*CI* 105; *SKS* 1:159). "Plato's sphere is not thought (*Tanken*) but representation (*Forestillingen*)" (*CI* 103; *SKS* 1:157); he has the "idea of dialectic, but not the dialectic of the Idea." The more the speculative interest of consciousness dominates in Plato, however —and this coincides with the movement from the "earlier" aporetic dialogues to the later "constructive" dialogues, e.g. the *Parmenides* and *Timaeus* —the more the mythical presentation is supplanted by reflection and transformed into "the image" (*Billedet*). Thus even in Plato's most speculative dialogues there is always a residue of estrangement marked by his recourse— not to concepts strictly speaking—but to images that *may be redeemed as* concepts. Plato never achieves pure concepts. He lacks a speculative logic.

Without a doubt, Kierkegaard has a personal attraction for the Platonic beginning that he does not seem to have for the Hegelian beginning: "Dear critic, allow me just one sentence, one guileless parenthesis, in order to vent my gratitude, my gratitude for the relief I found in reading Plato" (*CI* 27; *SKS* 1:89). What accounts for this is that in Plato's dialogues "the ideas themselves seem to know that there is time and an arena (*Tumleplads*) for all of them" (ibid.). The ideas are given a place to tumble about—to *play.* In other words, Plato's dialogues are not very well graphable onto a systematic, teleological development. True enough, from Hegel's perspective (which Kierkegaard to a certain extent shares) this is precisely the defect of Plato's thought. Hegel's thought remains systematically turned against a tumbling of ideas that does not have any internal, dialectical ordering. Moreover, since precisely the *mythical* is what tumbles chaotically out as a product of sensuously affected thought, Hegel's thought remains systematically aimed at a surpassing of myth.

If Kierkegaard aims at a critique of the Platonic beginning, and consequently at a critique of the mythical—or, I should more precisely say, the speculative-mythical[31]—he does not, however, entirely follow the lines of Hegel's critique.[32] The crux of Kierkegaard's critique is this: where it concerns being in and for itself, that is, the absolute or ground, *vision itself con-*

stitutes the essential myth. The originary myth that underlies every other myth in Plato, and which Hegel not only does not abandon, but actively completes, is that the absolute can be seen (speculatively grasped). From this point of view, it matters little that Plato is the mere "unripe fruit" of speculation and Hegel its ripe fruit. To the extent that Hegel also orients thinking radically around the presupposition that the absolute is the object of a vision, he too would be subject to Kierkegaard's critique.

What marks the difference between the Socratic standpoint and every speculative standpoint, then, is that it abandons the demand or expectation that the absolute can be brought to intuitive apprehension. Socrates allows a radical non-knowing. Indeed, knowledge as such, where it bears upon the absolute, is diagnosed as phantasmatic. To think the absolute, to apprehend it under its ideality, to grasp it as a principle, to render it present: all of these speculative moves are cut short by the thought of the radical contingency and finitude of all ontological determinations. The Socratic conception is one that regards the absolute as *radically free* of determinations (as nothing). Non-mythical thinking would thus be not a dialectical and conceptual discourse, as in Hegel, but a discourse that continually freed itself from the desire for determination concerning an ultimate ground. It would be a discourse that *un*-learned reliance upon ultimate grounds (but also that did not opt for the Sophist move of pluralizing and finitizing grounds): a "negative dialectic" rather than a positive dialectic. Such "authentic thinking" (*den egentlige Tænkning*) would withhold itself within a "skeptical reserve" (*skeptisk Paaholdenhed*), or εποχή (*CI* 220; *SKS* 1:265), from the speculative beginning. It would maintain the thought of ontological difference without giving in to the powerful desire to have nonbeing *be* something— even if only an intimated something. It would let the gap between essence and phenomenon, and consequently the condition of appearing, resonate.

The point of the critique of Plato and Hegel has thus been to separate the position of Socrates from its speculative appropriations. I have indicated the logic of these appropriations as one of allowing the interests of knowledge, which is to say the act of bringing to intuitive vision, or presence, to supervene upon a confrontation with nothing. Socrates withholds himself from thinking according to an ultimate ground. Or more exactly: though he initially thinks the ground or the Idea—one could almost say he postulates it—he ceaselessly turns toward the failure of every articulation of the ground. His thought exhausts itself in discovering the absence of grounds underlying positive phenomena. Is it, in the end, a case of negative theology? Not quite. Certainly, Socratic dialectic in Kierkegaard's terms is apophatic in the sense of stripping away positive predicates from the absolute. Nevertheless it is not exactly negative theology.[33] What Socratic dialectic lacks, and what Plato and Hegel both supply, is the positive or analogical moment of reconstruction. Plato bridges the gap mythically; Hegel, through the milieu of historical representation.

Mythic discourse succeeds where dialectical exertion fails to supply positive determinations for the absolute. The ultimate mythos, I suggest, is simply that the absolute can be *seen;* the absolute is Idea. With Hegel it is somewhat different. Hegel bridges the gap between the absolute and its representations through *history.* History is the milieu of representation par excellence. And Hegel regards philosophical discourse, conceptual discourse, as capable of recovering the ideal content of history (the Idea simply). Hence, Hegel systematically reads every philosophical position, for example, in light of a sense of the consummation of philosophy. Each moment is redeemable only vis-à-vis its placement in the "history of thought finding itself." *Finding oneself* is the very work of thinking, the very movement of reality. Yet Kierkegaard's Socrates has "no deeper speculative need." He does not proceed, along either theological or philosophical lines, to the positive work of recovering the positive meaning of the absolute. He does not become onto-theological, but sustains the thought of the absolute as absolute. He loses himself, succumbs to this thought.

Yet not having a deeper speculative need would not be a "natural" position; it would not be a question of the givens of Socrates' psychology. Rather, this would be precisely the work or outcome of Socratic thinking—understood, however, that the very terms of "work" and "outcome" must inevitably reverse their sense and flip into that of *gift* (at which point work becomes more like play). As Kierkegaard underscores, Socrates understood his own standpoint, his own irony, as a "divine gift" (*CI* 199; *SKS* 1:245).

THE INFINITE BEGINNING: SOCRATES IN "THE HISTORY OF THOUGHT FINDING ITSELF"

In every possible way, then, Kierkegaard insists upon the irreducible gap between Socrates' standpoint and *what seems to have been made possible* by that standpoint—namely, between irony and speculative thought. It becomes a question of rearticulating a beginning that falls always and essentially prior to the speculative beginning.

In one sense, to be sure, Kierkegaard grants, with Hegel, that Socrates opens the possibility of speculative thought as a discourse about the absolute in its distinction from givens. Socratic thinking breaks through to being in and for itself. And again, he grants that this position constitutes a radically new sense of interiority since the absolute can never be thought as objectively present in space and time. What he refuses, however, is to read Socrates as a mere moment in the "history of thought finding itself." A decisive qualification is the following: "Just as [Socrates] himself in a certain sense exists and yet again does not exist in world history, so his significance in the development of the world spirit is precisely to be and yet not to be, or not to be and yet to be: *he is the nothing from which the beginning must nevertheless begin* (*CI* 198; *SKS* 1:244; my italics). Socrates neither is nor is not part of the history of thought finding itself. His standpoint relates to speculative thought in terms of a non-dialectical difference.

Socrates' standpoint: the infinite beginning, nothing, what neither is nor is not, infinite absolute negativity. Every speculative beginning begins here, but the question will be whether the speculative beginning lets itself be measured by these. As becomes clear especially in the introduction to part one of *The Concept of Irony,* all of these notions gravitate toward a thinking of the event, the birth of a new present, the formation of a new phenomenal order. And if there is a single critical thrust to *The Concept of Irony,* it is to have forced a tension found already at the heart of Hegel's thought: between the *event* where something genuinely new comes into being and the *intelligibility* of the event.

Philosophically, what is at stake in Kierkegaard's effort to withdraw Socrates from speculative appropriation is the *Mellemværende,* the being-at-issue or *differend,* "between history and philosophy" (*CI* 10; *SKS* 1:72). History is "the Idea's temporality and fragmentariness" in such a way that even "the whole sum of historical existence is not the absolutely adequate medium of the idea" (*CI* 11; *SKS* 1:73). Hegel, too, could affirm this. For him, history as event is as such not the absolutely adequate medium of the idea; rather, history comes into its truth as recapitulated, as conceptually grasped, as fathomed. Thus Kierkegaard repeats, initially at least, a basically Hegelian account of the *differend* between history and philosophy according to which philosophy grasps the truth of history, the essence in the manifestation. Everything is grasped in light of the end (the Idea). Yet Kierkegaard moves on to complicate this in a double way: first, by pointing to a remainder that cannot be recapitulated in the conceptual transfiguration of an event; second, by noting the special difficulties attending the speculative recapitulation and appropriation of Socrates.

Though Hegel marks the difference between history and philosophy, between an event and its intelligibility, his dialectical logic aims to resolve this tension around the notion of determinate negation. An event negates only as its initial phase, but that very negation is, in reality, another determination. In this way Hegel reads Socrates and every other breakthrough in the history of thought finding itself.[34] But for Kierkegaard this procedure is surreptitious: what allows one to say that the meaning an event *comes to have* was precontained, as ideal potentiality, within that event prior to its happening? This, for Kierkegaard, is to substitute a constructed or illusory continuity, what he will call a "state" (*Tilstand*) or duration, within a temporality that is sudden. Kierkegaard's reading returns the figure of Socrates to the time of the event, a discontinuous time.

Although the massive apparatus of part one of *The Concept of Irony* performs this reinscription, in the introduction to that section Kierkegaard indicates with a single line the substance of his objection. History as eventful, or as the temporality of the Idea, he says, "longs for the repulse that emanates from consciousness, which looks back [at it], face over against face" (*CI* 11, my translation; *SKS* 1:73). Historical moments are not reducible to what seems to have been made possible by them; they are in excess to the meaning they receive in light of some end. More simply: history as eventful resists teleological reading. In Kierkegaard's rather strange phrase, historical moments have a face that *looks back* at the consciousness looking at them. They retain their alterity and exteriority.

From this point of view one can see how the infinite beginning of Socrates cannot, in spite of everything, be construed as a moment in a teleologically ordered process such as "the history of thought finding itself." He both is and is not a moment in this developing totality. He *is:* because speculative thinking secures its own origin, its own legitimating principle, by reference to the Socratic beginning—though in Kierkegaard's terms, it actually "conjures" Socrates in light of its *own* needs. He *is not:* because Socrates nevertheless remains alteritous to every ideal appropriation. The face of Socrates cannot be reduced to a moment in a totality. Irony always "walks again and haunts" (*CI* 258; *SKS* 1:296) in virtue of a reserve withheld from all ideal appropriation.

Kierkegaard captures the ambiguity of Socrates' relation to history in an image: "in a world historical sense [Socrates'] significance was that he set the ship of speculation afloat. . . . He himself, however, does not go on board but only prepares the ship for embarkation" (*CI* 217; *SKS* 1:261). *Not* going on board is precisely his positive act. Neither Plato nor, especially, Hegel was capable of thinking a preparation that would be superior to what it prepared for. Isn't preparing for a journey a mere moment in the journey itself? And isn't a journey defined precisely by its ultimate destination? Doesn't a telos command all preparation and dictate its very meaning?

Nevertheless Kierkegaard inverts the terms. His reading focuses on what does not go along on the speculative journey, what is *held back*. If the speculative move is to think the beginning only in light of its end, Kierkegaard, by contrast, estimates it in terms of what it will have presupposed: time as event, prior to intelligibility. An event signifies what is still underway, that whose meaning is not yet secured. It is structurally ironic in that its ideality is deferred; essence is held apart from manifestation. Idealism systematically turns the infinite beginning of Socrates, the event that *origi-*

nally enables thinking, into *something* thought, an ideal ground. An event becomes a content; the singularity of Socrates is erased in face of a transmissible result. It is a question of placing the Socratic standpoint back in relation to what every beginning in philosophy, as an ideal discourse, must presuppose, but which it can never grasp ideally: what originally enables thinking itself. Kierkegaard's interpretation of Socrates reinscribes the non-recollectable instant, prior to all vision or presence, in which thought is allowed vision. Via Socrates he pulls thinking back to the moment *prior to* the speculative journey, back to the preparations.

Hence, Socrates may indeed constitute the beginning of speculative thought, but not at all in the way speculative thought thinks. Speculative thought radically misunderstands, or rather erases, its own condition. To grasp Socrates is to grasp irony, and to grasp irony is to grasp the eventfulness presupposed in anything's becoming manifest (present). But for Kierkegaard, who apparently felt no deeper speculative need, this set him upon the course of a more and more rigorous thinking of the event. Time as event becomes the issue. In this sense, he never leaves the problem of total irony behind.

TWO

Endless Time
(Either/Or *1*)

It may at times have occurred to you, dear reader, to doubt somewhat the accuracy of that familiar philosophical thesis that the outer is the inner and the inner is the outer" (*EO* 1:3; *SKS* 2:11). So begins *Either/Or, A Fragment of Life* (1843). The editor of these texts, Victor Eremita, expresses reservations concerning what, for idealist metaphysics, constitutes the ground of phenomena: transcendental interiority. Whether it is Kant's unity of apperception, Fichte or Schelling's intellectual intuition, or Hegel's notion of self-mediating subjectivity, in each case idealism traces the possibility of experience back to some prior identity between subjectivity and objectivity, inner and outer. The work of philosophy, as system, is to grasp the totality of experience in light of this original identity, this "Idea."

Either/Or casts doubt on this egology through the elaboration of phenomena—such as grief, melancholy, anxiety, boredom, and decision—whose conditions seem rather to be found in an originary *non*-identity of inner and outer. These extraordinary analyses, all papers of a certain anonymous "A," remark especially upon an originary difference that continually undermines what, for idealism, is essential: self-consciousness as a power to keep itself present to itself, to re-present itself, to coincide with itself. The analyses draw thinking back to an originary failure of representation. Something is taken prior to being possessed; something is forgotten prior to being known; something is lost prior to being loved. The decisive event always happens in a time prior to the present, a time prior to time.

If *Either/Or* throws doubt on idealist metaphysics, it is by identifying a certain temporal lag that cannot be eliminated from the very possibility of self-consciousness. It makes urgent the radical failure of self-consciousness to stand present at its own inceptual instant. The principal account of subjectivity, as self-positing, undergoes displacement via a *prior* beginning.

This is the point of view from which I approach the series of fragments that is *Either/Or*. Delimitations are necessary for a text that is inexhaustible. I restrict myself to analyzing only as much of the text as necessary to clarify its break with the identity thesis via the problematic of temporality. The decisive moment in A's critique of idealism is his analysis of the unhappy consciousness. A thinks this theme, one explicitly appropriated from Hegel, through to the bottom, to the point where self-consciousness knows itself as chained to something irreparable. The representational movement of consciousness—which is what modern philosophy identifies as the "interior"—comes, according to A's analyses, always either "too early" or "too late."

With proper qualification, it is possible to speak of the elaboration of a "transcendental" problematic in *Either/Or*. It is not, of course, a question of performing a Kantian-type transcendental deduction to show the necessity of an originary synthetic activity. What needs to be explained is not identity, but difference; not spontaneity, but failure; not freedom, but exposure. Whatever strategies A adopts in order to cope with the originary failure of the ego, he nevertheless arrives consistently at the heart of the problem: the temporal instant is not an effect of the ego's activity, but rather the opening that first allows an ego. Here there is a paradox that finally, we shall see, receives the name gift.

Before coming to the texts themselves, however, a brief word is necessary concerning the history of reading *Either/Or*, especially the first volume.[1] Overwhelmingly, the papers of A have been read in light of a religious teleology, namely as expressions of an inauthentic "stage" of existence, the "aesthetic" stage. One discovers there, it is argued, only the contours of an existential comportment, a "life-view," that has in fact already been surpassed by an ethical and religious point of view—namely, by the analyses of part two. The *truth* of A's life-view would be recoverable only in light of the ethical and finally religious telos of human existence. As such it remains untrue.

This reading is not wholly wrong. The fragmentary jumble of what Victor Eremita calls, alternately, "Papers, Posthumous Papers, Found Papers, Lost Papers" (*EO* 1:13; *SKS* 2:20) is, no doubt, thoroughly entangled in the architectonic of the stages. Yet one has to be clear about the role of stages in general within Kierkegaard's problematic. What the teleological reading finally loses sight of is that the aesthetic, for example, is not a stage of the *religious*, but of *existence*. There is a tendency to regard the aesthetic only from the point of view of the ethical or religious, in terms of what it will have meant from the ethical or religious life-view (considered as telos). Yet, like both the ethical and the religious, the aesthetic emerges on the background of, and in response to, the event of existence itself. The question for all of the stages is not simply how they relate to one another, how one follows from or emends the other, and so on, but also how they qualify existence. Each stage bears an original and autonomous relation to existence itself. In this sense, the problematic of existence emerges as separable from and, indeed, more original than that of the stages.

Recognizing the priority of the problematic of existence to that of the stages allows a new approach, in particular, to the papers of A. A's "aestheticism," however it is regarded by an ethical or religious point of view, in fact translates as a truly radical kind of questioning of foundations. Far from being able to ignore or deflect this, the ethical and religious points of view will be constrained constantly to presuppose it. Neither the ethical nor the religious know any different reality than the aesthetic; they know only a different response to that reality, the reality of an existence that cannot be systematized or teleologically ordered. Any teleology is *between* the stages or *in* the representations of the stages, not in existence "itself." Subjects project ends and fashion teleologies, but as A knows well (a knowledge repeated in the religious), existence can deprive subjects of their very power to exercise their subjectivity. That deprivation and failure is central to A's deconstruction of the idealist identity thesis. To this I turn.

TAUTOLOGY AND EXISTENCE: DIAPSALMATA

The papers of A begin with a number of fragments entitled "Diapsalmata." These set the tone for the whole first volume and articulate the problematic of existence as well as a certain kind of aestheticism that responds to it. The longest and most important fragment is the one that repeats the title of the volume: "Either/Or: An Ecstatic Discourse." What is at stake in this discourse is a certain "grounding principle" (*Grund-sætning*) that can be formulated only in the most aporetic terms.

The fragment begins elaborating a series of double binds: "Marry, and you will regret it. Do not marry, and you will also regret it. Marry or do not marry, you will regret it either way. . . . Hang yourself, and you will regret it. Do not hang yourself, and you will also regret it. Hang yourself or do not hang yourself, you will regret it either way. . . . This, gentlemen, is the quintessence of all the wisdom of life" (*EO* 1:38; *SKS* 2:47). Either/or, it does not matter: this could go on ad infinitum. The double-bind situation A pushes to the extreme is a familiar one: to choose something will always also mean *not* to choose its opposite. Choice entails letting go a possibility just as much as taking one up. Unactualized possibility does not disappear; it haunts every subsequent moment, threatening the choice with the possibility of its repeal. The opposite of decision is not indecision, but regret, which threatens decision at its very core by insinuating itself between the subject who has decided and what he has decided about. It threatens to alienate the subject from his own decision. A's aesthetic "wisdom" constitutes an attempt to avoid this alienation by sublating it, or rather neutralizing it, in advance—namely, through the paradox of a suspension of all decision. Never to decide, neither deciding nor not deciding, leaves nothing to regret. A's either/or is thus in reality a neither/nor. It articulates a point of absolute indifference between opposites.

Such practical wisdom is one thing, but the basis of this wisdom is another. The discourse seeks to ground itself upon a grounding proposition (*Grund-sætning*). It seeks to grasp the double bind of regret vis-à-vis some deeper foundation. Here is where the problematic of existence opens up as inseparable from A's aestheticism, but nevertheless as distinct. A traces the double bind of regret back to a fracture in the very idea of beginning: there is an essential difference between beginning as something posited, a "departure point" for a deciding subject, and beginning as something that befalls one, something non-posited. These two cannot be synchronized, which will mean that to begin at an absolute origin, in full consciousness, is impossible. Nothing can ever be done without having first to backtrack. Hence, there will always be a remainder to feed regret.

At stake in the diapsalmata, then, will be something like the transcendental conditions for any departure (*Gaaenuderfra*), any choice. To choose signifies to inaugurate a temporality, a "before" and "after." Choice shapes the meaning of the past by casting it in light of a future possibility. The present emerges as time lived in light of choice, vis-à-vis a future expectation and in separation from a past state of affairs. This relationship between choice and the inauguration of a temporality leads A to formulate his own aesthetic solution to the double bind of regret in terms of a suspended, or sublated, temporality: "It is not merely in isolated moments that I, as Spinoza says, view everything *aeterno modo,* but I am continually *aeterno modo*" (*EO* 1:39; *SKS* 2:48). Radically suspending decision, A seeks to live a temporality without any inceptual instant, without the cut or discontinuity choice brings, without before or after. He exists in a suspended time, a quasi-eternity, or an eternity prior to any temporality: "for the true eternity does not lie behind either/or but before it" (*EO* 1:39; *SKS* 2:48).

One will object to A's wisdom: to suspend all choice, is that not itself a choice? Wouldn't the choice not to choose involve the same double bind of regret? Undoubtedly. Yet A makes a distinction between his "grounding proposition" and any "point of departure" (*Gaaenuderfra*): "[W]hen I say my fundamental principle is not a point of departure for me, this does not have the opposite of being a point of departure" (*EO* 1:39; *SKS* 2:48). A point of departure would signify a beginning whose meaning is controlled by a projected end, a principial beginning. In these terms, to suspend all decision would be a point of departure, a project. Yet the proposition that lies at the ground of A's thinking, he indicates, refers neither to a departure nor to a non-departure. It retreats to a point prior to departure and non-departure, prior to the opposition between choosing and not choosing.

One cannot say, then, that A chooses not to choose. Certainly A takes a path in thinking that can be characterized as a movement toward the ground. He departs, specifically, from a *certain conception of departure*. Thus A's "principle" can be formulated only in the most aporetic terms. He writes: "But for those listeners who are able to follow me, although I do not move, I shall now elucidate the eternal truth by which this philosophy is self-contained and does not concede anything higher. That is, if I made my maxim a point of departure, then I would be unable to stop, for if I did not stop, I would regret it, and if I did stop, I would also regret it, etc. But if I never start, then I can always stop, for my eternal starting (*Udgang*) is my eternal stopping (*Ophør*)" (*EO* 1:39; *SKS* 2:58). A moves back, then, to an event, an eternal departing that nevertheless eternally stops short of departing. His "principle" involves a parting that does not depart.

It would be tempting to read this identity of departing and stopping short, of beginning and ending, dialectically, so that every beginning would *in itself* be an ending and every ending would *in itself* be a beginning. A would be then pointing out, with Hegel, how the very notions of beginning and ending are necessarily co-implicated. Yet we have already been waived off from a Hegelian reading: "Many believe that they, too, [exist *aeterno modo*] when after doing one thing or another they unite or mediate these opposites. But this is a misunderstanding, for the true eternity does not lie behind either/or but before it" (*EO* 1:39; *SKS* 2:58). In fact, what lies at the ground for A—an eternal starting/stopping—explodes the dialectical, mediated notion of identity. Against mediation A raises a tautological principle, one purely "self-contained" and "self-comprehending," and so both uncontainable and incomprehensible from outside itself. It is a "principle," in reality a paradox or aporia, with no determinate or representable content: "If one or another of my esteemed listeners thinks there is anything to what I have said, it merely proves he has no head for philosophy" (*EO* 1:39; *SKS* 2:58). No speculative content can be drawn forth from this grounding proposition.

Nevertheless, one can think *around* the tautological identity of beginning and ending. For example, one could say A's principle—an eternal departure that nevertheless eternally stops short—signifies a beginning that is nevertheless *not* a beginning. A beginning without a beginning: in other words, a beginning that is nothing like the beginning a subject posits. A posited beginning is dialectically identical to its projected end: the beginning only really is once it shows itself as the beginning of a determinate, that is, concluded, process. Yet what attracts A's thinking is a beginning that never *departs toward* any end, a beginning doubled upon itself, a pure departure absolved from any determinate goals. Such would be an ab-solute or anarchic beginning.

One could think in proximity to this anarchic beginning in another way: one could say it enunciates the paradox of an eternal incipience, an "about-to-be" that never becomes. Suspended eternally between departure and arrival, beginning and ending, a *present* never opens up. An anarchic beginning would be prior to all presence. Or rather, what is at stake would be the very opening of the present. The instant of inception itself takes no time; it gives time. The initial opening of time could never itself become a moment within time. It would therefore be, precisely, a departure that would always already have ceased prior to, and as the condition of, the present: consequently, an eternal departure that is simultaneously an eternal stopping short.

A's "grounding proposition," then, does nothing other than enunciate the difference between the temporality of departures, where a subject projects an end and posits itself as the origin of a temporal process, and a more radical departure that cannot be formulated in temporal, representational, or subjective terms. That irreducible difference *is* his "principle." And it is also the ultimate root of the double bind of regret. Regret emerges as an essential and unavoidable possibility, afflicting the very possibility of decision and every either/or, only insofar as every intentional departure will discover that it always departs from something it did not posit—namely, with respect to an always prior ("eternal") departure. The effect of this is that, as soon as one chooses, one will be constrained to contend with much one did not choose. To choose will always also be to choose the non-chosen; there will always be a foundation for regret.

The difference between the beginning mediated by the intentionality of a subject and the always prior, anarchic beginning is at the origin of the characteristic moods enunciated in the diapsalmata: indolence, melancholy, boredom, anxiety, irony. All of these phenomena indicate the condition of a subject as subjected to the prior beginning, and thus deprived of its power to master temporality in project: "Time passes, life is a stream, etc., so people say. That is not what I find: time stands still, and so do I. All the plans I project fly straight back at me" (*EO* 1:26; *SKS* 2:34). Sensing its own radical failure to dominate time, the subject is drawn back, in mood, to the quasi-eternity of reality "standing still," as non-integratable into the temporality of projects—reality as a departure without any goal or end.

In this light, a teleological or archeo-teleological interpretation of reality, such as one finds with Hegel, can only appear as the effort to erect an ideal foundation *over* the anarchic beginning. Idealism places an intentionality, a projecting will, at the origin of the real; it thinks self-positing sub-jectivity as the re-presentable foundation. The crack between the beginning posited in project and the anarchic beginning, however, reappears in terms of a certain interminability: "Experience shows that it is not at all difficult for philosophy to begin. Far from it. It begins, in fact, with nothing and therefore can always begin. But it is always difficult for philosophy and philosophers to stop" (*EO* 1:39; *SKS* 2:58). Philosophy as a recovery of foundations is threatened with endlessness: which also means, threatened by an uncontrolled beginning.

The subtitle of these diapsalmata is *ad se ipsum,* "to himself." It starts to become clear that the beginning without beginning clarified in contrast to any ideal origin can be thought as the subject "itself." That is to say, A's di-apsalmata gesture to the way in which the subject is unable to execute a *de-parture from itself.* Subjectivity is a continual going-forth to meet the world that, nevertheless, remains absolutely unable to depart from itself. The sub-ject has the uniquely tautological characteristic of being stuck to itself. One can see here again the root of A's somber indolence: action into the world in the form of projects and resolutions does not constitute a true departure, but merely an unending return to the same. Either/or, it does not matter, for wherever one goes, one finds oneself.

A's ecstatic discourse, then, opens up the critical difference between the anarchic and ideal beginning. In so doing it brings to the fore something re-pressed in idealist texts: what is endless in reality, what resists incorporation into projects, what ruptures teleology. In the end, however, this may only be to insist upon the phenomenological ultimates of birth and death: "no one asks when one wants to come in; no one asks when one wants to go out" (*EO* 1:26; *SKS* 2:34). Natality and mortality, to invoke the terms of Reiner Schürmann, demand a thinking that respects an ab-solute, non-positable departure.[2]

These themes acquire greater concretion in the various papers of A. They are brought to their sharpest pitch, however, in the analysis of un-happy consciousness, to which I now turn.

UNHAPPY CONSCIOUSNESS

In the economy of Hegel's *Phenomenology of Spirit* the "Unhappy Con-sciousness" constitutes the final formation of self-consciousness before its transition to reason. Undergoing the experience of its own nonbeing, find-ing its essential being outside of it, consciousness finally breaks through to the experience of the certainty that it is "in itself Absolute Essence."[3] This formation therefore prepares consciousness for the breakthrough of the concept, the birth of idealism: "Reason is the certainty of consciousness that it is all reality; thus does idealism express its Notion."[4] The identity of inner and outer itself comes to consciousness.

In the history of Kierkegaard interpretation, especially on the issue of his relationship to Hegel, the question of the unhappy consciousness has always held an important place. Beginning with Sartre, Kierkegaard has been read as maintaining the essentially insurmountable character of the unhappy consciousness.[5] From this point of view, as Ricoeur points out, two different conclusions can be reached: either that Hegel pre-compre-hended the entirety of the Kierkegaardian position, thus sublating it, or that Kierkegaard comprehends the totality of the Hegelian position, ren-dering it incompletable.[6] This way of framing the issue is essentially cor-rect. What requires further consideration, however, is how Kierkegaard, for his part, thinks to penetrate more deeply into Hegel's position than Hegel himself had.

The essay titled "The Unhappiest One" explicitly recalls Hegel's discus-sion of unhappy consciousness. The aim of the essay is to push unhappi-ness beyond the point where it could be reintegrated back into a structure of satisfaction. "Ah! Happy," writes A, "is the one who has nothing more to do with the subject than to write a paragraph about it; even happier the one who can write the next" (*EO* 1:222; *SKS* 2:216). The implication is that the next paragraph in Hegel's *Phenomenology of Spirit*—the transition to the concept, to self-consciousness certain of itself—cannot be written if the unhappy consciousness is attended to with rigor.

As Alastair Hannay suggests, Kierkegaard's positive estimation of un-happy consciousness has a religious motive in the desire to maintain tran-scendence or alterity in face of Hegelian absolute knowledge.[7] Philosophical-ly what is at stake is the desire for phenomenological adequacy concerning the situation of existence. Specifically, A's essay "The Unhappiest One" traces the phenomenon of unhappiness back to the constitution of the tem-poral instant. Unhappiness affects consciousness, not merely as a contin-gent mood that befalls it now and then, but rather in terms of the very con-ditions for its possibility as temporal. This is finally why talk of surpassing unhappy consciousness is, for A, idle.

We can begin with Hegel's analysis in the *Phenomenology of Spirit*. He-gel follows the agony of self-consciousness in its sense of estrangement from the world through stoicism, skepticism, and the unhappy consciou-sness to the point, finally, where the dialectic turns and "the *existence* of the world becomes for self-consciousness its own *truth* and *presence*."[8] Con-sciousness at length understands the world, which is solid, determinate, and intelligible, as the scene of its fulfillment; the vagaries of alienation vanish before the hard and stable ground of worldly reality. Yet its sense of itself as irreducible to the world is the presupposition of this knowledge. The sense of irreducibility culminates in the unhappy consciousness. The latter is at bottom a religious formation for Hegel too insofar as, knowing its difference from the world, it grasps its essence—its fulfillment and its measure—as a "beyond." For the unhappy consciousness, absolute essence is strictly *transcendent:* "For the unhappy consciousness, the in-itself is the beyond of itself."[9] Unhappy consciousness knows itself explicitly as a lack of essential being, a void of essence. Yet, Hegel argues, this *knowledge* brings it into contradiction with itself: "*Unhappy Consciousness* is the consciousness of self as a dual-natured, merely contradictory being."[10] Consciousness is for itself contradictory: on the one hand it grasps the truth of its being in "the Unchangeable," while at the same time it knows itself precisely as the "protean Changeable." The essence of self-consciousness is to be identical to itself amidst the flux of existence. Kant had already formulated this necessity in terms of the unity of apperception. Nevertheless such identity cannot be grasped in any determinate way and so is pushed into a "beyond." Moreover, self-consciousness knows itself equally as a flux of sensations, the protean changeable.

The unhappiness of consciousness is not to be able to synthesize these two essential "facts" about itself into a coherent, unifying self-conception. Since it knows itself as both, consciousness cannot reconcile itself to itself. It becomes self-alienated and divided against itself: "since for it both are equally essential and contradictory, it is merely the contradictory movement in which one opposite does not come to rest in *its* opposite, but in it only produces itself afresh as an opposite."[11] Unhappy consciousness is thus unrest: it can *be* neither the one nor the other, since the consciousness of its protean changeableness continually interrupts its consciousness of its unchangeableness, and vice versa. It knows itself as both and neither. This unrest is its alienation. In Sartre's admirable formulation: it is what it is not and it is not what it is.

That is the general structure of the unhappy consciousness that A lifts out of the *Phenomenology of Spirit.* He writes: "The unhappy one is the person who in one way or another has his ideal, the substance of his life, the plenitude of his consciousness, his essential nature, outside himself. The unhappy one is the person who is always absent from himself, never present to himself. . . . The whole territory of the unhappy consciousness is thereby adequately circumscribed" (*EO* 1:222; *SKS* 2:216). The question will be how to evaluate this non-presence. Beyond the general structure of unhappiness, however, Hegel's account interweaves important intricacies that Kierkegaard alludes to. In particular, Hegel distinguishes between the Jewish and the Christian forms of unhappy consciousness.[12] The Jewish form rests in the sense of the absolute difference between divine and human, an alienation that is inscribed in the Law and historically effective in the exile.

The Christian form, by contrast, proceeds from the consciousness of the Incarnation as the moment of the mediation of the divine and the human, the Unchangeable and the Changeable. Unhappiness arises on the ground of the specifically Christian consciousness insofar as consciousness of the Incarnation is at first only "immediate," that is, it has its object in something merely historical, particular, and objective (the historical Christ). Christian consciousness knows that the Unchangeable divests itself of its beyondness and manifests in the reality of finitude; however, insofar as the Unchangeable appears under the form of its opposite, it is nowhere more hidden and nowhere more *beyond* that when it becomes near in this way. Thus Christian consciousness undergoes an exacerbation of estrangement.

Hegel follows this dialectic across Christian consciousness in its attempt to realize its unity with the object of its desire, that is, the Incarnation, which it grasps, correctly, as its true measure. However, at first it grasps its measure as something merely exterior, and thus it falls into the same contradiction with itself as before. Unhappy consciousness within Christian consciousness reaches its point of greatest contradiction, for Hegel, with the experience of the *disappearance* of the divine: the consciousness of the divine, absolute essence, as no longer present, already gone. To have vanished is a greater negation than never to have appeared. Self-consciousness, confronting the disappearance of its object, arrives too late to coincide with its essence. The *empty tomb* of Christ becomes the very emblem of this relation between consciousness and its essential truth: it stands over against emptiness; the very objectivity of its object has vanished, leaving it with absolutely "nothing" to hold to. The empty tomb of Christ is thus the "grave of its [i.e., consciousness's] truth";[13] the grave holds its truth, and its truth is nonbeing and alienation.

For Hegel, however, the experience consciousness undergoes with itself in being deprived of its support in an object, the experience of the "beyond," becomes the condition for the interiorization of truth. Losing its object, consciousness now understands *itself* explicitly as the locus of the mediation of "pure thought" (i.e., absolute self-consciousness) and "individuality." Mediation is driven to the interior of self-consciousness, becoming self-consciousness's concept of itself. Unhappy consciousness thus gives way, as indicated, to reason, "the certainty of consciousness that it is all reality."

Traversing this ground, "The Unhappiest One" presents a series of stages of unhappy consciousness, ending with a position that falls finally outside of the dialectic development Hegel traces. At the center of this presentation, once again, is an empty tomb, wherein lies the unhappiest one. Yet the empty tomb is no longer "the sacred sepulchre in the happy East, but the mournful grave in the unhappy West" (*EO* 1:220; *SKS* 2:213). Unhappiness cannot be dismissed as a figure of the past. Rather, it constitutes the reality of the present in the West.

At the outset, one should note the intrinsically contradictory nature of an *unhappiest* one. Who could claim to be the unhappiest? For any determinate situation of unhappiness, is it not possible to think of some even worse situation? The idea of an unhappi*est* one seems as contradictory as that of a maximal number. At issue, however, is not any "particular individual . . . [but rather] a class" (*EO* 1:222; *SKS* 2:215). In fact, a structure of consciousness is at issue. The unhappiness is not to be understood quantitatively, in terms of degrees, but qualitatively, in terms of the essence of consciousness. The push to discover the maximal formation of unhappiness, in other words, ought to be read as an effort to discover the conditions of any and all unhappiness. At stake are the conditions for the possibility of unhappiness in general.

A proceeds in this analysis by a process of separating and categorizing. He first rules out for consideration those who fear death: "we know of a worse calamity, and first and last, above all—it is to live" (*EO* 1:220; *SKS* 2:214). To fear death is simply to oppose life to death. Yet the unhappiness at issue involves a death that inheres in life itself, a death the self-consciousness cannot cease to undergo (a death that lives). In these terms Hegel had already, correctly in A's judgment, identified unhappiness as consciousness divided against itself, capable of representing its fulfillment only in an unattainable beyond. A appropriates Hegel, but translates his schematic in terms of temporality: "The unhappy one is the person who is always absent to himself, never present to himself. But in being absent, one obviously can be in either past or future time" (*EO* 1:222; *SKS* 2:216). One's life can be absent from the present by way of hope (*Haab*) or recollection (*Erindring*). Each relates to its object as absent. Nevertheless, the object of hope and recollection, though in one sense absent, can in another sense be present: namely, in the past present or future present tense. If consciousness can relate to a past moment as one in which it was present to itself, and hence as recollectable, or to a future moment in which it is present to itself in an anticipatory mode, it is not in the decisive sense unhappy: "strictly speaking, one cannot call an individuality unhappy who is present in hope or in recollection" (*EO* 1:223; *SKS* 2:216). Neither the past-present nor the future-present breaks up the basic structure of consciousness: *presence*.

For Hegel's phenomenological observer, we have seen, unhappiness, though constituting a tear in the fabric of presence, constitutes a dialectical transition to its certainty of itself, its presence to itself. A's perspective, though similarly taking shape as a phenomenological observation, differs sharply at this point. What interests A are phenomena that do not, and cannot, constitute a proper phenomenality, phenomena that remain indeterminate, at thresholds of presence, and so cannot properly be thought as *experiences* of a subject. Certain quasi-experiences become central.

Thus, unhappy consciousness comes to signify a relation in which consciousness, hoping or recollecting, is unable to bring its fulfilling object to determinateness, or to resolve an object at all. A cites an example:

> But if I were to imagine a person who had had no childhood himself, since this age had passed him by without real meaning, but who now, for example, by becoming a teacher of children, discovered all the beauty in childhood and now wanted to recollect his own childhood, always stared back at it, he would certainly be a very appropriate example. He would discover backwards the meaning of that which was past for him and which he nevertheless wanted to recollect in all its meaning. (*EO* 1:224–25; *SKS* 2:218)

The need to recollect a past that was never a present, never lived through and interiorized, is in the strict sense a formation of unhappiness because one recollects only a void. Recollected content, the substance of one's desire, remains in a beyond. In the example cited the unhappy one has lived a childhood without living it *as* a childhood—and now it is gone forever. What is recollectable is only the impossibility of recollection. One could imagine something similar relating to hope: for example, the scenario of hoping for what one can no longer regard as a real possibility.

Unhappiness, then, will refer to the failure of either recollection or hope to bring an object to presence. Yet even here, a delimitation is called for: the unhappiest one "will always have to be sought among *recollection's* unhappy individualities" (*EO* 1:225, my italics; *SKS* 2:218). This is because, he writes, "past time has the notable characteristic that it is past; future time, that it is to come. In a sense, therefore, one can say that future time is closer to the present than is the past" (*EO* 1:224; SKS 2:217). In the process of separating and categorizing forms of unhappiness, this constitutes an ontological intervention. Future and past are assigned fundamentally different regions of being: the future, though not present, has greater *proximity* to the present owing to its imminence. The past has less proximity simply because it will not return. In these terms, only one who has suffered the trauma of an irrecuperable event, whose life remains dominated by an event that cannot be interiorized—only such a one could qualify as the most unhappy. The discourse thus moves steadily toward thematizing an irrecuperable event that, as such, will always already have taken place, but that nonetheless will absolutely stamp the character of self-consciousness.

As A proceeds, it becomes clear where the misfortune lies: self-consciousness comes to forget or occlude "originary" temporality in favor of representable time and so puts itself out of alignment with the totality of time. A says: "[The unhappiest one's] calamity is that he came into the world too early and therefore continually comes too late" (*EO* 1:225; *SKS* 2:218–19). Consciousness undergoes an untimely birth in such a way that "it is turned the wrong way in two directions: what he is hoping for lies behind him; what he is recollecting lies ahead of him" (*EO* 1:225; *SKS* 2:218–19). Something of the destiny of the West, the unhappy West, is at stake here.

The unhappiest one recollects the future and hopes for the past. On the one hand, he relates to the future only in terms of what can be anticipated of it. He has always "already encompassed the future in thought" (*EO* 1:225; *SKS* 2:218–19). On the other hand, he continually hopes for a possibility that will always already have faded, a possibility now well past. Vincent McCarthy describes this condition as "suffering acutely from conflicting temporal ecstasies."[14] As A puts it: "it is recollection that prevents him from becoming present in his hope and it is hope that prevents him from becoming present in his recollection. . . . Thus, what he is hoping for lies behind him; what he recollects lies ahead of him. His life is not backwards but is turned the wrong way in two directions. He will soon perceive his trouble even though he does not comprehend the reason for it" (*EO* 1:225; *SKS* 2:218–19). It would not be inappropriate to consider the essay on the unhappiest one as a phenomenology of trauma. A traumatic rupture presents the kind of irrecuperability and secondary effects that this analysis elucidates. The trauma is less an experience than a quasi-experience, for what defines trauma is a tear in the fabric of presence itself. Consciousness is exposed to more than it can integrate and, unlike the experience of the sublime, does not recuperate itself in a secondary moment. The effect of the traumatic event is a dephasing of consciousness from its own temporality: the temporal "now" is no longer lived as an integral moment, relating to past-present and future-present, but placed out of time and out of being.

Or simply outside: and that means, without content or significance—and yet this "without," a forgotten element, dominates and dephases the present. So, for example, the traumatic past in the strict sense has not yet arrived since it was never experienced; it still lies in the future insofar as its meaning is not determinate. What it was is still to come. One thus hopes to be able to recollect. At the same time, the only future one has is a future that adheres to the past, an always prior future that no longer is; hope is a mere recollection. Memory annihilates hope, and hope memory. The present is voided of significance. One cannot *be* anything. Such dephasing constitutes a derangement, but the unhappiness lies precisely in that the person does not go mad.

If we, as phenomenological observers, come to the root of unhappiness, then, it will be seen as an originary failure to recollect, that is, to *establish presence*. Self-consciousness cannot recollect its own genesis; it cannot interiorize the temporality through which the present first comes to be. Originary temporality traumatically rests upon it. It comes to feel this rupture only in terms of a continual "misunderstanding [that] intervenes and in an odd way ridicules him at every moment" (*EO* 1:225; *SKS* 2:218–19). Temporality itself, namely, appears in its alterity as a "you" with whom he cannot come into agreement. His relationship to temporality as such and as a whole is identical in form to two people who are continually talking past each other. It is a ludicrous arrangement, enough to drive him mad, and yet his unhappiness is precisely that his is unable to *go* mad, that is, to tap the foundation of misunderstanding.[15]

The unhappiness of the unhappiest one, then, signifies a certain madness that persists at the very heart of lucid self-consciousness,[16] a madness that presents itself in the experience of the alterity of time. In fact, to be more precise, there is a remarkable irony here: the very power of self-consciousness to constitute reality, to recollect and anticipate, to keep itself present to itself amidst the displacements of time—the general power of re-presentation—renders self-consciousness powerless in face of originary or non-positable time. Its power is what renders it powerless. This is where something of the destiny of the modern West, that is, the metaphysics of the subject, is at stake.

A continues his presentation of the figure of the unhappiest one:

> His life knows no repose and has no content. He is not present to himself in the instant. . . . He cannot grow old, for he has never been young; he cannot become young, for he has already grown old; in a sense he cannot die, for indeed he has not lived; in a sense he cannot live, for indeed he is already dead . . . he has no passion, not because he lacks it, but because at the same instant he has the opposite passion; he does not have time for anything, not because his time is filled with something else, but because he has no time at all (*EO* 1:226, altered; *SKS* 2:219).

He has no time at all but lives within an endless quasi-eternity, continually *on the verge* of being and nonbeing, on the verge of a beginning, without ever beginning. The situation is "continually as someone giving birth" (*bestandig som en fødende*), who is yet "unable to give birth" (*EO* 1:226, altered; *SKS* 2:219). The unhappiness here is to be held back in a time prior to time, that is, prior to the formation of any ecstatic relation to future or past. The unhappiest one can neither be nor not be; his existence, in its very positivity, falls *between* being and nonbeing. To exist, in other words, would most originally mean *not* to be able to live beyond oneself. The structures of intentionality, project, ecstasis—which allow one to make a beginning, to inaugurate a temporality around oneself—are undercut by a more originary temporality that cannot be integrated within the re-presentational work of self-consciousness. Such originary time, involving the event whereby the subject is given to itself, would burden self-consciousness as an endlessness, a formlessness—namely, as something non-posited.

This figure of unhappiness, unlike Hegel's, does not turn a *dialectical* corner and give way to fulfillment. But why not? Here, the "dialectic" involves an endless production of contradiction, without telos, insofar as the temporality that begins in positing can never be reconciled with originary time. The beginning whereby there is existence and the beginning that posits a temporality (that is, a relation to a representable future and past) cannot be reconciled. The most basic contradiction of existence is not between the unchangeable and the changeable, or being and nonbeing, but rather between what falls prior to both being and nonbeing (originary time) and what can be captured in those terms (the temporality of project, or posited time). The unhappiness of the unhappiest one witnesses to this non-dialectical difference. And the unhappiest one lives bewildered by contradiction: every passion luring him into project must necessarily produce a counter-passion—namely, as the effort to supplement the failure of the project to deliver the ego from endless time. How helpless he is, trying to master originary time by positing and counter-positing, by making the contradiction dialectical! In spite of what Hegel suggests, contradiction does not promote development. There is no next paragraph.

Unless this is one: "Farewell, then, you unhappiest one! But what am I saying—'the unhappiest'? I ought to say 'the happiest,' for this is indeed precisely a gift of fortune that no one can give himself. See, language breaks down, and thought is confused, for who indeed is the happiest but the unhappiest and who the unhappiest but the happiest" (*EO* 1:230; *SKS* 2:223). In a note in his papers Kierkegaard added to this: "One may think the exclamation 'the unhappiest one is the happiest' is a rhetorical turn. By no means, it is a turn in the thought; for to be the unhappiest person is actually a gift no one can give himself" (*Pap.* IV A 227). This "turn in the thought," or "dialectical" reversal, has to be considered carefully. The *truth* of the unhappiest one is that he is the happiest one. But in what sense? Does this reprise the moment in Hegel's analysis of the unhappy consciousness in which self-consciousness discovers its relation to the absolute through the experience of its loss? That it discovers itself precisely amidst its own negation?

Not quite. Any critical distance from Hegel here is lodged in the word "gift." The absolute loss subjectivity undergoes is its exposure to originary time. Temporality cannot be interiorized within the representational work of self-consciousness. It remains a gift, which, registering the unrecollectable, cannot be appropriated within the ego's presence to itself. It is not here a question, as in Hegel, of an unhappiness that *gives way* to happiness, but rather of a happiness that is identical to unhappiness. Happiness *is* unhappiness and unhappiness *is* happiness. It is in these terms that "language bursts, and thought is confused" (*EO* 1:230, slightly altered; *SKS* 2:223). The bursting of language and the bewilderment of thought, rather than "the certainty of consciousness that it is all reality" (Hegel), thus culminate the movement of unhappy consciousness.[17]

If we are to think about this rupture in language and thought in terms of which the reversal happens, we can see it as moving thought back to a point prior to the distinction between happiness and unhappiness that self-consciousness itself draws as a work of language. Self-consciousness, along with the metaphysics that elevates it to the role of ground, can think of happiness only in terms of its fulfillment, its presence to itself. It prioritizes fulfillment over nonfulfillment. Indeed, fulfillment is taken as the very gesture of the real. Yet A thinks fulfilled self-consciousness to the end, where it shows itself as contentless, vacuous hell. The real is neither fulfillment nor nonfulfillment, but the gift of the present in which language bursts and thought is bewildered. A brings thought to the point where it becomes necessary to think unhappiness as a "gift of fortune," as itself the consummate moment. For beyond the polarity happiness/unhappiness, the gift of unhappiness, or of suffering, signifies the opening of self-consciousness to its outside: to the alterity of time. Such exposure constitutes simultaneously the condition for the possibility of all suffering and all joy. Idealist self-consciousness, interpreting subjectivity egologically, occludes this vulnerability and exposure; it turns the subject out of itself in the very effort to interiorize time. A madness is introduced under the surface of a vast normality.

BOREDOM:
REPRESENTATION RUPTURED

"The Rotation of Crops: A Venture in a Theory of Social Prudence" continues A's analysis of temporality and its relation to self-consciousness. The core phenomenon he meditates upon in the essay is boredom. Not unlike Heidegger later,[18] Kierkegaard's author treats boredom, albeit humorously, as a phenomenon in which the metaphysical problem of negation can be approached.[19] Boredom "has to the highest degree the repelling force always required in the negative" (*EO* 1:285; *SKS* 2:275). Not only this, but within boredom being *as a whole*, being as no-thing, is disclosed in its abyssal distinction from beings: "Boredom rests upon the nothing that interlaces existence" (*EO* 1:291; *SKS* 2:280). Inevitably, then, the essay becomes a commentary upon the problem of ontological difference and the beginning of philosophy.

In the "Rotation of Crops" the famous aestheticism of A becomes most apparent. The very decision to treat boredom, not only in light of the problem of negation, but indeed as the "root of all evil" (*EO* 1:285; *SKS* 2:275), betrays the interests of an aesthete. Yet it would be a mistake to treat the essay as the mere extravagances of an aesthete. In fact, A articulates a rigorous problematic: he thinks representational consciousness at its limit. What is at stake is to think the possibility of bringing temporality as such and as a whole under the "maximal supervision of recollection (*Erindringen*)" (*EO* 1:295; *SKS* 2:284). In other words, can one imagine the recollection, not of some past datum, but of the present itself? Can one imagine the present as reduced to re-presentation, as interiorized? Everything will depend upon "how one experiences actuality" (*EO* 1:293; *SKS* 2:282).

As a phenomenon, boredom discloses the abyss, or *Afgrund*, of being as a whole in its distinction from beings. In the language A employs, boredom is a qualification of pantheism: "Boredom is the demonic pantheism" (*EO* 1:290; *SKS* 2:279). This totality factor manifests itself in terms of an excess of subjectivity to the entire domain of *economy*, a domain constituted by the polarity of work (*Arbeid*) and leisure (*Moro*). Neither work nor leisure adequately addresses the root cause of boredom: the difference between the temporality of projects (of work and leisure) and temporality as such and as a whole, that is, the temporality of existence. In boredom temporality shows itself, initially at least, as in excess to the meaning it acquires through self-consciousness; it shows itself as nothing. One has "too much time," and this excess burdens self-consciousness.

"The Rotation of Crops" is acutely aware of temporal difference (the difference between projected time and originary time). Yet the whole thrust of the experiment is to consider whether and how this can be deflected, whether and how self-consciousness can retain its presence to itself, its founding relation to itself. In this sense A's "rotation method" signifies an effort to put the transcendentally self-present ego to work in a concrete way—namely, by repressing any temporality that cannot be brought under the power of re-presentation. A's aestheticism is nothing but a working out of the egology of modern metaphysics.

Thus the goal of the crop rotation method, to sketch it briefly, consists in avoiding becoming entangled in time by inwardly disengaging oneself from any experience that would make consciousness vulnerable to what it cannot posit. Specifically, this mandates an inward abstention from the commitments of friendship, work, and marriage[20]—not necessarily through a simple detachment, but through a detachment amidst these commitments. Each of these, which are exemplary of "the ethical," involves something like a promise: the ordination of oneself toward a future that cannot be wholly anticipated. Beyond deflecting these forms of ethical life, however, what finally must be "cultivated" through crop rotation is a detachment from the temporal instant itself. The temporal instant, time in its originary breaking forth, must be brought under the "maximal supervision of recollection (*Erindringen*)" (*EO* 1:295; *SKS* 2:284).

Recollection is time as *interiorized,* as re-presented. What A seeks to achieve with his method, then, is precisely what was diagnosed as the source of suffering of the unhappiest one: the reduction of temporality to the representative function of consciousness. Temporality is the deep threat to preserving a founding relation to self. As the previous essay has shown, temporality (originary time) is the non-negatable negation that rends consciousness from itself; it is the point at which the subject is exposed to the "outside" in general and thus the condition for the possibility of its being vulnerable. A does not propose a simple negation of temporality, but rather its "complete suspension" (*EO* 1:295; *SKS* 2:284). At least he grasps the problem radically.

The method he proposes involves shearing away, or letting go, whatever of time cannot be brought under the supervision of recollection. In other words, he proposes an originary forgetting, or a forgetting of the originary, as the obverse side of establishing the dominance of recollection. "It is between these two currents," between recollecting and forgetting, he says, "that all life moves, and therefore it is a matter of having them properly under one's control" (*EO* 1:292; *SKS* 2:282). Yet A grasps with full clarity that both recollecting and forgetting are threshold events, not entirely mediated by the intentional structure of consciousness. The instant of forgetfulness is a lapse, a stealing away. Similarly, recollection is subject to the nonvoluntary: beyond one's intention, a forgotten event can return "with the full force of the sudden" (*EO* 1:294; *SKS* 2:284).

Both forgetting and recollecting, then, are exposed to a temporality that withdraws from the present and thus from supervision of self-consciousness. This is exactly why they have to be taken in hand and put to systematic use. In this regard it is most essential to cultivate an originary forgetting, an exclusion, of everything that might interrupt the control over itself self-consciousness maintains. Toward this end a certain exertion is required: "to forget is an art that must be practiced in advance. To be able to forget always depends upon how one remembers, but how one remembers depends upon how one experiences actuality (*Virkeligheden*)" (*EO* 1:293; *SKS* 2:282). Avoiding exposure to time *as anarchy,* then, would require constituting actuality from the ground up. This would replay, at the level of a concrete praxis, the very movement Kant seeks to justify in the transcendental deductions of *The Critique of Pure Reason:* the production of the unity of self-consciousness, of experience, according to laws (a priori).[21] Indeed, although A's essay flagrantly violates Kant's strictures against conflating the transcendental and the empirical, he does seek explicitly to grasp that "Archimedean point," fashioned around a recollection that forgets, in terms of which inner and outer are identical: "In this way, forgetting and recollecting are identical, and the artistically achieved identity is the Archimedean point with which one lifts the whole world" (*EO* 1:295; *SKS* 2:284).

The identity of forgetting and recollecting expresses a work of the imagination, a work of poiesis: "The more poetically one remembers, the more easily one forgets, for to remember poetically is actually only an expression for forgetting" (*EO* 1:293; *SKS* 2:282). Poiesis, then, is meant to exercise an a priori function of *constituting* actuality: through it, one "reduces experience to a sounding board (*Resonansbund*)" and is able to "play shuttlecock with all existence" (*EO* 1:294; *SKS* 2:283). In short, the poetizing interiorization of reality allows a continual deflection of its alterity— that is, how it cannot be reduced to terms of representation. Concretely, the suggested "art of forgetting" proceeds by allowing a purely contingent element to function as an ideal origin, or ground, of a given phenomenal field. A's example:

> There was a man whose chatter I was obliged to listen to because of the circumstances. On every occasion, he was ready with a little philosophical lecture that was extremely boring. On the verge of despair, I suddenly discovered that the man perspired exceptionally much when he spoke. This perspiration now absorbed my attention. I watched how the pearls of perspiration collected on his forehead, then united in a rivulet, slid down his nose, and ended in a quivering globule that remained suspended at the end of his nose. From that moment on, everything was changed.(*EO* 1:299; *SKS* 2:288)

One's whole approach is organized around something arbitrary: "one considers the whole of existence from this [arbitrary] standpoint; one lets its reality run aground on this" (*EO* 1:293; *SKS* 2:282). The attempted reversal here is obvious: rather than allowing self-consciousness to run aground on reality (as happens in the threshold events of involuntary forgetting and remembering), reality is supposed to run aground on self-consciousness. Self-consciousness is to remain the constitutive origin of phenomena, the arché, via its poetic, interiorizing power.

I have already mentioned the Kantian background to this problematic (or, broadly, the idealist background). Introducing the role Kant cedes to the imagination in his transcendental deductions, especially in the first deduction, can help clarify the essay's deeper logic. For although A's intention to establish the grounding priority of poiesis is clear, what remains unclarified is how and why the phenomenon of boredom surfaces in such a radical way. This has to do, in terms of its logic, with the link Kant draws between the imagination and time consciousness. In other words, if we are to excavate the horizon of the problematic, we shall have to consider its relation to a shift inaugurated by Kant.

What I suggest is this: the method of crop rotation constitutes something like an existential repetition of Kant's effort to justify the unity of self-consciousness; in particular, it replays, under the notion of poetizing recollection, the transcendentally constitutive role Kant assigns to the "productive imagination." The repetition is an "existential" one precisely because Kierkegaard's author discovers a more radical threat to the unity of self-consciousness than its exposure to sensibility: namely, the encounter with the "nothing that interlaces all existence." This takes place in boredom. It should be noted too that boredom is a qualification of one's relation to temporality. Thus, what emerges is a confrontation with temporality *as* the nothing interlacing all existence—with time as *Afgrund* (abyss). If the identity thesis of idealism is to justify itself in the face of alterity, it will have to extirpate the root of boredom by staying present at the very origin of temporalization. The goal of the crop rotation method is nothing less than this continual uprooting of the very possibility of boredom.

In the *Critique of Pure Reason* the productive imagination, as a transcendental capability, and temporality, as the a priori form of "inner sense," are tightly related.[22] The productive imagination, to be exact, constitutes a "synthesis of apprehension," a priori, whose most radical function is to space out the instant of sense impression and enable a *consciousness of* time, that is, any possible experience of temporal sequence. Kant says: "For any presentation as contained in one instant can never be anything but absolute unity."[23] In order for there to be a consciousness *of* time, the instant, in which consciousness is simply passively struck by a presentation, has to be actively apprehended. That is, it must "first be gone through and gathered together."[24] What is at work here is something like a transcendental kind of re-presentation: the temporal instant is *re*-organized in terms that make consciousness of time, that is, the experience of sequence, possible. A certain repetition or re-presentation stands as the conditioning possibility of consciousness.

Nevertheless something more than a "synthesis of apprehension" is required: namely, a "pure transcendental synthesis of imagination that itself underlies the possibility of all experience."[25] The temporal instant must be primordially reorganized by the spontaneity of self-consciousness; yet this is possible, Kant argues, only vis-à-vis a general transcendental power to retain one instant and associate it with a further (earlier and/or later) instant. Kant calls this a "reproductive synthesis." He writes: "But if I always lost from my thoughts the preceding presentations . . . [for example, the different parts of a figure as I drew it] and did not reproduce them as I proceeded to the following ones, then there could never arise a whole presentation."[26] The imagination is the power of retaining and associating temporal nows. The productive imagination, then, acts as a kind of primordial memory: the instant does not merely strike; it is continually held, reproduced, and linked into other instants. In this way the imagination brings about the "necessary unity in the synthesis of appearance," without which "no concepts whatever of objects would meld in one experience."[27] Without the work of the imagination, in short, time would lack any determinate *meaning* (any ideality).[28]

One can think about the project of idealism—and at this level it doesn't matter whether it is Kantian, Fichtean, or Hegelian—as the effort to think temporality in terms of the genesis of the *meaning* of time. The identity of the inner and the outer that *Either/Or* ponders signifies here the co-extensiveness of the consciousness of time and the time of consciousness. To the extent that time is representable as a meaningful sequence of instants, idealism judges it as real. Kant's deductions provide the foundation for this reduction of time to represented time. Hegel's *Phenomenology of Spirit*, as I will indicate below, extends Kant's analysis.

Yet the "Rotation of Crops" goes beyond the Kantian problematic. The essential problem in Kant's analysis, that is, how the absolute unity of the instant gives way to the primordial reorganization by self-consciousness, returns in boredom. The transcendental synthesis is apparently incapable of effecting the reduction of time to meaningful time. Boredom, one could say, is nothing other than the excess of the temporal instant, as absolute unity, to its re-organization and re-production by self-consciousness. Boredom is a phenomenal indicator of time as resistant to the spontaneous, synthetic activity of self-consciousness. It indicates the temporal instant as absolute, predicateless, contentless, unity: time as nothing. The temporal instant, as such, overflows the sequencing, meaning-generating moves of consciousness. It ruptures representation.

Hence, after Kant, boredom points to *the* problem for idealist metaphysics: the alterity of time. I have already discussed A's "solution." Perhaps now the coherence of that solution becomes more apparent: A's praxis of forgetting by remembering otherwise, of turning existence into representation, simply extends the dream of a unified self-consciousness beyond its Kantian base. In effect, A absolutizes the re-productive synthesis by submitting the totality of experience to the "maximal supervision of recollection." Time only is as meaningful. It derives its reality from its origin in the spontaneity of the representing subject. A's rotation of crops takes representation to the limit.

Nevertheless the text ends up bearing witness against itself. It seeks a method with which to produce what Plotnitsky, in referring to Hegel, terms a *controlled transformation* of the temporal instant.[29] Yet what the essay actually ends up disclosing, whether self-consciously or not, is once again a radical failure to preserve the identity of inner and outer. The comical tone of the essay masks the profound pain of the subject exposed to an endless, absolute temporality that resists any incorporation into *its own* projects or method. Boredom is a phenomenological locus to consider a primordial kind of dispossession of the subject. In boredom the subject loses its own subjectivity, that is, its spontaneity, its principial status. Most painful is that the subject nevertheless has to live its own dispossession.

In these terms, A is only half joking when he raises the stakes of boredom to the maximal level: "Boredom is the root of all evil. It is very curious that boredom, which itself has such a calm and sedate nature, can have such a capacity to initiate motion. The effect that boredom brings about is absolutely magical, but this effect is not one of attraction but repulsion" (*EO* 1:285 *SKS* 2:275). Precisely because boredom introduces the subject to the negation that it itself *is*, that is, to itself insofar as it does not possess itself, it calls forth an effort on the part of the subject to reground itself, to dominate temporality as such and as a whole. This is why "boredom is the demonic pantheism" (*EO* 1:290; *SKS* 2:279). A elaborates: "Pantheism ordinarily implies the qualification of fullness; with boredom it is the reverse: it is built upon emptiness, but for this very reason it is a pantheistic qualification" (*EO* 1:291; *SKS* 2:279). Through boredom the subject is dislodged from the position of being able to posit itself; it finds itself expelled into a process that cannot be ordered according to beginnings or endings that it posits. It finds itself pulled into time as emptiness.

Boredom is demonic pantheism insofar as it solicits an effort to rule over this *Afgrund,* to master negation. This manifests itself as the self's effort to defer the instant of its dispossession through either work or amusement. Both are generally regarded as the cure for boredom, yet each only works the subject more deeply into it, for the alternating economy of work and leisure is what A calls, following Hegel, the "bad infinite" (*EO* 1:292, altered; *SKS* 2:281). Precisely because boredom exposes subjectivity to what cannot be organized teleologically, it cannot be addressed through projects. In boredom *everything* and *everyone* is boring—"or is there," A writes, "anyone who would be boring enough to contradict me in this regard?" (*EO* 1:285; *SKS* 2:275). The nothing that boredom discloses, and the way it dispossesses the subject of itself, cannot be contested on the basis of the subject's positings.

True, the method of crop rotation is supposed to defer the catastrophe of dispossession ad infinitum by the cultivation of a detachment from any temporality for which the subject is not the origin. And yet A himself recognizes with complete clarity that the only real cure would be a state of self-forgetful absorption into the whole, a state he refers to as a divine idleness: "idleness is a truly divine life" (*EO* 1:289; *SKS* 2:278). To be idle, without ends or goals, letting time temporalize—this would be to let go of the effort to master time.[30] Boredom here would be suspended in terms of its basic possibility. The catastrophe, however, is that such idleness cannot, in spite of everything, be taken in hand as the outcome of some method. Idleness no less than boredom remains fundamentally exposed to a temporality for which the subject is not the origin. Hence, the caveat the ruins everything: idleness is "truly a divine life, *if* one is not bored" (*EO* 1:289; *SKS* 2:278–79; my emphasis). In other words, one has to not be bored in order not to be bored.

The project of a rotation of the crops, then, witnesses more to the excess of time than to the possibility of reducing time to representable time. Idleness and boredom both manifest existence insofar as it falls beneath any method. Each manifests the *Afgrund,* according to which the subject loses its status as ground.

I have found in *Either/Or* 1 not only the confessions of an "aesthete," but the development of a "transcendental" problematic regarding temporality. The phenomena that interest A—indolence, melancholy, boredom—show an exposure of subjectivity to temporality as what overflows teleological arcs of development and continuums of meaning. They present the nothing in its positive meaning as no longer the dialectical opposite of being. Nonbeing is thus not taken principially, that is, as the condition through which being manifests itself, but rather as an *Afgrund* that interrupts the movement of manifestation. The problematic of negation that the papers of A present in this way cuts short the egological conception of the subject as a point of origin. More exactly, the basic schema of self-realization, the development of implicit being to explicit being through project and freedom, where the whole movement takes place from arché to telos, is challenged.

It would be possible to object to this reading of *Either/Or* 1 by pointing out that, in the letters of Judge William, a rigorous counterpoint is articulated in which teleology is fundamentally rehabilitated. The Judge posits, namely, the fundamentality of choice and the irreducibility of projects. Subjectivity is freedom, spontaneity, choice, the projection of itself onto a future in setting up ends for itself—and consequently the subject is inherently economic and teleologically oriented. Not to acknowledge this is to avert one's eyes from the deepest layer of the personality: engaged, committed freedom, inner activity, movement, development, *becoming oneself.* Thus with a strong paternal hand the Judge denounces the mystifications and dilettantism of A that prevent him from engaging his freedom in the world.

Ethical maturity signifies the assumption of responsibility for one's situation, posing the totality of one's situation as a task for freedom. The world is what we make it, and we are what we make ourselves. There are no excuses. For the Judge, A is ethically immature and, to his misfortune, a genius at constructing deep reasons for his detachment.

From this point of view, then, the question may be asked: Is it not the case that A's "metaphysics," in which subjectivity finds itself absolved from the order of ends, is mere ideological justification for an evasion of the decisive either/or: the choice of choice itself, choosing to choose, engaging one's freedom as a sovereignty of situation? As already suggested, A's aestheticism lies in the modality of his *response* to the excess of time, not in the clarification of that excess. To the extent that A deconstructs the identity thesis of idealism, or to the extent he clarifies an originary nonidentity that dispossesses subjectivity of its status as ground, his various studies are presupposed by the Judge—and, thus, by the entire "ethical" stage.

One can see this insofar as ethical choice, which is the self's choice of itself, is identical to its *despair* of itself, that is, the consent to its original lack of foundation within itself. Choice is not at bottom a spontaneity, an activity, but rather a receptivity and a consent. The Judge writes: "When around one everything has become silent, solemn as a clear, starlit night, when the soul comes to be alone in the whole world . . . then the heaven seems to open, and the *I* chooses itself or, more correctly, receives itself" (*EO* 2:177; *SKS* 3:183). The Judge's criticism of A thus departs from the same presupposition: the ab-soluteness of subjectivity, its lack of foundation. In consenting to this absolutely—which means to despair (*at fortvivle*)—the Judge overcomes the indolence of A. He accepts the absoluteness of the self: "When I choose absolutely, I choose despair, and in despair I choose the absolute. . . . I choose the absolute that chooses me" (*EO* 2:217; *SKS* 3:205). In the end, however, it will be necessary to ask whether the healthy ethical exuberance of the Judge really weighs the anarchy of the subject to its full measure. The Judge performs the quasi-Hegelian operation of grasping that anarchy—the "nothing interlacing all existence"—as the condition of the subject's being able to project itself, of its own accord, into the future. Groundlessness becomes, in the manner of Sartrean existentialism, the condition for the subject to make itself a ground. The question, however, is whether the endlessness subjectivity undergoes will not break forth again *after* the mediations of the ethical and thus, from a different point of view —a "religious" one—validate the guiding insights of A. We shall see this is very much what happens.

THREE

Entering into Philosophy
(De omnibus dubitandum est)

B etween the fall of 1842 and the spring of 1843 Kierkegaard wrote the small text *Johannes Climacus*, or *De omnibus dubitandum est*. It would appear that Kierkegaard envisaged something like writing a history of doubt,[1] in narrative form, in relation to modern thought. In particular, it was to be a consideration of the relation between doubt and the beginning of philosophy. It was an ambitious plan, but never completed. What survives is a work, introduced with a short narrative prelude (of autobiographical provenance), which has two parts.

Part one is titled "Johannes Climacus begins to philosophize with the aid of traditional ideas." At stake in part one is the effort to "enter into philosophy," which will mean, explicitly, to take up the standpoint of absolute knowing. Part two is titled "Johannes tries to think *propriis auspiciis De omnibus dubitandum est*." What exists of part two, however, is only a short chapter titled "What is it to doubt?" It is a transcendental analysis of the essential possibility of doubt within consciousness. Taken together, the two parts may be read as a meditation on the central issues within Hegel's *Phenomenology of Spirit:* namely, how natural consciousness is supposed to achieve the standpoint of absolute knowing, which concerns issues in Hegel's "Preface," and how knowledge is originally made possible through the constituting activity of consciousness, which relates to Hegel's discussion of "sense certainty."

The subtitle of the work, *De omnibus dubitandum est,* is an allusion to Hegel's discussion of Descartes in his *Lectures on the History of Philosophy.* Hegel writes: "Descartes expresses the fact that we must doubt everything (*De omnibus dubitandum est*); and that is an absolute beginning."[2] According to Hegel, the absolute beginning, opened with Socrates but repeated in Descartes, inaugurates "the culture of modern times" and the "thought of

modern philosophy."³ Descartes sets thought upon an egological foundation. This absolute beginning, namely the beginning as the setting of an
egological foundation, comes under critique in *Johannes Climacus.* Not
only does the phenomenon of doubt point, in terms of the conditions of
its possibility, to an originary difference fracturing consciousness, but the
very notion of an absolute beginning, so that thought would "begin with itself," shows itself as aporetic.

The critical meaning of *Johannes Climacus* is thus to point to a beginning that cannot be grasped as a principle, a beginning whose origin does
not lie in the self-positing movement of self-consciousness.

Part One: Becoming a Philosopher

GOING INTO THE ABSOLUTE: PARADOXES OF PRESENTATION

The horizon of part one of *Johannes Climacus* is Hegel's presentation of a
phenomenology of the absolute. According to Hegel, entering into absolute knowledge demands a total reversal and inversion of the everyday
standpoint of natural consciousness and a *climbing up* to another standpoint altogether. In the preface to the *Phenomenology of Spirit* Hegel writes:
"*Pure* self-recognition in absolute otherness, this Aether *as such,* is the
ground and soil of Science or *knowledge in general.* . . . Conversely, the individual has the right to demand that Science should at least provide him
with the ladder to this standpoint, should show him this standpoint within
himself."⁴ The standpoint of absolute knowledge—that is, "science" or
"system"—lies already within that of natural consciousness. The task of
philosophy as phenomenology is to present this standpoint to natural consciousness, to provide, as Hegel says, a *ladder* on which to climb up into the
absolute. The *Phenomenology of Spirit* as a whole is such a ladder.

The very title and name of the protagonist of Kierkegaard's work, Johannes *Climacus,* contains an allusion to this problematic: the name "Climacus" derives from the Greek *klimax,* that is, "ladder."⁵ What is at stake in
this text is the possibility or impossibility for natural consciousness to ele-
vate itself to the standpoint of absolute knowledge or to make an absolute
beginning. The very notion of bringing the absolute to presentation, however, involves certain antinomies. Hegel points to a certain violence presupposed as natural consciousness elevates itself to a dwelling in the absolute:
"When natural consciousness entrusts itself straightaway to science, it
makes an attempt, induced by it knows not what, to walk on its head too,
just this once; the compulsion to assume this unwonted posture and to go
about in it is a violence it is expected to do to itself, all unprepared and

seemingly without necessity."[6] Natural consciousness is basically dualistic. It regards itself as standing over against objects taken as simply other. It thinks everything with respect to its own (subjective and particular) point of view, it is certain of itself, and has no sense for the whole, the absolute, the way in which reality in itself is a self-building, self-sustaining whole.

The standpoint of science, however, opens up only vis-à-vis some prior ground in which subjectivity and objectivity, inner and outer, are identical. The prior identity of subjectivity and objectivity, however, is not itself—initially at least—presentable within natural consciousness. Natural consciousness must abandon its naturalness to gain the position of science. Thus of itself natural consciousness regards science as perverse; similarly, science regards natural consciousness as inauthentic. Each standpoint "appears to the other as the inversion of truth (*das Verkehrte der Wahrheit*)."[7] The goal of a *presentation* of science is to lead natural consciousness from its own standpoint toward absolute knowing by showing that the latter is already implicit in the former: "Let science be in its own self what it may, relatively to immediate self-consciousness it presents itself in an inverted posture; or, because this self-consciousness exists on its own account outside of science. Science must therefore unite this element of self-certainty with itself, or rather show that and how this element belongs to it."[8]

A phenomenological presentation of absolute knowing thus aims at showing how natural consciousness is, always already, within the standpoint of absolute knowledge; its very being is, always already, within the parousia of the absolute.[9] The task of science is not, violently, to insist upon its results; rather, it is to shepherd natural consciousness into its point of view by laying out the deep coherence between absolute knowing and self-certain consciousness. Science—the articulation of the whole in its wholeness as the whole—takes the trouble to prepare natural consciousness for its standpoint. In truth, however, this preparation or ladder into the absolute is necessary to the standpoint of science itself. It is no mere pedagogy. Hegel's guiding insight is that reality is in itself a system, that is, a self-relating whole in which dualisms cannot be fundamental. Yet preserving this standpoint means to confront the following antinomy: how can one present the fundamental wholeness of reality without, in the very act of presenting it, creating a division between reality and its presentation, and thus without reaffirming dualism? As soon as the absolute is made the object of a presentation, would not the standpoint of natural consciousness be reaffirmed? How can one then enter into philosophy?

The identity of self-consciousness's knowledge of the absolute and the absolute's knowledge of itself is the very heart of the *Phenomenology of Spirit*. Such identity, however, involves an aporia: on the one hand, the absolute *must be identical* to its presentation, otherwise dualism intrudes in the very act of presentation; on the other hand, the absolute *must not be identical* to its presentation, otherwise there would be no presentational space. The absolute must be and not be its own self-presentation, be and not be itself. Hegel resolves this aporia by understanding it in terms of a hermeneutical circle: the absolute "is the process of its own becoming, the circle that presupposes its end as its goal, having its end also as its beginning."[10] The absolute is absolute only insofar as it looks back upon its own development: "The true is the whole. But the whole is nothing other than the essence consummating itself through its development. Of the absolute it must be said that it is essentially a result, that only in the end is it what it truly is; and that precisely in this consists its nature, viz. to be actual, subject, the spontaneous becoming of itself."[11] Its movement toward awareness of itself is a movement whose end only makes explicit its beginning. The end is the beginning; the departure is the return.

For its part, natural consciousness must confront an aporia of presentation. If it is to be a presentation of the absolute as the absolute, natural consciousness must grasp its own movement or presentation in terms of a more fundamental movement that revokes it as *its* movement. For this reason, as Hegel says, the movement of the self-conscious I into the absolute is nothing other than a *recollection* (*Erinnerung*) of the absolute's own self-movement. Thus, to climb up to the standpoint of absolute knowledge for Hegel signifies the recollective gathering of a prior, and already determinative, foundation. Reality must already be self-gathering as the condition for the recollective gathering, or repetition, that consciousness itself produces in and for itself. Moreover, consciousness's repetition of the self-gathering of reality in and for itself must be graspable, by consciousness, as the culminating moment in the self-gathering of reality. The movement of the self-conscious I into the absolute must be grasped by that self-conscious I as the movement of the absolute into itself. In the precise phrase of John Sallis, the knowing of the self-conscious I "would be, as it were, appropriated to the self-knowing of the absolute."[12] Sallis continues: "if the absolute is absolute, then the I cannot have been initially outside it, so as then to undergo movement into the absolute. Rather, the I must already be in the absolute. It must be a movement by which the I, which takes itself to be outside the absolute, comes to the awareness that it is always already within the absolute."[13]

Presenting the absolute rightly, then, will mean to grasp the very act of presenting the absolute as the absolute's own act of self-presentation. As self-consciousness repeats, in and for itself, the self-gathering of the real, it must lean upon an initial anticipative insight into the whole, and it must, as it proceeds, revoke the act of presentation as having its origin in itself as a self-certain subject, and recognize it as the very movement of the absolute toward itself. Kierkegaard was attentive to these exigencies of presentation. In a section titled "A Presentiment," he formulates them in the following way:

> Thus, [to enter into absolute knowing,] the individual philosopher *must become conscious of himself and in this consciousness of himself also become conscious of his significance as a moment in modern philosophy; in turn modern philosophy must become conscious of itself as an element in a prior philosophy, which in turn must become conscious of itself as an element in the historical unfolding of the eternal philosophy. Thus the philosopher's consciousness must encompass the most dizzying contrasts: his own personality, his little amendment —the philosophy of the whole world as the unfolding of the eternal philosophy.* (*JC* 140; *Pap.* IV B1, 123)

This restates the spirals of mediation that are implied in absolute knowledge or in the presentation of the history of thought finding itself. The eternal philosophy would be the self-gatheredness of the foundation prior to, and as the condition of, its presentation (corresponding to Hegel's *Logic*). The historical unfolding of the foundation would be the *Phenomenology*. Modern philosophy, which we shall see repeats the foundation egologically, would signify the moment *in* the *Phenomenology* (and in history) in which self-consciousness becomes aware of its own significance in the historical unfolding that is the absolute's own self-presentation. And finally the individual I, the little amendment, would signify the existing individual ego who, presenting or repeating for himself the presentation of the absolute, recollectively gathers up the different strata while revoking the movement of gathering as its own movement. These spirals, culminating in absolute knowing, become the object of Kierkegaard's critique.

Kierkegaard's critique of absolute knowing emphasizes the element of nonidentity presupposed as the very condition for the possibility of presentation. Considered more exactly, this is the nonidentity between the whole and the parts, or between the process as a whole and its moments. The crux of Kierkegaard's criticism is this: absolute knowing could only mean the knowledge of an entire process, through all its moments and their interrelations, from the standpoint of its closure, for as long as the process is still underway, what every previous moment *will have meant* must remain open. Closure is the general condition for the knowledge of a process that would count as total. Hegel himself had indicated this in the idea that the beginning only is a beginning at the end. However, if one attempts to realize such closure with respect to human *existence*, Kierkegaard argues, it could translate only as a radically alienated relation to one's own temporal present, which is never closed. Yet absolute knowing was supposed to overcome precisely the alienation of self-consciousness. Hence, an aporia.

Kierkegaard frames the aporia directly in terms of temporality: "Philosophy . . . wanted to permeate everything with the thought of eternity and necessity [i.e., with the thought of closure], wanted to do this in the present moment (*præsentiske Øieblik*), which would mean slaying the present with the thought of eternity and yet preserving its fresh life. It would mean wanting *to see what is happening as that which has happened and simultaneously as that which is happening;* it would mean wanting to know the future as a present and yet simultaneously as a future (*JC* 142; *Pap.* IV B1 125; my italics). In short, the exigencies of presentation would demand a double and contradictory relation to one's own temporal present: to relate to it as something already gathered into the eternal self-gatheredness of the foundation, and thus as closed; *and* to relate to it as something still open, something with a future. Thus to think absolute knowing, which means dwelling in the parousia of the absolute in the present moment, it would be necessary to think the antinomies both of a future that is simultaneously open and closed and of a present that is simultaneously finished and unfinished.

Here, then, we come to a strange result: if one takes rigorously the exigencies of presentation as Hegel understands them, one comes to the notion of existence as *between* openness and closure, beginning and ending, or rather as their contradiction. One arrives at the understanding of the temporal instant as the coincidence of life and death. Now, on the one hand, this is exactly the understanding of temporality Kierkegaard's various authors bring to light. On the other hand, however—and here is where the critique in *Johannes Climacus* begins—it is necessary, Kierkegaard indicates, to allow this simultaneity of life and death to remain aporetic. Hegel, in short, does not respect the existential rupture that his *own position* imposes. Hegel does not remain faithful to the exigency of presentation. To be exact, he does not do so where he does not attend to the essential difference between the anticipative sense of the parousia of the absolute (i.e., the moment of closure) and that parousia itself. Hegel had sought to resolve the antinomies of a closed future and a posthumous present—ideas that are inextricable from a presentation of absolute knowing—by thinking them in terms of an *anticipative* sense of the whole. Before realizing absolute knowledge existentially, actually "dwelling in its element," one would necessarily have a prior sense of it—otherwise absolute knowledge would not be knowledge of the absolute in which one already stands.

Yet Hegel's position, which demands *actually living* in the parousia of the absolute, would seem to require redeeming this presentiment of the whole within the present. At some moment, in other words, the eternity of the foundation, that it must always already have been gathered into itself, must be made real in a particular instant of time. Outside of this instant of realization, the absolute could never become identical to its presentation. Hence, the present instant would at some point have to be marked with a temporality characterized by full presence, or full closure. This is where Hegel would pass beyond the simultaneity of life and death that his own position implies in favor of something like absolute life.

In reply, Kierkegaard's Johannes offers a thought experiment to test out the notion of a moment in life lived absolutely, that is, in full self-presence: "if someone beginning a specific period of time in his life wants first to become conscious of this in its eternal validity as an element in his life [i.e., what it will have meant], he will precisely thereby prevent it from acquiring significance, for he will nullify it before it has been by wanting that which is a present to manifest itself to him in that very instant as a past" (*JC* 142; *Pap.* IV B1, 125). Full meaning, exposed to no loss, opacity, or death, would not even be meaning. Meaning requires precisely *not knowing* what the beginning will have meant. The present and its meaning, in all strictness, do not coincide. Life and death, opening and closure, though simultaneous, cannot be harmonized. It is this that Hegel's absolute knowing must finally obscure or even deny.

This would be to say that one could never get beyond the presentiment of absolute knowing; or, more exactly, it would point to a presentiment that was not *of* anything. As Johannes himself tries to move from the elaboration of the exigencies of presentation to an actual dwelling in the parousia of the absolute, he witnesses to what cannot be erased: "[Johannes] then decided to let the thought work with all its weight, for he made a distinction between the laboriousness of thinking and the weight of the thought. As a historical thought, he thought the thought with ease. He had collected new strength, felt himself whole and complete; he put his shoulder, as it were, to the thought—and look, it overwhelmed him and *he fainted*! (*JC* 141; *Pap.* IV B1, 123). The lapse of consciousness as a narrative element here is no mere contingent effect. Rather, it points to the general necessity of loss of presence, lapse, delay, and death for the constitution of meaning. To deny this necessity would produce, paradoxically, a vacuous, dead life, already over and done with before it had even begun. If there is a presentiment of life in the absolute, then, it will inevitably be inseparable from a presentiment of the undoing of self-consciousness, a presentiment of a radical outside. Something like an absolute future, a future beyond the power of self-consciousness to posit, or an absolute past, thought as a beginning impossible to recollect, will be named. Such a presentiment would, however, be close not to a presentiment of full self-presence, but to one of derangement: "[Johannes] hardly dared turn his attention to that thought [of absolute knowing]. It dawned on him that it could drive a person to madness, at least someone who did not have stronger nerves than he had"

(*JC* 141; *Pap.* IV B1, 123). Here the coincidence of life and death remains as non-dialectical contradiction.

SLIPPAGE OF THE FOUNDATION:
MODERNITY AS BEGINNING

The primary issue of part one of *Johannes Climacus,* to repeat, concerns the possibility or impossibility of *becoming* a philosopher (*at blive en Philosoph*). The question is how to begin with philosophy, how to take up the stand-point of thinking philosophically. Within the Hegelian horizon of the text, the question of the beginning of philosophy is not only a conceptual question involving the issues of presentation, but also a historical question concerning the moment in the "history of thought finding itself" at which the authentic consciousness of the beginning of philosophy itself begins.

In his *Lectures on the History of Philosophy* Hegel presents any number of moments in which the absolute beginning of philosophy becomes historically manifest. Nevertheless, he does cede a certain founding privilege to modernity—in particular, to Descartes. The significance of Descartes according to Hegel is to have inaugurated the philosophical culture of modern times: "with Descartes the culture of modern times, the thought of modern Philosophy, really begins to appear, after a long and tedious journey on the way which has led so far."[14] Hegel continues: "Descartes expresses the fact that we must begin from thought as such alone, by saying that we must doubt everything (*De omnibus dubitandum est*); and that is an absolute beginning."[15] Descartes's *ego cogito,* which like Fichte's intellectual intuition "directly involves my being," is the "absolute ground of all Philosophy" (*das absolute Fundament aller Philosophie*).[16]

Descartes's unveiling of the absolute ground of philosophy is conditioned, however, by a movement of doubt. Suspending all its judgments about reality as simply given, it discovers a domain of absolute givenness: its givenness to itself, the certainty that it *is*. It is not this or that particular thing it is certain of, it is certain of itself. In thinking itself, its thinking and its being are identical: it *is* its own self-thinking. Self-conscious self-certainty, as the identity of thought and being, constitutes the true element of the real. Descartes hits explicitly upon the egological interpretation of being. He inaugurates the new and essential foundation. Such is Hegel's reading of Descartes.[17] Yet for Hegel the absolute beginning inaugurated in Descartes, opening properly modern thought, has to be situated with respect to the larger narrative of the history of thought finding itself. The position of modernity involves therefore an ambiguity: on the one hand it constitutes the result of a historical process, the outcome and indeed culmination of an entire history; on the other hand it is indeed an absolute beginning, a beginning in and with itself alone. Thus, for Hegel, modernity inevitably involves a self-consciousness that knows itself simultaneously as absolute and relative, contingent and necessary, temporal and eternal.[18]

The question *Johannes Climacus* raises, however, is whether it is possible to secure the historical and conceptual distinctiveness of the modern beginning in these terms. To what extent, in other words, can self-consciousness offer itself as a foundation? The effort of *Johannes Climacus* is to show that the modern beginning, conditioned by doubt and a retreat into the egological, must run aground on the aporias that cling to any beginning. Strictly thought, beginning and foundation are incompatible. Partly this has to do with general conditions for grasping a beginning determinately, and partly with difficulties about the role of doubt in the modern beginning.

In order to clarify these difficulties, and thus to problematize the stability of an egological foundation, Kierkegaard formulates three of his own "theses." They are: "(1) *philosophy begins with doubt;* (2) *in order to philosophize, one must have doubted;* (3) *modern philosophy begins with doubt*" (*JC* 132; *Pap.* IV B1, 116). These three theses are designed to draw out the ambiguous position of the modern beginning, that is, that it must be simultaneously absolute and relative. So, for example, to the extent that the modern beginning is an absolute beginning, but is nevertheless conditioned by doubt, does this imply that *all* philosophy properly speaking begins with doubt (thesis 1)? Or is it only *modern* philosophy that begins with doubt, and thus only modern philosophy that is truly philosophical (thesis 3)? And in what sense could an absolute beginning, as absolute, be conditioned by the *prior* movement of doubt (thesis 2)?

Theses one and three both try to expose a certain slippage in Hegel's discussion between philosophy as such, philosophy as departing from an absolute beginning, and modern philosophy, which begins at a certain moment. If in modernity an absolute beginning opens, would this not have decisive retrospective and prospective force on the very meaning of philosophy? Kierkegaard writes: "if, because of its beginning, modern philosophy has excluded for all future time the possibility of another beginning"—that is, insofar as self-consciousness is regarded as an unsurpassable horizon—"this suggests that this beginning is more than a historical beginning, is an essential beginning" (*JC* 134; *Pap.* IV B1, 117). The predicate "modern," in other words, must not really be a historical predicate, but a philosophical one. It signifies autonomy, egology, absolute beginning as interiority. In these terms, however, as soon as modernity opens, it must manifest itself in terms of what it always already will have been: essential philosophy. The entire future of philosophy and its entire past will have to be rethought in light of this "Idea." This, of course, is exactly what Hegel sets out to accomplish in his *Lectures on the History of Philosophy.* From Hegel's standpoint, explicitly egological, "the history of philosophy is itself scientific, and thus becomes the science of philosophy."[19] Philosophy is the history of philosophy (as the self-gathering of thought to itself): "The study of the history of philosophy is the study of philosophy itself."[20]

Hegel is also of course aware of the paradox that, on the one hand, philosophy concerns only "true, necessary thought . . . [which] is capable of no change,"[21] but that, on the other hand, it constitutes a "totality which contains a multitude of stages and of moments in development."[22] He resolves this paradox, we have seen, in the idea that the development is nothing other than the recollective regathering of the "same" truth—it is, precisely, that truth becoming *conscious of itself.* The becoming conscious of itself *is* the development, is the history. Hegel was perfectly aware of the real issue here: "It is a question as to how it happens that philosophy appears to be a development in time and has a history. The answer to this question encroaches on the metaphysics of time."[23] History, and more generally time, signifies precisely the movement of self-consciousness toward itself. Presupposed in the idea that philosophy, whose content is eternal, has a history is the notion that time coincides with the *consciousness of* time.

According to Kierkegaard, however, this understanding of temporality founders in the aporia of beginning:

> Modern philosophy must be assumed to be even yet in the process of becoming; otherwise there already would be something more modern, in relation to which it would be older. Is it not conceivable that modern philosophy, as it advanced and spread, became aware of its wrong beginning, which, regarded as a beginning would prove not to be a beginning? By what authority is this beginning declared to be a beginning for all modern philosophy? This can be correct only if the beginning itself is the essential beginning for modern philosophy, but, historically speaking, this cannot be decided until modern philosophy is concluded in its entirety. (*JC* 135; *Pap.* IV B1, 118)

In Hegel's own terms it is possible to posit a beginning only on condition that one knows determinately what that beginning was the beginning of. A beginning can be posited only on condition of closure. As long as one cannot say what the beginning will have been the beginning of, one cannot *posit* the beginning as the beginning (i.e., bring it to consciousness). Before the moment of closure, a certain indeterminacy clings to the beginning— the possibility that it was not the beginning at all, but only a "misunderstanding." Unless modern philosophy—the epoch of the egological—has concluded, one cannot speak of its having been a beginning. On the other hand, if one can speak of its closure and so enunciate determinately what it was the beginning of, then one will already be beyond that beginning and outside that history. Hence: one can stand *in* the beginning only on condition that one not take it *as* the beginning; or, one can take it as the beginning, but only on condition that one no longer stands within *that* beginning. In either case, self-consciousness does not coincide with the beginning, does not know itself in its beginning. It is either *too early* or *too late* to bring the beginning in which one stands to full self-consciousness.

For Hegel, modernity has definite priority as a moment in the history of thought finding itself precisely because it presents self-consciousness as foundational. Grasping self-consciousness as foundational allows Hegel to think reality as a movement of self-gathering, that is, as the movement wherein substance becomes subject, or attains to a consciousness of itself. But if it is the case that, for any process, the beginning cannot be determined except on condition of its end, and if in the very act of thinking a process as complete one steps beyond it, this suggests that the instant of beginning cannot be formulated ideally. Put differently, temporality is not adequately analyzed on the horizon or foundation of self-consciousness. To take temporality and history seriously is not to know from where one departed, or where one is heading. But if that is the case then the "history of thought finding itself" loses its ground in the ego.

DOUBT AS CONDITION

A second major issue in part one of *Johannes Climacus,* which spills over into part two, concerns doubt as a condition for beginning absolutely in and with self-consciousness. The difficulty here is twofold: first, to think how an absolute beginning could be conditioned by anything at all; and second, to think how precisely doubt could issue in a beginning. Kierkegaard addresses the first problem by asking "Was it by necessity that modern philosophy began with doubt?" (*JC* 137; *Pap.* IV B1, 120). The question here is how modern philosophy understands itself to have emerged from previous philosophy. On the one hand, it must understand itself as the outcome of a previous tradition, otherwise the predicate "modern" would be meaningless; on the other hand, it must understand itself as founded in nothing prior to it, otherwise a beginning in doubt could not be absolute. Doubt plays its role here in clearing the ground so that a beginning with nothing other than itself becomes possible; doubt is the condition for beginning absolutely. Nevertheless, one can still ask about the *history of the condition* whereby an absolute beginning is possible: is doubt the outcome of a previous tradition or itself an absolute beginning? If doubt is the outcome of a previous tradition, then modern philosophy's beginning with doubt will be subsumed under a prior beginning and hence not be absolute:

"If modern philosophy by necessity begins with doubt, then its beginning is defined in continuity with an earlier philosophy . . . [so that] the beginning of modern philosophy would only be a consequence within an earlier beginning" (*JC* 138; *Pap.* IV B1, 121).

Nevertheless this cannot be the case, Kierkegaard suggests, insofar as doubt by its very nature is a "reflection category" and a "polemic against what went before" (*JC* 145; *Pap.* IV B1, 127). Doubt cannot *follow from* anything, but is exactly a rupture of continuity; it is a severance or "tearing loose" (*Løsriven*) (*JC* 138; *Pap.* IV B1, 121). In this sense, though doubt always orients itself by what precedes it (otherwise there would be nothing to doubt), it indeed constitutes a new departure point, a new beginning.

The category of doubt, then, seems to fulfill the conditions of a historically conditioned absolute beginning: it not only situates itself with respect to a previous historical movement, but also tears loose from that and begins from itself. Doubt is an absolute beginning. On Hegel's reading of Descartes, however, doubt *conditions* an absolute beginning. The absolute beginning is thinking beginning with itself and unfolding what lies in it.

Evidently, Kierkegaard has reversed the very meaning of an absolute beginning. It now signifies a severance, a tearing loose, a leap: "It [the absolute beginning conditioned by doubt] would have to be a unique kind of consequence—namely, a consequence by which the opposite results from something. This is ordinarily called a leap" (*JC* 138; *Pap.* IV B1, 121). The necessity arises here for thinking according to another kind of logic altogether than the developmental or archeo-teleo-logic of Hegel, in which a process moves to the point of recovering what has been implicit within it. Here, if one thinks doubt as what conditions an absolute beginning, and thinks doubt in terms of its own historicity, then one has to think a historical movement whose end is not a return to the beginning always already present within that movement, but rather a break from that very historical movement. That is, one has to think a process culminating in its own negation, undoing itself.

This is to think according to "a leap" (*et Spring*). It is to think the beginning—of whatever sort, whether the Socratic beginning or the modern beginning—not *retrospectively* in light of its end, but *prospectively* as a departure without a goal. At work in the historical movement of philosophy is not a self-gathering, a recovery of the foundations, but rather a continual tearing loose from what has served as the foundation. Doubt, then, cannot be confined, as Hegel would like, to serving simply as the condition for the absolute beginning of modernity; it cannot be periodized, but must be seen at work in all thinking. For this reason, we shall see, Kierkegaard understands doubt as precisely "the beginning of the highest form of existence" (*JC* 170; *Pap.* IV B1, 149). As an absolute beginning in this sense (as leap or tearing loose), doubt is simply the power to sever, to begin all over again from the beginning—but never to get beyond the beginning, never to make a beginning (i.e., one that is determinate or founding). For this reason, Kierkegaard argues that doubt cannot become a method or praxis, not a principle, which one could communicate, receive, develop. It is nothing one could organize a community around. There is no history of doubt in the same way there is no history of irony. Hence, it cannot become a *property* of the human spirit in the way that, for example, the invention of the wheel or mathematics can.

More to the point, doubt cannot be one of the "formative stages of universal spirit" that would constitute the *inheritance* of the past to contemporary times. For Hegel, to realize absolute knowing is to live through, to recollect, past stages of spirit. He writes: "The individual whose substance is the more advanced spirit runs through this past just as one who takes up a higher science goes through the preparatory studies he has long since absorbed, in order to bring their content to mind: he recalls them to the inward eye, but has no lasting interest in them. . . . This past existence is the already acquired property of universal spirit which constitutes the substance of the individual."[24] The standpoint of doubt, however, cannot be numbered among acquired property of spirit because, as soon as it is, it is original, a discontinuity, an absolute severance from what precedes it. But in that case it is not a beginning that self-consciousness can take up within itself—it does not intrinsically issue in anything, nor can it be converted into a principle. Kierkegaard concludes: "*Aller Anfang is schwer*—he had always agreed with the Germans on that, but this beginning [with doubt] seemed to him to be more than difficult, and to call it a beginning and to designate it by this category seemed to him to be akin to the way the fox classified being skinned in the category of transition" (*JC* 155; *Pap.* IV B1, 138). It is a beginning, but not a beginning whose basic movement is already determined in light of its end. To contain it that way is akin to the fox's classifying "being skinned" as its development to another stage of its life.

Part Two: Doubt and Originary Duplicity

From part one to part two of *Johannes Climacus* Kierkegaard moves from the paradoxes of presenting absolute knowledge to an analysis of consciousness. Though he wrote only a few pages before abruptly breaking off the manuscript, these pages are especially important for clarifying his appropriation and critique of idealism. He pursues the question "What is it to doubt?" by asking concerning the general possibility of doubt within self-consciousness. Hegel's discussion of "sense certainty" in the *Phenomenology of Spirit* is explicitly referenced. Indeed, part two can be regarded as a deconstructive reading of Hegel's discussion—a discussion, one may recall, that constitutes the real beginning of the *Phenomenology of Spirit*.

The general or essential possibility of doubt within self-consciousness, it will turn out, constitutes the "secret of human existence" (*JC* 256; *Pap.* IV B 10). To clarify this secret and to think according to this secret is to point to an irremediable gap between consciousness and itself. What is at stake is "the coming into existence of consciousness . . . [which] is the first pain of existence" (*JC* 257; *Pap.* IV B 14:9). Here again it is a question, in dialogue with Hegel, of a rigorous thinking of the beginning: "The principal pain of existence is that *from the beginning* I am in contradiction with myself, that a person's true being comes through an opposition" (*JC* 253; *Pap.* IV B 10a; my emphasis). Consciousness is born in a painful tearing loose from immediacy. The question is whether this instant of severance can be recuperated. The aim of Kierkegaard's analysis is to show the impossibility of a thinking of the beginning. Self-consciousness shows itself as conditioned by an originary "duplicity" (*Dupplicitet*) that cannot be overcome.

DOUBT AS TRANSCENDENTAL PROBLEMATIC

In part one of *Johannes Climacus* Kierkegaard treated doubt in its relation to the beginning of philosophy, especially modern philosophy. In part two he considers doubt as a phenomenon whose possibility within consciousness must be clarified. To clarify doubt according to its essential possibility is a forthrightly transcendental problematic.[25] To pursue this problematic is to step back to "consciousness as it is in itself, as that which explains every specific consciousness, yet without being itself a specific consciousness" (*JC* 166–7; *Pap.* IV B 145). At issue then is pure consciousness, consciousness as that which is presupposed in every *consciousness of* something determinate. This is a "pure" problematic in Kant's sense: it concerns how a subject constitutes phenomena as doubtful; or rather, how in general a phenomenon can become doubtful for a subject. Kierkegaard is perfectly idealist in asserting that doubt cannot be explained on the basis of what is doubtful about a particular object—that is, on an empirical basis rather than a transcendental basis. An empirical answer "would offer a multifariousness that would only hide a perplexing diffusion over the whole range of extremes" (*JC* 166; *Pap.* IV B 145). What has to be explained is how, in general, something can *appear* doubtful, not how it can *be* doubtful.

As a phenomenon, Kierkegaard notes, doubt has to be distinguished from mere uncertainty: doubt "is a higher moment of uncertainty—I determine my relation to the thing—which I do not do in uncertainty" (*JC* 262; *Pap.* IV B, 10:18). Uncertainty is an indetermination that belongs to the object; doubt is an indetermination that belongs to the subject's relation to an object. Some uncertainty in the object *matters,* something is at stake in that uncertainty for a subject—that is where doubt arises. Strictly speaking, then, doubt arises only where consciousness is *interested,* where a person is trying to clarify not merely something about the object, but rather something about his own relation to the object. In this sense, doubt is strictly speaking a mode of consciousness' *self-relation* rather than its relation to an object. To doubt is always to doubt over oneself in relation to an object. But the precise difficulty of doubt is that the one who doubts cannot distinguish the object from his interest in the object. The distinction between the subject and the object undergoes blurring; the doubter, to the extent he doubts, cannot know to what extent he is being objective. This inability to separate from the object so as to determine its objectivity, where something is at stake, is the pain of doubt.

Phenomenologically, Kierkegaard notes, doubt is not set at rest by more knowledge concerning the object. Doubt has a "paradoxical dialectic" (*JC* 166; *Pap.* IV B 144) that knowledge does not have. The effort to render an object doubtful, for example by producing reasons against it, can produce the opposite result, that is, belief: "for if someone were to discourse on doubt in order to arouse doubt in another, he could precisely thereby evoke faith (*Tro*), just as faith, conversely, could evoke doubt" (ibid.). The reason for this is that what consciousness loses in doubt is not knowledge, but a criterion of its knowledge. Doubt means not to know what my knowledge means, not to know what it means to know. Uncertainty is elevated "a whole rank" from the sphere of knowledge of the object to the sphere of the relation consciousness has to its knowledge. In this sense, doubt is the interiorization of uncertainty, the subject's loss of certainty concerning itself. Where doubt in this sense has taken hold, more knowledge only gives more to doubt.

What the phenomenon of doubt presupposes, then, is interest. If one is to clarify the general possibility of doubt, however, it is necessary to explore how interest is itself possible. It is possible, Kierkegaard will say, only vis-à-vis the structure of consciousness itself as "being between" or *inter-esse:* "Consciousness, however, is the relation and thereby is interest, a duality that is perfectly and with pregnant double meaning expressed in the word 'interest' (*interesse*)" (*JC* 170; *Pap.* IV B1, 148). Consciousness "is" as being-between: neither a subject nor an object, but what is between the two, the very relation of the one to the other. Only in these terms could the uncertainty of an object contaminate the subject's relation to itself.

The movement of Kierkegaard's argument will thus be the following: from doubt as phenomenon to some interest (the ontic level); from some interest to consciousness as *inter-esse* (the ontological level); from the structure of *inter-esse* to an originary duplicity in terms of which one can speak of an "inter" at all (the pre-ontological level). Only insofar as consciousness shows itself as originarily duplicitous, or in some basic way "untrue," will it be possible to explain the general possibility of doubt within consciousness. This will conflict directly with the affirmations of idealism, whether in Kant's unity of apperception, Fichte's intellectual intuition, or Hegel's mediation, that consciousness must originarily be identical with itself—in other words that it must constitute *the truth of being*. In these short pages, departing from the very problematic that opens the epoch of egology (i.e., doubt), Kierkegaard turns idealism inside out.

IMMEDIACY AND MEDIATION

And he does so precisely through a rereading of Hegel's chapter on "sense certainty" in the *Phenomenology of Spirit*.[26] The aim of Hegel's extraordinary chapter on "sense certainty" is to show that the immediate, the "here" and "now" in their simple givenness, is in fact always already mediated. Concerning the temporal "now," for example, Hegel writes: "To the question, 'What is Now?,' let us answer, e.g., 'Now is Night.' In order to test the truth of this sense-certainty a simple experiment will suffice. We write down this truth; a truth cannot lose anything from being written down, any more than it can lose anything through our preserving it. If now, this noon, we look again at the written truth we shall have to say that it has become stale."[27] What Hegel means to show with this "experiment" is that the truth of immediacy cannot be stated at all except on condition of its being mediated. That is, to grasp the *truth* of the immediate is to render it in language, to idealize it, and as soon as one does so, one translates the immediate particular into something *universal*. "Now" intends to grasp some singularity, but it *means* any now. The truth of the now as singular has no duration, no being; it is a truth that is purely ephemeral and so always becomes stale. Of itself, the "Now" could not even be a "Now." It becomes a "Now" only vis-à-vis a series of "Nows" that are held together, or synthesized, in light of some concept: "The pointing-out of the Now is thus itself the movement which expresses what the Now is in truth, viz. a result, or a plurality of Nows all taken together; and the pointing-out is the experience of learning that the now is a *universal*."[28] The immediate "Now," in short, is not singular, as it initially seems to be, but universal.

Thus, in any effort to express the immediate a contradiction arises, according to Hegel, between the singularity one *intends* to say and the universal one *actually* utters. Regarding this contradiction, Hegel writes: "But language, as we see, is the more truthful; in it, we ourselves directly refute what we mean to say, and since the universal is the true [content] of sense-certainty and language expresses this true [content] alone, it is just not possible for us ever to say, or express in words, a sensuous being that we mean."[29] Language is the more truthful because it is within language, and through language, that being in its truth is constituted. To be means to be for consciousness; and to be for consciousness means to become expressed within consciousness through language. Being is here identical to representation: something *is* to the extent it is presentable within consciousness. Outside of that, it can claim only apparent being, purely vanishing being, not true being.[30]

Kierkegaard begins his clarification of consciousness by pointing to the essential contradiction Hegel had found. He writes: "Immediacy is reality; language is ideality; consciousness is contradiction. The moment I make a statement about reality, contradiction is present, for what I say is ideality. . . . When I express [reality] in language, contradiction is present, since I do not express it but produce something else" (*JC* 168; *Pap.* IV B, 146). Like Hegel, he saw the contradiction between reality and ideality as one between particularity and universality: "Intrinsically there is already a contradiction between reality and ideality; the one provides the particular defined in time and space, the other the universal" (*JC* 257; *Pap.* IV B 10:7). As soon as I want to express sensation, then, contradiction is present, for I do not express it, but "produce something other."

In these terms, what I *call* the immediate, that is, the determinate sense experiences of this or that, is in fact not at all immediate. The immediate as determinate sense experience is already the product of a prior work of mediation or determining, a prior work of language. Like Hegel, Kierkegaard recognizes that language does not merely reflect given reality, but rather constitutes reality in its givenness for consciousness. And, like Hegel, Kierkegaard suggests that this prior, constituting work of language is generally occluded within natural consciousness. Natural or everyday consciousness considers the *determinate* givens (e.g., colors, trees) to be the immediate when in fact, strictly speaking, the immediate "is precisely *indeterminateness*" (*JC* 167; *Pap.* IV B 1, 145).

Now Hegel, for his part, considers language to be the truer: in other words, he considers the truth of being to lie within the expressive work of self-consciousness. The truth of being lies in its becoming determinate in and for self-consciousness. Sense determination as a function of self-consciousness is precisely the beginning of absolute knowing, for if the immediate "Now" (or what initially seems to be immediate) is always already mediated, then self-consciousness in principle must encompass the totality of being. This is where Kierkegaard's analysis differs radically. He writes: "I cannot express reality in language, because I use ideality to characterize it, which is a contradiction, an untruth" (*JC* 255; *Pap.* IV B 14:6). Thus for

Kierkegaard, language is not "the truer"; in fact, it is fundamentally untrue. But here one has to be precise: if language is untrue, it is not because it measures itself against some pure experience of immediacy that counts as truth. On the contrary, for Kierkegaard there can be no such thing as a pure experience of immediacy. The immediate, as the indeterminate, is rather what consciousness will always already have lost in its expression of the real. Even more precisely, the immediate is what will always already have been canceled by consciousness as consciousness. Consciousness loses its relation to immediacy in the very act of expressing it, and then becomes forgetful of this loss. It mistakes reality as represented for reality as reality—that is its untruth. But it overlooks this: "Yet consciousness is not clear about this; it believes that it expresses reality" (*JC* 256; *Pap.* IV B 14:7). Consciousness fails to see its own duplicity: that reality is, for it, what it expresses *as* reality. Consciousness doubles reality in the very act of expressing it, but it sees only "reality."

Kierkegaard thus holds two things simultaneously: first, with Hegel, that determinate sense experience is always already mediated, so it is illusory to speak of an experience of immediate being; and second, against Hegel, that mediated being (being as expressed in language) is nevertheless in some basic way "untrue" or duplicitous. This is to say that he refuses to identify being with being-for-consciousness, or representation, even though he affirms the irreducible priority of representation. True being, or reality, is not being-for-consciousness, but rather *what is presupposed* by that. True being lies always prior to the present. True reality is originary time, but consciousness occludes this as its basic act. That is its "untruth"—an untruth, one should note, that coincides with its truth.

Kierkegaard locates his objection to Hegel's idealism, then, at the transition from immediacy to mediation. Hegel's strategy is to show how immediacy is an illusory beginning point. The beginning is mediation and mediation is the beginning. This is why, as Jean Hyppolite points out, Hegel's thought constitutes a radical critique of the ineffable.[31] Nothing of real being remains finally unsayable because, as the analysis of sense certainty shows, real being signifies precisely being as sayable. For Kierkegaard, though, this is not to attend to the essential pain of existence: that consciousness will *always already*, at its very first moment, have lost its relation to reality (i.e., immediacy) and so become "untrue." Indeed, this loss and untruth is the very condition, the very "truth" one could say, of consciousness. Kierkegaard writes:

> Cannot consciousness, then, remain in immediacy? This is a foolish question, because if it could there would be no consciousness at all. But how, then, is immediacy cancelled (*hæves*)? By mediation, which cancels immediacy by *pre*-supposing it (*ved at forudsætte den*). What, then, is immediacy? It

is reality itself. What is mediation? It is the word. How does the one cancel the other? By giving expression to it, for that which is given expression is always presupposed. (*JC* 168; *Pap.* IV B 1, 146; slightly altered)

Consciousness is in itself a suspending of immediacy. If there is consciousness, mediation has already taken place. Consciousness *is* that mediation. Yet consciousness is a suspending of immediacy only inasmuch as, and to the extent that, it expresses it. So much expression, so much consciousness: consciousness lives in language from its inceptual instant. Consciousness is, one could say, *apophansis:* its basic function is to introduce ideality, to bring things to determination, to truth, to express something as something. It is within this doubling of reality that doubt becomes possible.

Within the relation of immediacy as such, doubt would be impossible simply because "*immediately . . . everything is true*" (*JC* 167; *Pap.* IV B1, 146). Nevertheless, as Hegel already pointed out, such truth is purely momentary, and hence "this truth is untruth the very next moment, for *in immediacy everything is untrue*" (ibid.). The immediate is the purely momentary, what has no duration. The work of consciousness, expressing the immediate, is to constitute a duration, an extended now, by re-presenting the immediate in consciousness's own terms, according to its own ideas. The immediate acquires duration, that is, only in its *repetition:* "The first expression for the relation between immediacy and mediation [i.e., for the expressing-canceling of the immediate] is *REpetition* (**Gjen**tagelsen)" (*JC* 260; *Pap.* IV B 10:8). Kierkegaard himself highlights the "re-" in repetition: reality acquires determination and permanence only in being taken up *again* by consciousness, that is, re-presented. The present is not original, but rather a re-presenting.

Reality is simultaneously gained and lost in its repetition. As repetition, consciousness itself interjects duplicity into reality by opening the distinction between appearing and being. As repetition, consciousness is not a domain of certainty and identity, but rather of duplicity. For as soon as there is consciousness, a gap has already been opened up between reality as reality (immediacy), and reality as expressed (mediation): more simply, between reality and its repetition. The "thing" is duplicated: it is something in-itself and something for-us; it is, *and* it appears as what it is. It is precisely in terms of this originary duplicity, inseparable from the function of consciousness itself, that doubt finds its general possibility.

THE COMING INTO EXISTENCE
OF CONSCIOUSNESS

To be means to be repeated. Strictly speaking, for consciousness, something is only in being taken again—that is, in being reconstituted within consciousness in its own terms and according to its own laws. In this sense, again, Kierkegaard's analysis reaffirms the egology of idealism. But with one decisive difference: in re-constituting reality for itself, which means in constituting its own original moment, consciousness does not simply render reality transparent, but "produces something other." Something genuinely new comes into being with consciousness: a present. At the same time, however, this originary present comes into being only through, and as, a *re*-presenting. Thus the very first moment of consciousness already depends upon a prior movement. Consciousness must already in some way be before it can be. The question is really this: Can consciousness think its own coming into existence? Is it possible to think the transition *to* consciousness as itself a movement *of* consciousness? Can consciousness occur prior to itself? There is a familiar circle here: "The old question of which came first, the tree or the seed—if there were no seed, where did the first tree come from; if there were no tree, where did the first seed come from" (*JC* 255; *Pap.* IV B 10:14).

But the passage from real-reality to ideal-reality, from immediacy to mediation, according to Kierkegaard, cannot be analyzed as a movement within a single duration. Repetition indeed has the same structure as mediation: reality is cancelled (*hæves*) and set into the light of ideality at the same time. The real is made plastic for consciousness. However, the "sublation" is not continuous, but a leap. In fact, even talking about a transition from immediacy to mediation is misleading insofar as it prompts one to imagine a moment of consciousness prior to the present but continuous with it. The transition from immediacy to mediation, however, is not a transition from one moment of consciousness to another moment of consciousness, but rather a transition *to consciousness* in the first instance. What is at stake is precisely "the coming into existence of consciousness" (*JC* 257; *Pap.* IV B 14:9).

Fichte, who opened the path for Hegel and post-Kantian idealism, thought this circularity in terms of consciousness as *self*-positing.[32] He takes consciousness as a point of absolute origin and embraces the paradox of an act that would precede any one who acts. Fichte writes: "The I reverts *into itself*. Does this not imply that the I is already present for itself, in advance of and independently of this act of self-reversion? In order for the I to be able to act upon itself, must it not already be present for itself in advance? . . . By no means! The I *originally* comes into being for itself by means of this act, and it is only in this way that the I comes into being at all."[33] Consciousness is only as self-reversion; nothing is prior to this. Self-reversion or self-positing *is* the origin. For Kierkegaard, however, this is to sidestep the "principal pain of existence, that *from the beginning* I am in contradiction with myself" (*JC* 253; *Pap.* IV B 10a). What is original to consciousness is not its identity with itself or its reversion into itself, but rather its contradiction of itself or its difference from itself. In relation to itself, consciousness does not *posit* itself (*sætter sig selv*), as Fichte said—that is, not as pure origin. Rather, "consciousness pre-sup-poses itself (*for-ud-sætter sig selv*)" (*JC* 255; *Pap.* IV B 10:14): that is, it posits itself not as origin, but in relation to a prior instant that it cannot posit. The originary suspension of immediacy is not, in this case, simply an act of consciousness (pure self-reversion). Consciousness does not simply condition itself.

To suggest that consciousness posits itself would be to say that it initiates, through its own absolute spontaneity, the break from immediacy. This would be to say that consciousness speaks some absolute word, that it brings itself into being through speaking itself. In that case, its "word" would be precisely the truth of being; it would be its own word, its own expression. If that were the case, however, it would not be possible to account for the essential possibility of doubt. Hence, the break from immediacy must be thought not as pure self-positing but in terms of some prior disruption, a certain "collision" (*Sammenstødet*), which will have befallen consciousness as immediate: "for consciousness emerges precisely through the collision, just as it presupposes the collision" (*JC* 171; *Pap.* IV B, 149). What conditions the emergence of consciousness, then, is a certain *interruption* of immediacy: consciousness finds itself, it posits itself, only in finding itself interrupted.[34] It would not be a collision between consciousness and something else, of course, because at issue is that whereby there is consciousness in the first place. In terms of the origin of consciousness, then, Kierkegaard points to a passive condition: consciousness comes into existence through an interruption of itself. It comes into existence, from the beginning, in pain. Its first moment is a moment of loss, not positing. From the beginning it is not present to itself, but divided from itself. As interrupted, consciousness both does and does not posit itself. This originary self-division or duplicity is the radical condition of doubt.

The "untruth" or originary duplicity of consciousness, which makes doubt possible, thus arises in two ways: "The possibility of doubt, then, lies in consciousness, whose nature is a contradiction that is produced by a duplicity and that itself produces a duplicity" (*JC* 168, altered; *Pap.* IV B 1, 147). On the one hand, consciousness itself introduces duplicity insofar as, expressing the real, it opens the distinction between reality in itself and reality for it. The whole of Hegel's dialectic, of course, aims to show how this duplicity is one that consciousness itself posits; it is a duplicity within an identity: "The distinction [between what is in itself and for us] falls within it," Hegel says.[35] Yet according to Kierkegaard consciousness emerges only on condition of a duplicity having already opened. Duplicity is not simply a distinction that consciousness itself enacts, but is the distinction whereby consciousness enacts itself.

Kierkegaard takes up the circularity of consciousness also with respect to the question of reflection. It may be thought that reflection, for example, is the origin of doubt. Kierkegaard, however, denies that this is so. "We could not," he says, "say that reflection produces doubt, unless we would express ourselves in reverse; we must say that doubt pre-supposes reflection, without, however, this *prius* being temporal" (*JC* 169–70; *Pap.* IV B, 147). Reflection is the condition for doubt, so doubt cannot be the *effect* of reflection. This points, however, to an ambiguity about reflection.

On the one hand consciousness *reflects* upon reality and represents it to itself. It draws a distinction between itself and its object. But this is not what conditions doubt. Rather, the condition for doubt lies in a reflection that precedes consciousness as its condition. Kierkegaard writes: "Reflection is *the possibility of the relation* [between reality and ideality]; consciousness is *the relation, the first form of which is contradiction*" (*JC* 169; *Pap.* IV B, 147). Though consciousness reflects, it does so only on condition of reflection. In other words, reflection—like the collision—occurs both prior to and after the emergence of consciousness. Reality and ideality must already have been set off reflectively vis-à-vis one another in order to account for the representational capability of consciousness. This refers to a difference that cannot itself be represented only because it serves as the general condition for representation.

Thus, consciousness is produced by and produces duplicity, emerges through and presupposes the collision, is and is not the origin of reflection. One cannot reduce consciousness, in terms of the conditions of its possibility, to any pure principle or ground, neither in the Fichtean transcendental-archeological way, nor in the Hegelian archeo-teleological way. What is "originary" is that consciousness just as much undergoes negation (difference, duplicity, contradiction), whereby it loses its self-originating status, as it controls and produces it. It is in the ambiguity between these two, the positing and non-positing, that doubt has the conditions of its possibility.

Consciousness is thus, from the beginning, not at one with itself—it is, in this sense, basically "untrue." As repetition, consciousness is itself the gap between reality and its re-presentation. It begins within this gap and it continually brings about this gap. For this reason, the possibility of doubt cannot be eliminated. That possibility rests in the gap between reality and its repetition, a gap that consciousness *is*. If one stuck to reality in all strictness simply *as it appeared,* then one would never be deceived or fall into doubt. For example: "I believe the one is an egg, the other is something resembling an egg" (*JC* 254; *Pap.* IV B 10:1). As long as I do not go beyond the statement that it resembles an egg—that is, that it appears to be an egg, whatever it might really be—I cannot be deceived. Such certainty recurs as the naïveté of consciousness, where it lives naively within its linguistic determinations, taking them for reality. Only when this naiveté is interrupted, where the gap between reality and its representation manifests itself, does the question of true being in the strict sense arise: "In the question of truth, consciousness is brought into relation with something else, and what makes this relation possible is untruth" (*JC* 167; *Pap.* IV B 1, 146). In the failure of representation and the consequent experience of untruth, consciousness, however, becomes attentive to its own role in the constitution of truth. And it catches sight of the ineliminable possibility of doubt: namely, that its relation to reality is structured through its own act of taking it up *again*. It catches sight of the fact that its immediacy is always already mediated and that the movement of mediation itself has opened the distinction between reality for it and reality in itself.

Consciousness is between reality and its re-presentation: it is, once again, *inter-esse*. This is what Kierkegaard means in thinking consciousness as "spirit" (*Aand*), but in a sense entirely different from Hegel's. He writes: "Consciousness is spirit, and it is remarkable that when one is divided in the world of spirit, there are three, never two" (*JC* 169; *Pap.* IV B 1, 148). In the break from immediacy something threefold opens. There are (1) the I who expresses or represents reality, (2) the thing expressed, or reality *as* represented for consciousness, and (3) the thing "itself" prior to its re-presentation. If there were not three terms, doubt would be impossible: "If there were nothing but dichotomies, doubt would not exist, for the possibility of doubt resides precisely in the third, which places the two in relation to each other" (*JC* 169; *Pap.* IV B 1, 148). Consciousness is the relation between the expression and the reality lost in that very expression. It is between the sayable and the unsayable; it is a need to say, a tension, an interest. For this reason, one cannot identify consciousness with the ego. Consciousness is a reference to alterity (the "third" term). Nor can one reduce consciousness, as the whole of Hegel's *Phenomenology* attempts to do, to self-consciousness. For if at any point, at either its beginning or its ending, consciousness lost its relation to alterity, if it could reduce reality to the domain of immanence and eliminate the possibility of doubt, it would cease as consciousness.

The possibility of doubt, in other words, is inseparable from the very possibility of consciousness. This implies that consciousness exists as fully actual only in the experience of doubt: "doubt is the beginning of the highest form of existence, because it can have everything else as its presupposition" (*JC* 170; *Pap.* IV B 1, 149). Doubt brings one into relation with what is *unconditioned:* not, as in Descartes, Fichte, or Hegel (though in very different ways!), a milieu of identity, but rather one of duplicity. Doubt points to that difference whereby consciousness is originally enabled. Thus the transcendental exploration of the essential possibility of doubt within consciousness has led to an opposite conclusion than one finds in idealism. Positing, synthesis, identity—and along with these knowledge and determination—are not originary and grounding. They are themselves conditioned by duplicity, a gap between the real and its representation. To summarize: Kierkegaard takes doubt as a transcendental clue for the clarification of the structure of "pure" consciousness. Doubt is a modality of the subject's relation to itself. Unlike both Descartes and Hegel, Kierkegaard considers doubt not as a moment in self-consciousness's becoming certain of itself, but precisely as "the highest," an unsurpassable condition. It is unsurpassable insofar as it points to a condition without which there could not be any *consciousness of* at all: the opening of a certain gap between consciousness and itself, an "inter" as the condition for any *inter-esse*. Without such a break, nothing could explain the inter-est located at the heart of the phenomenon of doubt. Outside of consciousness's having undergone an interruption before even being, as its very condition, self-consciousness could not feel itself vulnerable in the way that it does in doubt: vulnerable to itself. Moreover, doubt—whose dialectic is interminable—shows this vulnerability to be without measure, limitless. Doubt, then, is a phenomenon in which non-negatable negation "manifests" itself; it points to a subjectivity that does not originally have a hold on itself, but is rather exposed to transcendence as the very condition for its self-relation. Yet such a condition is occluded within any transcendental apperception or intuition.

REPETITION AND RECOLLECTION

At the end of part two, Kierkegaard takes up a question that becomes important in *Repetition:* the difference between repetition and recollection. He writes:

> Here the question is more specifically one of a repetition in consciousness, consequently of recollection. Recollection involves the same contradiction. Recollection is not ideality; it is ideality that has been. It is not reality; it is reality that has been—which again is a double contradiction, for ideality, according to its concept, has been, and the same holds true of reality according to its concept. (*JC* 171–72; *Pap.* IV B 1, 150, slightly altered)

Repetition and recollection set forth the characteristic moves of consciousness. Each involves the contradiction of reality and ideality touching each other—that is to say, coming together in such a way that their difference is not overcome. Within neither ideality nor reality as such could there be anything like repetition or recollection. The principal problem, however, is to grasp both the intervolvement of repetition and recollection and their difference from one another.

In the language already used in this chapter, recollection sets forth the nature of consciousness as *apophansis*. Recollection in itself involves repetition—namely that of determining something as something. To this extent recollection repeats the thing, that is, is in itself repetition. It repeats the thing by grasping it ideally. In this way the thing is retained and *held inwardly*, as a datum of consciousness, against the pure passage of time. Only through such a retention of the moment, a block on its passage, could there be a comparison of one moment with another to allow one, for example, to see two eggs as two instances of "the same." Without recollection, that is, the power to retain the moment from its slippage into nonbeing, there would be no consciousness. Recollection, then, which involves a repetition, is the more precise word to express the re-presenting function of consciousness. Under the category of recollection Kierkegaard is really thinking of representation. How then is repetition to be distinguished from representation?

Kierkegaard says, however, "only a repetition of what has been before is conceivable" (*JC* 171; *Pap*. IV B 1, 150). This is ambiguous. The question is: *where* or *when* has it been before? In the case of recollection, the point is that apophansis requires at least two moments separated by an interval. To determine an egg as (yet another) egg is necessarily to have recourse to a prior moment in which the same content was given. In the case of repetition, however, one is not speaking about a prior moment as to its presence, that is, as to what is given as the content of the moment, but rather about the very possibility of the moment. Here, then, the element of the "before" is entirely different: "before" signifies an anteriority that is the condition of presence—hence, refers not exactly to a prior moment, but to a priority that allows the moment to be. Such a "before" is not recuperable within any moment, and the moment of consciousness, the time of the present, thus always finds itself within a belatedness. Consciousness is repetition only insofar as it undergoes itself or finds itself passively related to itself. It is, but then discovers it must already have been. It is a repetition *of itself*.

These themes, barely outlined in part two of *Johannes Climacus*, are given a more extensive discussion in *Repetition*. One can already see, however, that the structure of the transcendental unity of self-consciousness has for Kierkegaard become problematic through a reflection upon doubt and its transcendental conditions. Self-consciousness, as spirit, discovers its enabling possibility in an alterity it cannot integrate, an alterity against which it "collides." In these terms, doubt emerges as a more absolute relation to the absolute than is possible within knowledge, which is always disinterested.

Johannes Climacus marks an important turn in the authorship. In this text, I have shown, Kierkegaard addresses two fundamental problems within

Hegel's thought: absolute knowledge and the nature of consciousness as "spirit." On the one hand, he clarifies an aporia clinging to the very idea of achieving total knowledge of any process still underway. The condition for absolute knowledge, he has said, could only be an alienated relation to one's own temporal instant. One would have to relate to one's own temporal instant in the modality of a future present (what it will have meant). Yet such a relation would annihilate the precise character of any *instant:* that it is underway, still open. The critique of absolute knowledge, then, leads one back to a consideration of temporality. On the other hand, Kierkegaard has appropriated Hegel's analysis of sense certainty. As I have shown, he basically endorses Hegel's point that immediacy (or reality) is never something simply given, but rather itself the result of mediation (ideality). *For consciousness* immediacy will always already have been suspended (presupposed).

The question with Hegel, however, has been whether or not this rupture with immediacy implies a difference that cannot be taken back. For Hegel, the very dialectic of consciousness, beginning with the contradiction between the saying and the said at the level of *sense certainty*, leads to the recovery of lost immediacy. The difference that consciousness undergoes in experience, becoming the very experience of despair, is for Hegel at bottom a moment in a larger teleological unfolding toward the reconciliation of consciousness with itself.

Kierkegaard, however, understands the rupture from immediacy in a radically different way: it is the ongoing and hence ineradicable condition of consciousness. What enables consciousness originally is what also disables it. While the very movement of consciousness is to suspend immediacy by positing it (determining it) in relation to itself, and hence taking itself as a radical origin of phenomena, it nevertheless remains exposed to what interrupts positing, an even prior origin. Consciousness is and is not the origin, the principle. It is between. And in this between there lies the essential possibility of doubt.

FOUR

Repetition (Repetition)

R*epetition: A Venture in Experimenting Psychology,* by Constantin Constantius, was written in 1843, immediately following *Johannes Climacus.* It was published on the same day as *Fear and Trembling* (October 16, 1843). At the center of the book's concern is the delimitation of a new category, "repetition" (*Gjentagelsen*), which is supposed to contrast with both Platonic recollection and Hegelian mediation. As a category it is supposed to "play a very important role in modern philosophy" (*FTR* 131; *SKS* 4:9). I have already briefly considered the notion of repetition as it appeared in *Johannes Climacus.* In that work, Kierkegaard understands consciousness itself as repetition: reality itself is doubled in and for consciousness so that it *appears* (is re-presented), and consciousness will always already have broken with its immediate relation to the real, and to this extent will always precede itself and consequently be a repetition of itself. *Johannes Climacus,* however, mainly aimed at clarifying this originary and ineradicable duplicity of consciousness, its basic "untruth." *Repetition* meditates the question: is a recovery of lost immediacy possible? To put it in different terms: now, once modern thought has grasped the thoroughly mediated character of the most immediate, is there anything like a second immediacy? Is it possible to relate to reality on the other side of its being-for-consciousness, so that "all things are new"?

More than anything, however, *Repetition* extends the critical problematic of *Johannes Climacus.* At stake is the event of coming-into-existence: not only of consciousness, but of the worldly context as a whole. The world, just as consciousness, is in itself a repetition. This means that the world cannot be thought without also thinking the path of its coming-into-existence. Yet here, just as with consciousness, a certain aporia lurks: the event of coming-into-existence does not itself unfold within time—it has no duration or continuity—but happens "in the instant." The critical problematic Kierkegaard's early works pursue is to keep clear about the distinction between the instant and the present, that is, between "originary" time and the time consciousness re-presents to itself. From Kierkegaard's perspective, idealism is founded as the very erasure of this distinction.

The event of coming-into-existence, or repetition, is simultaneously the interest of metaphysics and the interest upon which it founders: "[R]epetition is the *Interesse* of metaphysics, but also the *Interesse* upon which metaphysics comes to grief; repetition is the watchword in every ethical view; repetition is the *conditio sine qua non* for every issue in dogmatics" (*FTR* 149; *SKS* 4:25). In John Caputo's words, "the full range of onto-theo-logic —of metaphysics, ethics, and theology—is here delimited. There can be no mistaking the character of Kierkegaard's project. If it is 'religious,' as it certainly is, it proceeds by way of a religious delimitation of onto-theo-logic."[1]

Though *Repetition* is primarily literary in form—detailing a failed love affair and a failed return trip to Berlin—the notes to the text from Kierkegaard's *Papirer* contain invaluable hints and clues about its conceptual genesis. In order to provide the proper orientation toward the narrative of *Repetition,* then, it is important first to clarify its conceptual horizon as much as possible. The problem of repetition arises in quite determinate ways from certain aporiae found within the idealist treatment of freedom as absolute spontaneity. Fichte's *Vocation of Man* and Schelling's *Philosophical Investigations into the Essence of Human Freedom and Related Matters,* both studied closely by Kierkegaard—and in fact Kierkegaard studied Schelling's text just prior to writing *Repetition*—are especially important here in shaping the problematic Kierkegaard takes up.

I will begin then by laying out the conceptual horizon of *Repetition* as reconstructable from the notes.

REPETITION AS THE INTEREST OF FREEDOM: THE MODERN METAPHYSICS OF SUBJECTIVITY

Fortunately for readers of *Repetition,* Kierkegaard's contemporary J. L. Heiberg wrote a review of the book, which appeared in his little "New Year's Gift" *Urania.* Kierkegaard wrote but never published a response. What prompted Kierkegaard to write a response was Heiberg's critical comment that the category repetition is not applicable to the domain of self-consciousness or spirit, as implied in *Repetition,* but only to that of nature. Repetition refers, according to Heiberg, most properly to the circular rotation of the stars, which, when grasped in terms of its ontological significance, signifies nature's conformity to law. The repetition of natural phenomena is precisely what manifests the being of their being—namely, their sameness, their lawfulness. Thus Heiberg writes that in the repetition of natural phenomena we "should see the resting eternity, the fixedness, the security and infallibility, that specifically allows repetition to continue in order to be able to manifest itself through it" (*FTR* 380). According to Heiberg, when applied to the domain of spirit or consciousness, the proper category in terms of which to grasp the being of beings is not repetition, but "development" or "mediation." The latter explicitly places the emphasis upon the way in which spirit is capable, through its freedom, of assimilating its past and "achieving genuinely new beginnings" (*FTR* 379).

In responding to Heiberg's critique Kierkegaard distinguished between three kinds of repetition and their relation to freedom:[2] (1) Where freedom is qualified simply as desire, the repetition of the object of desire is avoided —one avoids, for example, having the same meal every evening. (2) Where freedom is qualified as "sagacity" or calculative thinking (*Klogskabet*), the repetition of phenomena is presupposed, but freedom knows how to introduce variation and diversion into the monotony. (3) Finally, where freedom is qualified only "in relation to itself" (*FTR* 302; *Pap.* IV B 112), everything is reversed: it becomes a question not of avoiding repetition or bearing up under it, but rather of producing repetition. Kierkegaard writes: "Now freedom breaks forth in its highest form, in which it is qualified in relation to itself. . . . Here emerges the issue: *Is repetition possible?* Freedom itself is now the repetition" (*FTR* 302; *Pap.* IV B 112).

Strictly speaking, then, the repetition at issue in *Repetition* concerns the possibility for freedom to take itself back to itself, to absolve itself to itself and preserve its capability from out of the circular rotations of being. The question is whether, in the midst of being's monological sameness, ever reproducing itself—which can express itself also within consciousness as the habitual or the addictive—freedom can retain a relation to itself that is absolute: "If it were the case that freedom in the individuality related to the surrounding world could become so immersed, so to speak, in the result that it cannot take itself back again (repeat itself), then everything is lost" (*FTR* 302; *Pap.* IV B 112). Repetition, in this sense, contrasts precisely with every return movement that has its foundation in the generality of law.[3]

Strictly qualified, then, the problem of repetition is a problem of freedom. As such, as Constantin has said, it is a category of *modern* philosophy. The modern metaphysics of subjectivity—partly retrieved and partly contested in *Repetition*—takes shape as the effort to show how the ego, as spontaneous thetic power, constitutes the radical ground of experience. Freedom takes on all the predicates of unconditioned or absolute being. In this sense, freedom is the interest of modern metaphysics and, if one is to follow Constantin, the interest upon which it founders. What *Repetition* will seek to show, then, is that even though the modern metaphysics of subjectivity generates the interest in repetition, that very interest will lead to its undoing.

Repetition signifies freedom's accessing of its own power, its absolvence to itself. For freedom to be qualified only in relation to itself, however, is precisely for it to posit itself. In this sense, the Fichtean idea of the self-positing ego is embedded in the very formulation of the problem of repetition. To clarify this stratum is essential for grasping the foundering of first philosophy at issue in the text. Fichte discovers the root of freedom—and in fact the very root of life itself—within the ego's originary presence to itself. Thus, Fichte writes that intellectual intuition (the ego's presence to itself through the act of self-reversion) "contains within itself the source of life, and apart from it there is nothing but death."[4] Life is absolute freedom, pure thetic power, absolute beginning. The domain of finite or empirical experience, however, is "accompanied by a feeling of necessity," being bound within time and space and subject to necessity. It is in the context of experience, then, that Fichte presents freedom as the "supreme interest" of the self and the ultimate object of philosophical justification. "First philosophy" comes to signify the philosophical justification of freedom—or rather, of the *interest* in freedom. Philosophy is to acquire, in direct contrast to "dogmatic" thinking, an essentially practical and ethical horizon.[5] Fichte writes: "One's supreme interest and the foundation of all one's other interests is one's *interest in oneself.*"[6] Moreover, as Fichte makes clear, the interest in oneself is an interest in *retaining oneself* as a freedom amidst the dispersion of time. What threatens freedom according to Fichte is the possibility to become "dispersed and attached to objects,"[7] that is, inextricably entangled in finitude, to the point of losing any originary connection to itself.

This Fichtean interest in the ego's remaining present to itself amidst the dispersions of time, which states an ethical as much as metaphysical interest, shapes the conceptual background of a quotation like the following: "The issue [of repetition] will arise at this point again and again, insofar as the same individual in his history makes a beginning many times, or the question will again be whether each individual is capable of [beginning], or whether he is lost through his initial beginning, or whether what is lost through his initial beginning is not recoverable" (*FTR* 288; *Pap.* IV B 110). One can see, then, how profoundly Fichtean the interest in repetition is: it is a question, for both Fichte and Constantin, of clarifying the supreme interest of freedom and of establishing the priority of this interest over ontology. In addition, Fichte is very clear that the problematic of freedom must finally acquire a religious expression. In his *Vocation of Man,* a text Kierkegaard had studied as early as 1836, Fichte argues that the subject has its reality only in the act of faith (*Glauben*), which is an enactment toward the future.[8] The subject is perpetually on its way to being, or between being (*inter-esse*); it never *is* its being. Faith, then, as an act, is itself a matter of continual renewal (repetition).

This ethical-religious horizon is embedded within the problematic of *Repetition*. Nevertheless, Kierkegaard reshapes the problematic fundamentally by placing it in relation to its limit, or foundering. For Fichte, the "initial beginning"—the ego's transcendental presence to itself—constitutes the ground of its futural being. The "inter" of *inter-est* is that the ethical-religious subject hovers between an originary (transcendental) and a consummate moment of pure presence: between the "absolute I" and the "ideal I." For this reason, the movement of freedom, though separable from circular rotations of nature, itself becomes the repetition of general law—the moral law. Repetition as faith thus finally signifies, for Fichte, the particular losing itself in the universal, or returning to its foundation.[9] Faith is endless return to the foundation of presence, endless realization. This is the point at which Constantin will consider it necessary to think through the foundering of freedom. It will be a question of clarifying an "initial beginning" that *cannot* be recovered; and of thinking in terms of a future that exceeds the horizon of positing.

REPETITION AS JOY

The interest of freedom in *Repetition* is, then, finally the inverse of the interest Fichte identified: it is not an interest in oneself or in a return to self, that is, in the recovery of an originary presence to self, but rather in a departure from self. Although the supreme interest of freedom is in freedom itself—for "only in freedom's relation to the task of freedom is there earnestness" (*FTR* 292; *Pap.* IV B 111, 268)—freedom now signifies, inversely, a freedom *from* self rather than a freedom *for* self or a return to self. Freedom will mean breaking the autism of return.

A phenomenological marker for freedom as departure from self, one indicated in the text, is joy. Repetition constitutes the "blissful security (*salige Sikkerhed*) of the instant" (*FTR* 132, altered; *SKS* 4:10). In joy there is a breaking of return insofar as the instant itself constitutes a new departure point. One is "lifted out" of the circuit of mundane rotations in an instant that is not substitutable with any other, but singular. Joy is a departure—not toward any telos/ground—but departure simply. In a significant passage Constantin describes a certain ecstatic departure:

> At one time I was very close to complete satisfaction. I got up feeling unusually well one morning. My sense of well-being increased incomparably until noon; at precisely one o'clock, I was at the peak and had a presentiment of the dizzy maximum found on no gauge of well-being, not even on

a poetic thermometer. My body had lost its terrestrial gravity; it was as if I had no body simply because every function enjoyed total satisfaction. . . . My being was transparent, like the depths of the sea, like the self-satisfied silence of the night, like the monological stillness (*Monologisk Stillhed*) of midday.(*FTR* 173, altered; *SKS* 4:47)

Although there is nothing to suggest any direct link, this passage has curious resonances to the *Enneads* 4.8.1.[10] The allusions to the Neoplatonic experience of the plenitude of being, or rather of the One beyond being, the "All-Highest," are remarkable: not only does Constantin repeat that the event happened at precisely *one* o'clock, but the event itself is an entrance into *monological* stillness—that is to say, into pure transparency, pure interiority, the exclusion of everything exterior, the suspension of dualisms, the pleromatic presence of the absolute. This would seem to be the Neoplatonic experience of joy (which Hegel transforms into the experience of absolute knowledge). It is the moment of ab-solution, the liberation from the generality of law, from being and nonbeing.

Within Neoplatonism, the event of repetition would signify the return (*epistrophe*) to the absolute. The joy of surpassing being and nonbeing, which coincides with the liberation from projects and ends, and from knowledge, culminates the movement of intellection. Yet, as Plotinus underscores, it is a moment by its very nature sudden and paradoxical, arriving not as the outcome of a process, but essentially as a grace. It is never the object of an achievement.[11] Such joy cannot be produced, anticipated, or fabricated. It is beyond poiesis, not even registering on the "poetic thermometer." This is a significant notation insofar as, later in the text, Constantin draws a decisive distinction between the poetic and the religious. The above experience is beyond the poetic, beyond representation.

And yet in the end the representational movement of consciousness consumes, as it were, this excess from the inside: "As stated, it was one o'clock on the dot when I was at the peak and had presentiments of the highest of all; when suddenly something began to irritate one of my eyes, whether it was an eyelash, a speck of something, a bit of dust, I do not know, but this I do know—that in the same instant I was plunged down almost into the abyss of despair, something everyone will readily understand who has been as high up as I was and, while at that point, was also preoccupied with question of principle as to whether in general it is possible to achieve absolute satisfaction" (*FTR* 173, altered; *SKS* 4:47). A chance speck of dust in the eye occasions the fateful return to consciousness. It is hardly accidental that the *eye* is afflicted. In Neoplatonism vision, a cipher for intellection, is still the dominant faculty—even if vision is finally only of light itself. In the *modern* context of *Repetition,* the eye stands as a cipher for intellectual intuition or self-positing. As soon as self-consciousness awakens, immediacy is killed. The whole experience plays out doubly: living it, and being aware of living it. And self-consciousness cannot be evaded even at the highest moments of ecstasy.

Constantin draws the essentially modern conclusion from his experience that absolute satisfaction is impossible: "As soon as I asked myself or there was a question about perfect satisfaction for even a half an hour, I always [thereafter] declared *renonce*" (*FTR* 174; *SKS* 4:47). What I wish to underscore is this: Constantin says "it was after that time [i.e., after the *renonce*] that I turned to and began to get excited about repetition" (*FTR* 174; *SKS* 4:47). The genesis of the *question* of repetition, then, may be found in the need for a rearticulation of the kind of event Plotinus mentions in the experience of a departure from being. It is a question of rearticulating the event of transcendence, the inbreaking of the absolute into time, in its suddenness.[12] There is a vestige of this theme in *Repetition,* even if it is transformed and made more difficult by the modern metaphysical context of subjectivity.

REPETITION AND MEDIATION

The author of *Repetition* provides a fundamental coordinate for the interpretation of the category repetition in the following: "If one knows anything of modern philosophy and is not entirely ignorant of Greek philosophy, one will readily see that this category precisely explains the relation between the Eleatics and Heraclitus, and that repetition proper is what has mistakenly been called mediation" (*FTR* 148; *SKS* 4:25). Repetition names what mediation would have liked to name, but did not. In the notes to *Repetition* Kierkegaard expands upon his mention of the Eleatics and Heraclitus:

> Movement is dialectical, not only with respect to space (in which sense it occupied Heraclitus and the Eleatics and later was so much used and misused by the Sceptics), but also with respect to time. The dialectic in both cases is the same, for the point and the moment correspond to each other. Since I could not name two schools in which the dialectic of motion with respect to time is expressed as explicitly as Heraclitus and the Eleatics express it with respect to space, I named them. (*FTR* 309; *Pap.* IV B 112)

In order to account for Constantin's framing of the problem in this way, it is necessary to refer to Hegel's reading of what he calls, in his *Lectures on the History of Philosophy,* "the Eleatic School" and its relation to Heraclitus. Though Kierkegaard's author does not cite Hegel's discussion explicitly, there are strong indications that he had this in mind.[13]

According to Hegel, the relation between the Eleatics and Heraclitus involves the transition from "being to becoming."[14] This is the transition from the monism of the Eleatics, according to which "only Being is, non-Being is not," to the conception of Heraclitus, in which the reality of nonbeing—which is to say motion, negativity, finitude—is firmly grasped. According to Hegel, what one finds in Heraclitus is "a perfecting of the Idea into a totality, *which is the beginning of Philosophy,* since it expresses the essence of the Idea, the Notion of the infinite . . . as that which is, i.e. as the unity of opposites."[15] Heraclitus grasps in an original way the speculative idea, which is that the Absolute is precisely the identity of being and nonbeing, or that being is, originally, becoming. The absolute is not, as in Parmenides, being in absolute, self-identical simplicity, exclusive of all movement, but precisely the dialectical or *mediated* identity of being and nonbeing. Hegel writes of this: "The recognition of the fact that Being and non-being are abstractions devoid of truth, that the first truth is to be found in Becoming, forms a great advance. The understanding comprehends both as having truth and value in isolation; reason, on the other hand, recognizes the one in the other, and sees that in the one its 'other' is contained."[16] Each pole—being and nonbeing, the whole and the part, finite and infinite, subject and object, and so on—*is* only as the other of *its* other, and thus as dialectically identical to it: "since each is the 'other' of the 'other' as its 'other,' we have here their identity."[17] That is the "great principle," Hegel says, "that can be found in the beginning of my Logic."[18] Like Socrates and Descrates, then, Hegel interprets Heraclitus in terms of a beginning that would be redeemed only in terms of his own thought—which is to say, from the perspective of the history of thought finding itself. The first truth, that with which philosophy begins, is the dialectical intervolvement of being and nonbeing, or movement.

Like Constantin, moreover, Hegel resituates the issue between the Eleatics and Heraclitus in relation to the modern problem of temporality: "If we were to say how that which Heraclitus recognized as principle, might, in the pure form in which he recognized it, exist for consciousness, we could mention nothing else but time; and it quite accords with the principle of thought in Heraclitus to define time as the first form of Becoming."[19] Recalling his discussion of sense-certainty, Hegel writes: "It is not that time is or is not, for time is non-being immediately in Being and Being immediately in non-being: it is the transition out of Being into non-being, the abstract Notion (*Begriff*), but in an objective form, i.e. in so far as it is for us."[20] Time, in other words, is movement as re-presented, or "being becoming as perceived."[21] For Hegel, then, the relation between the Eleatics and Heraclitus was that the latter apprehended the thoroughly mediated character of all immediately given being: "Not this immediate being, but absolute mediation, Being as thought of, Thought itself, is the true Being."[22]

Kierkegaard's author, however, suggests that this is to misconstrue Heraclitus's advance beyond Parmenides. Heraclitus discovered not mediation, we may assume, but repetition. What is the difference? Simply put, mediation implies that movement is always the movement of logos, that is, of self-consciousness. Hegel's move to interpret the Heraclitean beginning as the beginning of his own *Logic,* where it is a question of justifying "self-knowing truth" as the "sole subject matter and content of philosophy,"[23] is emblematic of his effort to think movement as the movement of consciousness coming to itself. Movement falls within consciousness's presence to itself; the dialectic of movement is the dialectic of self-consciousness. Kierkegaard regards this as an aberration in the tradition: "for the very reason that movement is dialectical with respect to the category of time, it has been assigned a place in the philosophy of spirit in both ancient and modern philosophy, but, please note, has been mistakenly applied to logic only by Hegel" (*FTR* 322, *Pap.* IV B 1 309).

If repetition is not mediation, then, that is because it presents the movement of coming-into-being as, indeed, originary, but not as recuperable in and for self-consciousness. In short, it presents movement as precisely transcendence, not immanence. The concept of mediation, Kierkegaard judges, has "helped to make the transcendence of movement illusory" (*FTR* 308; *Pap.* IV B 117, 289). The task of *Repetition* is thus to present, in an experimental way, the transcendence that belongs to movement, or to temporalization, as precisely the real. Its aim is to undo and unlearn certain conceptions of movement.

REPETITION AS CREATION

One of the more suggestive ways Constantin presents the category of repetition is to say that it signifies the event of creation itself: "If God himself had not willed repetition, the world would not have come into existence. Either he would have followed the superficial plans of hope or he would have retracted everything and preserved it in recollection. This he did not do. Therefore the world continues, and it continues because it is a repetition" (*FTR* 133; *SKS* 4:10–11). Repetition here clearly signifies the event in which the world as a whole first comes into being and continues in being.[24] It is the condition in and by which there is world at all, what Ed Mooney refers to as "transcendental world-bestowal."[25] In this sense, then, repetition is no merely ontic, nor even existential, problematic. It suggests an event, which it characterizes as repetition in order to contrast it to hope and recollection, in terms of which there first is a worldly context. Moreover, it is no less essential that God *wills* repetition. The world emerges through no necessity, but on condition of a freedom that is absolute.

It would not be altogether wrong to interpret the above quotation in light of the theological doctrine of *creatio continua*. Yet this would fail to grasp the specificity of the notion of repetition in its contrast to (a divine) hope and recollection. That God neither hopes nor recollects would be to say that the instant of creation, as repetition, is to be thought as the emergence of transcendence or alterity vis-à-vis divine self-consciousness. Repetition would point to something paradoxical: that the *world itself transcends God,* even though God creates it. God does not "contain" the context of worldliness, and therefore God cannot, strictly speaking, constitute its ground. If creation is repetition, it must be possible to think God as a creative non-ground or un-ground of the world.

Kierkegaard had an immediate precedent for this thought: Friedrich Schelling's *Philosophical Investigations into the Essence of Human Freedom and Related Matters.* Kierkegaard's notes show that he had read Schelling's treatise just prior to writing *Repetition.*[26] The influence of Schelling's 1809 treatise on *Repetition* (as well as *The Concept of Anxiety*) is decisive. Schelling's treatise is in part an effort to show on what condition one could think human freedom, in its radical meaning as autonomy or self-positing, as capable of coexisting with an absolute, divine will. Schelling solves this problem, relying on Jacob Boehme, through appeal to the notion of a divine "ground." He writes:

> Absolute causality in one being leaves nothing but unconditional passivity for all others. This leads to the dependency of all the world's beings upon God, so that even their sustenance is but a constantly renewed creation in which the finite being is produced not as an undetermined generality, but as this determined, particular being, having these and no other thoughts, strivings, actions. To say that God restrains his omnipotence explains nothing: if God withdrew his power for an instant, man would cease to be. Since freedom in contradiction to omnipotence is inconceivable, is there any other alternative to this argument except to save man with his freedom in the divine being itself, to say that man is not outside God, but in God, and that his activity belongs to the life of God?[27]

An autonomous, self-positing creature, Schelling explains further, is possible in relation to divine omnipotence only if it has its ground "in that which is God, but *is not God himself,*" i.e., in that which is the ground of his existence."[28] Schelling links the possibility of freedom in the radical sense as self-positing to that in God which is not God: not to God as absolute existence, but to God as the (abyssal) ground of existence.

Schelling grasps the divine ground, which neither is nor is not God, in figurative language as "the longing felt by the eternal one to give birth to itself"; or, in more conceptual language, as "everything that lies beyond absolute identity."[29] The ground is an eternal about-to-be, an eternal beginning that remains at its beginning. Schelling also characterizes the ground as a groundless, eternal, self-affirming will—but a "will in which there is no understanding, and which therefore is not autonomous and perfect will."[30] The divine ground, then, is an indeterminate potential to be, that which is presupposed in every act of existence—whether human or divine. What God creates must, precisely as created, transcend God. The creature expresses the divine ground, that of God which is nevertheless not God. Schelling writes: "The consecution of things from God is a self-revelation of God. God can reveal himself only in what is like him, in free beings that act by themselves, for whose being there is no ground except God, but who are as God is. He speaks, and they are there. Even if all the world's beings were only thoughts in the divine mind, for this very reason they would have to be living."[31] For God, to think is not to represent, but to create. Hence the creature, as a creature, would be simultaneously absolute and relative: "The concept of a derivative absoluteness or divinity is so little contradictory, that it is far more the central concept of all philosophy."[32] Yet this would only be to say that, as an absolute-relative or relative-absolute, the creature constitutes precisely a *repetition* of the divine life.

In Kierkegaard's text, God's willing of repetition is the condition in which there is a world at all: "the world continues, and it continues because it is a repetition" (*FTR* 133; *SKS* 4:11). The world as a whole is not to be thought starting from presence or being but, from its very inception, as a recommencing. Every present, every span of duration, refers to a prior instant that does not fall within a continuum of presence. Each instant starts with itself, or is an absolute beginning.[33] Yet what the Schellingian background of the text allows us to see is that the absolute beginning at issue here is anarchic, an eternal about-to-be, departing without *departing toward*. Creation as repetition presupposes this abyssal ground (or *Afgrund*). If God's act of creation contained no moment of excess, no creative insanity, as it were, then creation would not be what it is: the birth of something *other* than God (a self-positing freedom). Creation is the breach of divine immanence, the instant wherein God abandons both hope and recollection, the instant in which God relates to an other that cannot be taken back into identity.

In the letters on Job in part two of *Repetition* this creation as alterization is mentioned: "[Job] knows that despite his being frail, despite his withering away like a flower, that in freedom he has something of greatness, *has a consciousness that even God cannot wrest from him even though he gave it to him*" (*FTR* 208, my italics; *SKS* 4:76). Self-consciousness, in other words, is simultaneously relative and absolute: something simultaneously bestowed by God and, for that very reason, abandoned by God (let go). These are the conditions, the conditions of a birth, in which the tormenting "ordeal" of self-consciousness, an event at the very heart of *Repetition,* becomes essentially possible.

Highlighting the Schellingian background of the text also serves to clarify its difference from Hegel: creation as repetition would not be mediation, that is, the movement of God's own self-othering. The creaturely order, particularly finite self-consciousness, cannot find its ontological meaning, as repetition, in that it is a moment of divine self-exposition. On the contrary, the creaturely must be able to claim its own paradoxical autonomy vis-à-vis God—not merely as a necessary moment in divine self-exposition, but as something non-collapsible to divine life. Here again, the difference between Hegel and Schelling—and *Repetition* definitely follows Schelling in this regard—is that Hegel finally erases anything like an abyssal ground to reality. In terms of his archeo-teleo-logic, he could never maintain the idea of an indeterminate divine will, or a divine longing, except as the mere beginning of a process of self-determining and self-discovery.

Kierkegaard's reliance upon Schelling apparently also reflects his positive relation to the sources of Schelling's thought: above all, the thought of Jacob Boehme. In a note Kierkegaard refers to this reliance: "Thus movement plays a major role in the whole Schellingian philosophy, not only in his philosophy of nature . . . but also in his philosophy of spirit. So, also, in his treatise on freedom, where, moving partly in Jacob Boehme's expressions and partly in his self-made paraphrases, he constantly struggles to include movement" (*FTR* 322; *Pap.* IV 117, 7). Schelling never mentions Boehme in the treatise, and yet Kierkegaard saw clearly, on the basis of his own reading of Boehme, the profoundly Boehmean nature of it—to the point of seeing Schelling's treatise as paraphrase.[34] For Boehme, as with Schelling, the creature cannot be a mere moment in the self-exposition of divine life;[35] it can claim real alterity. God's *self*-revelation, in this sense, signifies not God's discovery of himself in otherness, but the bestowal of another self, a bestowal that keeps nothing in reserve. For God to will repetition is thus, in Boehmean-Schellingian terms, to let go of the function of grounding so that genuine and radical otherness, that is, freedom, can be.[36]

RECOLLECTION AND REPETITION
AS EXISTENTIAL CATEGORIES

All of the above has been an effort to fill out the conceptual horizon of the category of repetition. In the strict sense, however, repetition must be thought as an *existential* category: that is, it refers to a relation, as Constantin said, that freedom has toward itself. A certain self-relation, then, is named in repetition. Is freedom capable of retaining itself? Earlier I showed this problem was paramount for Fichte as well. Fichte marked a difference between entangled, ontic freedom and ontological freedom (the will as pure self-positing, absolute origin). The task of existence was to retrieve one's ontological freedom amidst one's finitude, an essentially infinite task. *Repetition*, too, raises freedom as an initially ontological problem. Only here the problem is radicalized: the possibility is raised that freedom may be entangled in itself, that it may not be a pure positing, a pure origin, but might refer essentially back to some even prior origin. What if freedom is not an origin, but an effect; what if it finds its enabling condition in something transcendent? If so, then the modern metaphysics of the subject, centered upon its original thetic power, would founder. At the instant of foundering, the interest in repetition must turn from the task of infinite self-realization (Fichte) to the work of *patience*: waiting upon an event that cannot be produced through the subject's thetic power. The work of freedom is essentially a work of patience, not positing. That is the reversal at issue in *Repetition*.

Constantin defines the category "repetition" in a way that may seem, at first, to be dialectical. He says repetition and recollection are the "same" movement, but they move in opposite directions. He writes:

> Repetition and recollection are the same movement, except in opposite directions, for what is recollected has been, is repeated backward, whereas genuine repetition is recollected forward. Repetition, therefore, if it is possible, makes a person happy, whereas recollection makes him unhappy—assuming, of course, that he gives himself time to live and does not promptly at birth find an excuse to sneak out of life again, for example, that he has forgotten something. (*FTR* 131; *SKS* 4:9)

Is repetition *possible*? This is not given; in fact to problematize repetition as a possibility offered to freedom is what *Repetition* accomplishes. Nevertheless, the structure of repetition can be defined more closely by contrasting it with recollection. Recollection, then, is in itself a repetition, and repetition is in itself a recollection. The two movements, though opposite, presuppose one another. Outside of these two, no meaning emerges: "if one does not have the category of recollection or of repetition, all life dissolves into an empty, meaningless noise" (*FTR* 149; *SKS* 4:25). What then is the identity in difference, or difference in identity, between the two? First of all, it is necessary to distinguish between an ontic and an ontological meaning of the terms. One can recollect a content or repeat an action, but such acts do not refer to the essential problem. More than particular acts, recollection and repetition refer to the structure of consciousness itself.[37] Recollection refers to the ontological conditions of *knowledge*, repetition of *life*.

Kierkegaard's understanding of recollection probably derives from Hegel's reading of Plato in his *Lectures on the History of Philosophy*. Hegel comprehends recollection according to its ontological significance: "Knowledge of the universal is nothing but recollection (*Erinnerung*), a going with-in self, and that we make that which at first shows itself in external form and determined as a manifold, into an inward, a universal, because we go into ourselves and thus bring what is inward in us into consciousness."[38] Recollection thus states the ontological meaning of the movement of knowledge as a relation to ideality, where ideality constitutes both the "inner," universal side and the real being of the immediate. In terms of its ontological meaning, then, recollection does not signify a mere memory of something past. As a backward repetition, constituted fundamentally as a movement of knowledge, it signifies bringing to presence the *truth* of temporality—which is to say its ideality. This is the sense in which, as Constantin says, for the Greeks "all knowing is recollecting" (*FTR* 131; *SKS* 4, 9). To recollect is to come to the ground of a phenomenon, a retreat back to what is *ontologically* prior—the essence, the idea, the principle. It is to go past the outside surface of a phenomenon to its inside, past its particularity to its universality, past its eventfulness to its meaning. The ideality of an event (its meaning) can be known only on condition of its pastness. The owl of Minerva, Hegel says, flies only at dusk. Recollection is therefore less an act of knowledge than the ontological condition of any knowledge.

In addition to the meaning of recollection as what constitutes the ontological ground of knowledge, however, there is another meaning more closely related to a Platonic mythos. In the *Symposium* dialogue, for example, Plato presents the movement of recollection in terms of the pre-philosophical experience of desire, or eros, in the presence of beauty. The movement of erotic desire leads from particular to more and more general instances of beauty and finally culminates in the vision of absolute beauty —that is, beauty "that neither comes nor goes, neither flowers nor fades."[39] Yet beauty is still interpreted as the object of vision, and hence as ideality and as that which remains constantly present. In this sense, it is the object of recollection, and what binds the Hegelian and Platonic versions is the shared presupposition that what is real of anything lay in its ideality; moreover, that ideality is that of a thing which remains constantly present and thus capable of being brought back to presence (known). Recollection presupposes the coincidence of ideality and reality in the movement of knowledge.

The "young man" in the narrative of *Repetition*, who will exemplify the movement of recollection, we shall see is neither a Hegelian nor a Platonist.

He shares with both an orientation that grasps the reality of the real in terms of its ideality. Yet the Idea is for him the object of a poetic meditation. Thus, recollection becomes an act of poiesis—or rather, poiesis is thought as an act of recollection. Hence, a *third* meaning to the term recollection: poiesis. All three of these meanings are in play in the text.

Repetition, in contrast to recollection, signifies *recollection forward*. Whereas recollection articulates the radical conditions structure of knowledge, repetition expresses those of life: "all *life* is a repetition." Life is here opposed to knowledge as "transcendence" is to "immanence."[40] As with recollection, it is necessary to free the category from its merely ontic meaning. There is no repetition, it should be evident, in the mere iteration of things, for there is no forward movement in that. The forward direction of repetition signifies a relation to the future. However, repetition must be sharply distinguished from hope: "Hope is a new garment, stiff and starched and lustrous, but it has never been tried on, and therefore one does not know how becoming it will be or how it will fit. Recollection is a discarded garment that does not fit, however beautiful it is, for one has outgrown it. Repetition is an indestructible garment that fits closely and tenderly, neither binds nor sags" (*FTR* 132; *SKS* 4:10). Hope is a relation to the future *as represented*, to the future under a definite ideal aspect, to what one can envision, calculate, move toward, the future as the realization of possibility articulable in the present. If repetition is a relation to the future, then, it is to the future as what escapes anticipation, foresight, calculability, and so on. Hence, quite simply, repetition is a relation to the *absolute future* (the future that remains unpresentable).

In what sense, however, is repetition precisely a *recollection* forward? Here one must attend to the significance, noted by Hegel in his discussion of Plato, of the etymological link between *Erindringen* (Danish) or *Erinnerung* (German) and the movement of interiorization. As an existential act, repetition thus names the movement whereby the absolute future is interiorized—something nevertheless impossible. Insofar as the absolute future withdraws from any anticipative foresight or calculation, insofar as the modality of its coming is always "sudden" and interruptive, the act of repetition thus translates a work of patience: learning, in other words, the essential finitude of freedom. At the same time, however, the recollective act at the heart of repetition also translates as holding to a certain expectancy aimed at the absolute future—not the expectation of any representable content, but the expectation of a certain renewal (the "all things have become new").[41]

Summarizing, one could say repetition, as existential act, signifies a becoming receptive toward temporality. Receiving time is the most basic work of the *living* subject. But to receive time—that is, to take it up always again

—entails learning the distinction between posited time (the time of projects) and originary time (the time undergone in patience). More exactly, it means affirming the temporality that cannot be posited, the temporality in which the thetic power of the subject is interrupted. To receive time is to affirm existence beyond the fulfillments dreamed of by the self-realizing subject. It would be an unconditional affirmation of existence, the "earnestness of existence" (*FTR* 133; *SKS* 4:11) itself.

I turn now to the narrative portions of *Repetition*, where these themes are experimentally in play.

Experimenting with Repetition

Repetition is a "venture in experimenting psychology." The category repetition can be presented only in a "venture" (*et Forsøg*) because it is subjected to the same dialectic it states: it does not preexist its presentation, but emerges in the very act of presenting it. In the end it is a matter of rendering visible the *question* of repetition—whether repetition is possible? Constantin pursues this question through two narratives: that of a failed return trip to Berlin and that of a failed romance. In each case repetition appears under a deferral, as what has not yet taken place. Part one of the book details the trip to Berlin, while part two considers the "young man's" failed love affair. I consider each in turn.

FARCE: THRESHOLDS
OF REPRESENTATION

Introducing his experiment in the possibility of repetition and its relation to recollection, Constantin writes: "When I was occupied for some time, at least on occasion, with the question of repetition—whether or not it is possible, what importance it has, whether something gains or loses in being repeated—I suddenly had the thought: You can, after all, take a trip to Berlin; you have been there once before, and now you can prove to yourself whether a repetition is possible and what importance it has" (*FTR* 131; *SKS* 4:9). The heart of the experiment of part one is Constantin's return to the Königstädter Theater in Berlin. There is a nested series of repetitions: the return to Berlin, the return to the theater in Berlin, and the theater as a site precisely of repetition. The theater, in fact, constitutes a site in an emblematic sense: it signifies the space of interiority itself, the space in which freedom relates to its own possibility. In these terms an analogy opens up, fundamental for the whole text, between the theater and existence. It becomes necessary to speak of the "play of existence" (*Tilværelsens Skuespil*). Through this analogy the long digression in part one on the theater, along

with the analysis of farce—for "farce is performed at the Königstädter Theater, and in my opinion superbly" (*FTR* 161; *SKS* 4:36)—shows itself to be
anything but a digression.[42]

The bulk of part one, then, is dedicated to the analysis of farce. One
has to ask why precisely farce? The answer is that "every aesthetic category
runs aground on farce" (*FTR* 159; *SKS* 4:34). The foundering of aesthetic
categories, however, points toward a foundering of the underlying concept
of the *subject* of aesthetic experience. The critique of farce becomes a critique of the subject thought, as in idealism, in terms of its power to represent reality to itself. It is a critique of the faculty of judgment, which identifies subjectivity with its power to determine the real on the basis of its
spontaneity. Those are the metaphysical stakes in the analysis of farce.

In his *Critique of Judgment* Kant lays out two forms of aesthetic judgment: the beautiful and the sublime. Judgments about beauty claim a universality they cannot demonstrate and so rest, in terms of their possibility,
upon a *sensus communis*—a shared experience of the world.[43] Yet farce does
not "succeed in producing a uniformity of mood." Constantin continues:
"For a cultured person, seeing a farce is similar to playing the lottery, except
that one does not have the annoyance of winning money. But that kind of
uncertainty will not do for the general theater-going public" (*FTR* 159;
SKS 4:34). Farce involves an incalculable, singular element whose effects
cannot be anticipated: "Seeing a farce can produce the most unpredictable
mood, and therefore a person can never be sure whether he has conducted
himself in the theater as a worthy member of society who has laughed and
cried at the appropriate places" (*FTR* 160; *SKS* 4:35). This fundamental
uncertainty undercuts any stable aesthetic consensus and, hence, the basis
of aesthetic judgment.

The "subject" of farce is not a subject capable, in Kant's terms, of assuming particulars under universals (in a "determinate judgment"), or ab-
stracting universals from particulars (in a "reflective judgment"). Rather,
the subject becomes much more fluid, much less like a subject in the idealist sense at all: "Thus did I lie in my theater box, discarded like a swimmer's
clothing, stretched out by the stream of laughter and unrestraint and ap-
plause that ceaselessly foamed by me" (*FTR* 166; *SKS* 4:40). This ceaselessly foaming Heraclitean stream leaves the subject discarded "like swim-
mers clothing." Closer to farce is the sublime. In the judgment of the
sublime there is a negative or indirect presentation of the absolute. Strictly
speaking, the sublime refers to no object, for it relates to the formless, the
unbounded, what the imagination cannot contain—in general, to what appears "contra-purposive" to the faculty of reflective judgment.[44] All we are
entitled to say, Kant writes, is that the object we call sublime "is suitable for
exhibiting a sublimity that can be found in the mind."[45] The mind itself,

that is, the spontaneous subject, is the locus of sublimity; the sublime is found in the judgment of sublimity.

In terms of this judgment, a certain dialectic ensues whereby the faculty of judgment—the subject—is first ungrounded by what it cannot contain and then regrounded. Kant says:

> The quality of the feeling of the sublime consists in being a feeling, accompanying an object, of displeasure about our aesthetic power of judging, yet of a displeasure that we present at the same time as purposive. What makes this possible is that the subject's own inability uncovers in him the consciousness of an unlimited ability which is also his, and that the mind can judge this ability aesthetically only by that inability.[46]

The moment of ungrounding is that in the sublime the imagination encounters an "abyss in which [it] is afraid to lose itself"; the presentational powers are torn up by an excess that seems counter-purposive to judgment. Re-presentation approaches its limit. And yet, as Kant says, this rupture is purposive on a different order: it is in fact reason (*Vernunft*) exerting its dominance over sensibility. The sublime shows that nature in its totality cannot exhibit the Idea and thus shows the priority of a supersensible or "rational vocation"—ultimately a moral vocation—over that of sensibility.[47] The judging subject is thus regrounded within a rational, supersensible order, the token of which is a feeling of elevation.

Like the sublime, farce relates to what "can no longer be contained in forms or lines"; it is "sheer lunacy," "sheer abandonment" (*FTR* 164; *SKS* 4:38). It is excess, a "plunge into the abyss of laughter." The difference from the sublime, however, is that the subject loses itself in this abyss, discarded like swimmer's clothing. The dialectical turn of regrounding on the basis of an intelligible order where, more precisely, the subject rediscovers itself as its own, autonomous ground, does not quite take place. Laughter takes the place of moral seriousness—but in laughter one does not have full possession of oneself. Farce is the sublime without regrounding. If the sublime exhibits the inadequacy of nature to present the Idea, farce exhibits the inadequacy of the faculty of judgment to contain the subject. The subject shows itself as more than a spontaneity or positing. Farce, then, constitutes a phenomenon that cannot be accounted for in terms of, and thus delimits, the work of representation. Farcical artists are geniuses who turn away from "faithful representation" (*tro Gjengivelse*) and "ideal reproduction" (*ideale Reproduction*). They are, Constantin says,

> not so much reflective artists who have studied laughter as they are lyricists who themselves plunge into the abyss of laughter and now let its volcanic power hurl them out on the stage. Thus they have not so much calculated

what they will do as let the moment and the natural power of laughter supply everything (*raade for Alt*). They have the courage to venture what the individual makes bold to do only when alone, what the mentally deranged do in the presence of everybody, what the genius knows how to do with the authority of genius, certain of laughter. They know that their hilarity has no limits, that their comic resources are inexhaustible, and they themselves are amazed at it practically every moment. They know that they are able to sustain laughter the whole evening without its costing them any more effort than it costs me to scribble this down on paper. (*FTR* 161; *SKS* 4:36, slightly altered)

Farce represents nothing. It is *essentially* performative, supplied entirely from resources of the moment. Its effect lies unpredictably and incalculably between the performers and the audience in the total accidentality of the situation. Like every performance, it is a repetition, but the movement of repetition in farce lies within a relation to the temporal moment *as* the incalculable (*uberegnelig*). Farce lives off temporality in its character as "accidental concretion," time as sudden, the absolute future as the incalculable. The farcical actor is necessarily surprised at himself. His movements are not grounded in any faculty of judgment or representation. The idea of what he will do arrives in the doing itself.

Constantin focuses his analysis of farce particularly upon the actor Beckmann: "[Beckmann] is not only able to walk, but he is also able to *come walking* (*komme gaaende*). To come walking is something very distinctive, and by means of this genius he also improvises the whole scenic setting" (*FTR* 164; *SKS* 4:38). The peculiar construction in Danish, *at komme gaaende* (to come walking), would perhaps be better rendered, though less literally, as "to arrive already under way." The genius of Beckmann is that he does not merely come into the scene as a space already constituted and fit into its context; rather, in arriving, he introduces the space or context into which he himself arrives as an element. He is the whole and the part. Beckmann does not merely arrive *into* the scene, he is the arrival *of* the scene. He appears along with the context in which he appears, and so is "sheer economy for a theater, for when it has him, it needs neither street urchins nor scenery" (*FTR* 164; *SKS* 4:138).

This analysis of Beckmann's performance points to the more general structure of coming into appearance: the "here and now," the scene of appearing, is self-presupposing and unto itself. The instant always takes itself "by the scruff of the neck" (*FTR* 164; *SKS* 4:138). Beckmann's dance presents the general character of *movement*. Movement is not within space and within time, but is rather the movement of space and time: the site of appearing and the appearing of what appears. Moreover, such coming into appearance is "sheer abandonment" that can "no longer be contained in forms or lines," excess. As a phenomenon, then, farce discloses the limits of representation: the here and now cannot be contained within the re-pre-senting, synthetic work of consciousness. The here and now are not con-tainable as *mediation*. At this point the whole problem of repetition—that is, whether a return to immediacy is possible—flips. The phenomenon of farce shows an immediacy that clings to representational consciousness in the form of something uncontainable. Aiming at a return to immediacy, consciousness discovers that the immediate returns to it in every possible way, but in precisely such a way that positing, representational conscious is continually undermined.

Hence, the comical result of Constanin's return trip to Berlin, where nothing turns out to be the same: "there simply is no repetition," something which he verifies "by having it repeated in every possible way" (*FTR* 171; *SKS* 4:45). The problem is that the judging, representing subject cannot re-tain all of its content. Life, as repetition, *gives* to consciousness more than it can keep, and so it *takes* away from consciousness what it would like to keep, that is, posit. Excess appears as lack. Consciousness finds itself in a double bind: life "unremittingly and treacherously retakes everything it had given (*tage Alt igjen*) without providing a repetition (*Gjentagelse*)" (*FTR* 172; *SKS* 4:45). Immediacy ceaselessly returns, not as consciousness re-turning to itself, but as the impossibility of return. Repetition turns out to be the exact opposite of what Constantin initially supposes: not the gather-ing of consciousness to itself, but the continual undoing of consciousness.

The true "subject" of part one is thus not the subject of modern meta-physics, but rather time itself: "Travel on, you fugitive river! You are the only one who really knows what you want, for you want only to flow along and lose yourself in the sea, which is never filled!" (*FTR* 176; *SKS* 4:49). Time is an absolute subject—not gathering itself into itself, or knowing it-self to be all reality, but continually losing itself. If there is repetition, it is this mortal undertow—giving all and taking all—that will have to be ad-dressed.

As a souvenir of his failed experiment and as an emblem of his view of life, Constantine adopts the stagecoach horn:

> Long live the stagecoach horn! It is the instrument for me for many reasons, and chiefly because one can never be certain of wheedling the same notes from this horn. A coach horn has infinite possibilities, and the person who puts it to his mouth and puts his wisdom in it can never be guilty of a repeti-tion, and he who instead of giving an answer gives his friend a coach horn to use as he pleases says nothing but explains everything. (*FTR* 175; *SKS* 4:48)

The only thing that repeats is the lack of repetition. A subject is what con-tinually loses itself to the sudden, to the incalculable, but without losing it-

self. The infinite possibilities for surprise played out in (or as) time continually undo the possibilities a subject can project for itself, that is, represent
to itself.

THE "YOUNG MAN":
A STUDY IN RECOLLECTION

The other narrative of part one, intertwined with the experiment of repetition, is that of the "young man" whose love has become stalled out in poetic
recollection. Just as Constantin attempts to stage-manage repetition, un-
successfully, he tries to "handle" the dilemma of the young man. This story
is the counterpoint to Constantin's experiment. The trip to Berlin ends in a
moment of dissemination rather than self-gathering. In face of this, Constantin retreats to stoicism. The young man follows a different path: that of
recollection or inwardization, the retreat to ideality, presence.[48] The two figures are as perfectly suited to one another as analyst and analysand.

The position of the young man recalls certain themes in Plato's dialogue *The Symposium*. The latter expresses a fundamental link between the
absolute—that which *is* in the strictest sense—and erotic desire. In the
Symposium the absolute appears as beauty, at once the object of longing and
of intellective vision. Particularly in the Diotima portion of the *Symposium*, eros is conceived as the medium of ideality or idealization, the very
link between the mortal and the divine, the temporal and the eternal. One
relates to the order of being through the experience of desire. Desire is the
"mean" between being and nonbeing, and for this reason Diotima describes
it as the child of penia and poros, poverty and abundance.

In the narrative of the young man, in which Kierkegaard's biography is
evident,[49] Constantin observes that "the idea was indeed in motion" (*FTR*
140; *SKS* 4:18). What idea? Simply the idea of the idea, the experience of
eidos. In many respects, the young man replays the transition analyzed in
chapter one with respect to *The Concept of Irony:* Plato opens philosophy as
metaphysics in the moment he abandons Socratic irony by, mythically, interpreting the absolute as the object of vision. As we shall see, the young
man lacks an "ironic resiliency" (*FTR* 137; *SKS* 4:15), a readiness for non-
vision and absence. His standpoint is mytho-poetic.

His conflict irrupts insofar as he relates to "the girl," the "border of his
being," not as other, but as an occasion for an experience of ideality. Constantin, who has installed himself as the confessor and confidant of the
young man, writes of him: "He was deeply and fervently in love, that was
clear, and yet immediately in one of the first days he was in a position to
recollect his love. He was essentially through with the entire relationship. In
beginning it, he took such a tremendous step that he leaped over life. If the
girl dies tomorrow, it will make no essential difference" (*FTR* 136, slightly

altered; *SKS* 4:14). The young man falls in love but, in the moment of rec-
iprocation, succumbs to the *idea* of love rather than to "the girl" herself.
The ideality, or poetry, of love overwhelms its reality. The girl becomes for
him merely an "occasion" in which he finds himself in a transfigured world,
in contact with the medium of ideality as such. In other words: "The young
girl was not his beloved: she was the occasion that awakened the poetic in
him and made him a poet" (*FTR* 138; *SKS* 4:15). She is the other whom he
needs to consolidate his own relation to the Idea. Once he awakens to the
poetic, however, she becomes the occasion who will not disappear, an alba-
tross around his neck.

If this narrative of failed love is somewhat banal, its analysis is not. The
essential problem, according to Constantin, is that "in the very first moment he became an old man in regard to the entire relationship" (*FTR* 136;
SKS 4:13). Niels Eriksen has called attention to the fascinating note in
Kierkegaard's *Papirer* where the complexity of this movement is evident.
Kierkegaard describes the dialectic of the poetic in this way: "[The poet]
first dreams that he is old in order to suck in through the funnel of a whole
life the most aromatic moment of his earliest youth" (*Pap.* III A 95; *JP*
804).[50] In this sense, recollection is the poetry, or rather the poetized. At a
limit, the poet would imagine himself dead in order to draw the plenitude
of meaning out of the present moment. Remarking on the situation of the
young man, Constantin observes: "His mistake was incurable, and his mistake was that he stood at the end instead of at the beginning, but such a
mistake is and remains a person's downfall" (*FTR* 137; *SKS* 4:14). The
problem is that the young man's love takes root within a beginning in which
the love is basically abrogated, a beginning in which, as Constantine says,
"he took such a tremendous step that he leaped over life" (*FTR* 136; *SKS*
4:13). It is only vis-à-vis a certain distance, a becoming older of the moment, that the truth or meaning of the moment becomes manifest and
thus—on idealist presuppositions—that the moment acquires reality. The
real is what consciousness can interiorize, that is, recollect. Recollection is
conditioned by a certain lapse, a forgetfulness, a death, in which the moment is nevertheless stored away. Such forgetfulness is the filter that separates out the ideal content of the moment from its mere appearance.

The young man's position as recollection involves the desire to suck *all*
of the meaning out of the present moment. He demands total meaning,
pure life. This can be had, however, only on condition of death: only if the
relationship is finished is it possible to grasp in its ideality, or to relate to poetically. It is no surprise, then, that he secretly dreams about the death of his
beloved: "if the girl dies tomorrow, it will make no essential difference"; "he
could almost have wished her dead." The death of the beloved—real or
imagined, it would hardly matter—allows the object of desire to be trans-

figured and converted into pure immanence. In pure immanence, the girl acquires virtual or represented reality: "In a sense, her existence or non-existence was virtually meaningless to him" (*FTR* 138; *SKS* 4:15).

There is a complicated erotics at work in the young man's position. On the one hand, there is a reinscription of Plato's *Symposium,* where erotic desire demands the death of its object and even of itself. Desire ascends always past the object that awakens it, past the satisfactions offered by the object, toward a more separate object. In the *Symposium* desire finally intends the absolutely separate, absolute beauty, to the utter *exclusion* of everything finite and changeable. Ontologically, desire is contact with the absolute that draws it past its satisfactions to the point where it becomes a desire of desire—that is to say, where it regards longing as higher than any satisfaction. Such longing is conditioned by a sacrifice of satisfactions, of life, even of erotic love itself: "if necessary, one must sacrifice life for it, yes, what is more, sacrifice erotic love itself, even though actuality lavished it with favors" (*FTR* 140; *SKS* 4:18). Erotic desire realizes itself in doubling itself, in sacrificing itself, in denying itself. Such desire of desire is what Constantin calls an "intensified recollecting" (*potenserede Erindren*), which he maintains is "erotic love's eternal expression at the beginning . . . the sign of genuine erotic love," which is "eternity's flowing back into the present" (*FTR* 137; *SKS* 4:14–15). Erotic love suspends its satisfaction as the condition to sustain its longing, and "anyone who has not experienced this mood at the very beginning in his own love has never loved" (ibid.).

The young man's position replays the eros of the *Symposium,* but subtly shifts it by thinking it in the egological context of modern metaphysics: it becomes less a question of sustaining the transcendence of desire in face of the absolute than of opening a field of pure immanence, of pure poetry. It is not a question of moving past the object toward the absolute, but rather of preserving the object of desire (the girl) as present, yet only as poetically re-presented. The poet desires an infinite object, that is, an object purely constituted through his own positing, an object reducible to its being-for-consciousness: an object not different from consciousness itself. In these terms his poetic desire reduces the reality of the girl to the status of an "occasion that awakened the poetic in him and made him a poet" (*FTR* 138; *SKS* 4:15). At best she would be something counter-posited, posited as suspended by poetic re-presentation.

What the young man lacks, Constantin notes, is a certain "ironic resiliency" to sustain a relation to the girl insofar as she cannot be posited: in other words, to sustain a relation to the girl *as other*. To do this would mean allowing the death of the desire for pure meaning. Yet insofar as pure meaning could be acquired only by the death (immanentization) of its object, what would be necessary here would be something like a death of death: "It may be true that a person's life is over and done with in the first moment, but there must also be the vital force (*Livskraft*) to kill this death and transform it to life" (*FTR* 137; *SKS* 4:15, altered). That vital force, bringing about the death of death, would no doubt signify the movement of repetition—which has *mistakenly* been called mediation.

What will be at stake is a "logic" of double negation that follows the exact opposite trajectory of mediation: not thinking the emergence of life out of death, where death would constitute the condition for life's intensification (inwardization) and self-presence, but rather thinking the simultaneity of life and death: that is, letting go of pure life and pure meaning, allowing death to be. As we shall see, allowing death to be will constitute the religious movement par excellence: it will mean allowing the death of the conception of the self as an origin of meaning, or allowing the metaphysics of the subject to founder.

The young man has been driven up to the cusp of this reversal (this transcendence). He is caught by a unique circumstance: he did not realize the extent to which he was already a poet, had already grasped the real only in its being-for-consciousness, until he fell in love. He "becomes a poet," but only in the sense that he realizes his relation to actuality was already purely poetic. The girl is simultaneously the occasion for him to become a poet and an interruption of his poetic relation to the real. She is the interruption through which the poetic becomes conscious of itself, through which it constitutes itself as poetic. She awakens and defeats the poetic in the same moment; in short, she is the breach of immediacy. The young man, then, can neither retreat to his prior naiveté nor press forward to the undoing of the poetic. This ambiguity is caught in the question of guilt: "He was aware that he made her unhappy, and yet he was conscious of no guilt; but precisely this, in all innocence to become guilty of her unhappiness, was an offense to him and vehemently stirred his passion" (*FTR* 138; *SKS* 4:15). In the experience of a guilt that cannot be traced back to an intentional act, of a guilt that *surprises* and confounds, he discovers a freedom entangled in itself. Such undergoing Constantin calls "the ordeal." We find the explication of this category in part two, in the young man's exposition of the *Book of Job*.

THE ORDEAL

Part two contains a series of letters from the young man to Constantin, who had offered to intervene and help free the young man from his entanglement. He had suggested an elaborate ruse to make the young man look like a seducer so that the girl, through her indignation, might find a measure of self-respect again; and so that he would find his freedom and ease his conscience. The young man declines the suggestion and flees to Stockholm, where he writes a series of letters on the case of Job. He takes the position of Job as his own: "If I did not have Job!" (*FTR* 204; *SKS* 4:72). The core of these letters is the presentation of an entirely new category: "the ordeal." The young man writes: "How, then, is Job's position to be explained? The explanation is this: the whole thing is an ordeal (*Prøvelse*)" (*FTR* 209; *SKS* 4:77).

The turn toward the *Book of Job* serves to place the ordeal of the young man in light of a more radical and fundamental crisis. The ordeal is a phenomenological category similar to boredom, melancholy, and anxiety. It refers, briefly, to the undergoing of originary time, or to the "experience" of the difference between the temporality that appears on the horizon of representation and time as coming-into-existence, or origination. In the ordeal the subject undergoes its own lack of ground. The young man's letter of Oct. 11 speaks from the heart of the ordeal:

> What does it mean to say: the world? What is the meaning of that word? Who tricked me into this whole thing and leaves me standing here? Who am I? How did I get into the world? Why was I not asked about it, why was I not informed of the rules and regulations but just thrust into the ranks as if I had been bought from a peddling shanghaier of human beings? How did I get involved in this big enterprise called actuality? Why should I be involved? Isn't it a matter of choice? (*FTR* 200; *SKS* 4:68)

This passage thematizes what Heidegger will later call "thrownness" (*Geworfenheit*) or facticity.[51] It points to an exposure to reality prior to any consciousness of it, to an event that is not *of* or *within* the world. Rather, the event here is that *whereby* there is a world in the first instance. An event of this order will always already have transpired, leaving the self-conscious *I*— the "who am I?"—infinitely belated with respect to itself and its world. This manifests itself in a fundamental indolence and nausea: "I am nauseated by life; it is insipid, without salt or meaning. If I were hungrier than Pierrot, I would not choose to eat the explanation people offer" (*FTR* 200; *SKS* 4:68).

The ordeal expresses something altogether transcendent: "This category, ordeal, is not esthetic, ethical or dogmatic—it is altogether transcendent" (*FTR* 210; *SKS* 4:77). One will completely miss the character of this transcendence, however, unless one sees the ordeal as the category, not for the eternal, but for what lies *between* time and eternity. Between eternity and time is the event of coming into existence, or originary time—to be radically distinguished from time as represented, which it makes possible. Originary coming into existence happens in the instant, without duration, prior to presence. For consciousness, however, time signifies its *own* time, the world its own project. Originary time breaks through to consciousness only in suffering. Only suffering rivets consciousness to what is, in the strictest sense, an undergoing. The young man can hardly express the violence of origination strongly enough: to be is to have been shanghaied into being, forced to serve. It is as though freedom were violated prior to its first awakening.

The ordeal expresses an event that is neither temporal nor eternal. It is not the direct presence of the eternal within time, which would annihilate temporality, but rather an interruption of it. In the letter from Dec. 14 the young man writes: "That this category [the ordeal] could tend to cancel out all actuality by defining it as an ordeal in relation to eternity, I readily perceive. But this doubt has not gained the upper hand over me, because, inasmuch as ordeal is a *temporary* (*midlertidige*) category, it is *eo ipso* defined in relation to time and therefore must be annulled in time" (*FTR* 210; *SKS* 4:77). That the ordeal is defined in relation to time does not mean, however, it would fill out a certain finite duration, as if it were simply a matter of lasting a number of hours, days, and so on. On the contrary, the ordeal means that hours and days, the anticipation of the future and recollection of the past, no longer hold meaning. Time as represented time is undone by originary time. How *long* does Job's ordeal last? To count the days or assign it to a period of life is no measure of it. Without being eternal, an ordeal is ineffaceable.

ORIGINARY GUILT

The ordeal initially refers, then, to suffering. More exactly, it refers to a suffering of the very possibility of suffering, that the self finds itself exposed to the world prior to its possession of itself. If Fichte, for example, could trace "empirical" consciousness back to a prior act of self-positing, the opposite appears here. What is prior is an event of undergoing in which consciousness is given over to itself, unable not to be. Yet the ordeal finally doubles upon itself and becomes an experience of guilt: not guilt over this or that, but a guilt that lies at the very origin of consciousness. The self discovers itself as already guilty, or guilty in its very innocence. Why? In the sense that to be, as consciousness, is to have already betrayed the real. Consciousness posits itself—this is not its truth, but precisely its untruth, or originary guilt. Yet it is also its innocence, for otherwise it would not be. Guilty *and* not guilty is the very structure of consciousness.

The question of an originary guilt emerges in Job's case in his discussion with the three friends. The main argument of Job's friends is that his suffering must have some intelligibility, some ground, and on this basis it

becomes irresistible to see Job's calamity as the just punishment for trans-
gression. Because Job suffers he must be guilty, they argue; "he must repent,
beg forgiveness, and then all will be well again" (*FTR* 208; *SKS* 4:76). According to the young man, however, Job's greatness is to have maintained
his innocence: "The secret in Job, the vital force, the nerve, the idea, is that
Job, despite everything, is in the right" (*FTR* 207; *SKS* 4:75). The young
man continues:

> On the basis of this position, [Job] qualifies as an exception to all human
> observations, and his perseverance and power manifest authority and autho-
> rization. To him every human interpretation is only a misconception, and to
> him in relation to God all his troubles are but a sophism that he, to be sure,
> cannot solve, but he trusts that God can do it. Every *argumentum ad*
> *hominem* is used against him, but he undauntedly upholds his conviction.
> He affirms that he is on good terms with God; he knows that he is innocent
> and pure in the very core of his being, where he also knows it before the
> Lord, and yet all the world refutes him. Job's greatness is that freedom's pas-
> sion in him is not smothered or quieted down by a wrong expression. (*FTR*
> 207; *SKS* 4:75)

What is the basis of Job's claim to innocence? He maintains the innocence
of self-positing; this is his "spiritual thrust of freedom." The three friends
aim directly at this point without, however, raising any ultimate questions
concerning self-positing itself. They do not raise freedom into any radical
problematic. If there is a problem, it must be something particular in the
use of freedom.

Yet Job insists on his innocence, not only vis-à-vis his friends, where it is
a question of defending himself against guilt in relation to positive law, but
more decisively vis-à-vis God, where he insists on the outrage of having
been exposed to being (created) at all. He presents, "so to speak, the whole
weighty defense plea on man's behalf in the great case between God and
man" (*FTR* 210; *SKS* 4:77). In so doing Job sets himself "in a purely personal relationship of opposition to God, in a relationship such that he cannot allow himself to be satisfied with any explanation at second hand"
(*FTR* 210; *SKS* 4:77). A "first hand" explanation would be one that Job
himself could authenticate, one he could produce himself (that is, posit).
Job maintains the *right* of self-consciousness—that is the "spiritual thrust of
freedom." He seizes consciousness as something that "even God cannot
wrest from him even though God gave it to him" (*FTR* 208; *SKS* 4:76).[52]
How, then, does Job's position turn to guilt? It does so in the position "before God" (*for Gud*). In a letter from January 13, referring to the denoue-
ment of the *Book of Job,* the young man declares: "The storms have spent
their fury—the thunderstorm is over—Job has been censured before the

face of humankind—the Lord and Job have come to an understanding. . . . Was Job proved to be in the wrong? Yes, eternally, for there is no higher court than the one that judged him. Was Job proved to be in the right? Yes, eternally, by being proved to be in the wrong *before God*" (*FTR* 212; *SKS* 4:79). "Before God" Job is simultaneously guilty and innocent. One should not underplay the sharpness of the paradox: he is guilty where he is innocent and innocent where he is guilty. Self-consciousness, positing itself but also thrown, *cannot but* be both guilty and innocent. It is guilty insofar as, positing itself, it must betray and occlude originary time. The guilt lay, consequently, in relating to itself as origin of itself, exchanging reality for its representation. Yet it is also innocent to the extent that there could be no self-consciousness otherwise than through a self-positing. Before God, in relation to its original enablement, self-consciousness lives itself as contradictory, simultaneously guilty and innocent.

In Job this contradiction is loosed, in a manner, for he receives everything back double—with the exception of his children, for a "human life cannot be redoubled that way" (*FTR* 221; *SKS* 4:88). A crucial caveat, for repetition, then, is impossible. A human life cannot be repeated; there is absolute loss. Or, if there is repetition, it can be only, impossibly, of the non-repeatable, the singular.

THE BIRTH OF A POET

Job's ordeal explains the situation of the young man in the sense that it grasps the deeper possibility of it in the event of coming-into-existence. Like Job, the young man finds himself—before the beloved if not before God—guilty and not-guilty. In the letter of October 11th he writes: "My whole being screams in self-contradiction. How did it happen that I became guilty? Or am I not guilty? Why, then, am I called that in every language? What kind of miserable invention is this human language, which says one thing and means another? Has something happened to me, is not all this something that has befallen me?" (*FTR* 201; *SKS* 4:68–69). Even more brutally he asks: "must I perhaps repent that the world plays with me as a child plays with a beetle?" (*FTR* 202; *SKS* 4:69). Language calls him unfaithful. It classifies the whole affair under a general notion. Yet to the extent that language trades in general notions (universals), it occludes what is singular or exceptional. As a discourse of universals, it considers only *what is;* it does not attend to the *path* of something's coming-into-being. It is in regard to the latter where exceptionality has its home. The young man suddenly discovers that he has *already* become guilty, prior to any intentional exercise of freedom. Guilt befalls him. Does language make no allowances, then, for an event, a becoming guilty, that would occur prior to the present?

Is it unable to hold guilt and innocence simultaneously together? For the young man this is primarily a crisis of language. As guilty/not-guilty the young man's existence has no determinate relation to language. He cannot come to an understanding of himself—he is an exception.

This is where repetition becomes a need and a question: "The issue that brings him to a halt is nothing more or less than repetition . . . [but] repetition is and remains a transcendence" (*FTR* 186; *SKS* 4:56–57). For the young man a repetition would mean beginning all over again from the very beginning, starting new, erasing the past. Concretely, it would mean expressing the universal by marrying the girl. This is where he stalls.

Nevertheless, a certain quasi-repetition occurs in that the girl, surprisingly, marries another, thus releasing him and allowing a return to himself. The young man writes: "I am myself again. This 'self' that someone else would not pick up off the street I have once again. The split that was in my being is healed; I am unified again. . . . Is there not, then, a repetition? Did I not get everything double? Did I not get myself again and precisely in such a way that I might have a double sense of its meaning?" (*FTR* 220–21; *SKS* 4:87). The young man understands the event as a repetition in the precise sense that he undergoes a "raising of his consciousness to the second power" (*FTR* 229; *SKS* 4:94). Here, however, Constantin will interject: a raising of consciousness to the second power, that is, the emergence of self-consciousness in the strict sense, is precisely *not* repetition. On the contrary, it is representation or recollection. In fact, the young man interprets the event of his coming back to himself entirely in accordance with an aesthetics of the sublime:

> Three cheers for the flight of thought, three cheers for the perils of life in service to the idea, three cheers for the hardships of battle, three cheers for the festive jubilation of victory, three cheers for the dance in the vortex of the infinite, three cheers for the cresting waves that hide me in the abyss, three cheers for the cresting waves that fling me above the stars! (*FTR* 221–22; *SKS* 4:88)

Not only do the images call to mind the sublime—the wild ocean, battle, the abyss, the stars—but there is also the same movement: a plunge into the abyss is followed by infinite elevation. The only difference between this and the Kantian sublime is that the idea to which he belongs does not signify, as in Kant, the supersensible vocation of the human being, but rather the exceptionality of the poet. The sublime is here the romantic sublime, to which corresponds an infinite poetic striving. The young man is born a poet.

The birth of the poetic has a dialectic that mimics repetition. Each case involves "the dialectical battle in which the exception arises amidst the universal" (*FTR* 226; *SKS* 4:92). A poet becomes a poet, that is, achieves voice or singularity as a poet, only in "conflict with all existence (*Tilværelse*)" (*FTR* 228; *SKS* 4:94, altered). The poet must find a unique relation to language in order to be truly creative. Literally all of existence is at stake, for the language the poet takes up has already determined the world in its totality. The poetic word draws its power from the originary secret of human existence, that is, the exceptional path of coming into existence as it falls always prior to the present. The poet draws from a time prior to time, originary time. He concerns himself with ordeals of language, with events. This brings the poet near to the religious: the poetic exception "constitutes a transition to the truly aristocratic exceptions, to the religious exceptions" (*FTR* 228; *SKS* 4:93). To think through the dialectic of the poetic is to catch sight of the religious: each inaugurates a "new order of rank" (*Rangsorden*) according to which the exception is prior to the rule, the event prior to what becomes present in the event. Each thinks the universal through the exception, not the exception through the universal: "There are exceptions. If they cannot be explained, then the universal cannot be explained, either" (*FTR* 227; *SKS* 4:92). Hence, the exception "explains the universal in that he explains himself" (*FTR* 227; *SKS* 4:92). The universal does not explain; it is rather what needs to be explained.

Consequently, the poetic and the religious both think the mediations of language vis-à-vis a "dialectic" not equivalent to mediation: the movement of coming-into-existence. Strictly speaking, only exceptions exist; universals do not exist. Nevertheless—here is the dialectic, which bears more on the poetic than the religious—exceptions can sustain themselves, that is, become conscious of their exceptionality, only in the "wrestling match" and conflict with the universal. The exception can be thought only through itself. As such, the exception has no language, for language is precisely mediation and universality (thinking something through something else). Thus the exception has to create a language, or "affirm himself as justified" (*FTR* 226; *SKS* 4:92) in face of the universal. This is the work of the poet. The poet uses the universal to consolidate himself as the exception.

If the poetic and the religious have a common bond, in the end they remain antithetical. Thus, in a "concluding letter" Constantin, who hints that he has himself invented the young man in order to explore the concept repetition,[53] attempts to clarify the originary "untruth" of the poet. He writes:

> [The young man's] dithyrambic joy in the last letter is an example of this . . .
> for beyond doubt this joy is grounded in a religious mood, which remains
> something inward, however. He keeps a religious mood as a secret he cannot
> explain, while at the same time this secret helps him poetically to explain actuality. . . . In the earlier letters, especially in some of them, the movement

was much closer to a genuinely religious resolution, but the moment the temporary suspension is terminated, he gains himself again, but as a poet, and the religious founders, that is, becomes a kind of inexpressible substratum. (*FTR* 228–29; *SKS* 4:95)

This presents poetic joy, the self's experience of itself or doubling upon itself, as an occlusion of the religious. The poet understands himself, consolidates himself as an exception, only in face of an inexpressible substratum. The poetic act, whereby consciousness raises itself to the second power, reduces the event of coming-into-existence to a horizon of the inexpressible: a background. The poet treats the ordeal, then, dialectically: as the tension necessary for consciousness to discover itself, to experience itself as exceptional. Expressing what has no proper place within language, the very happening of reality itself, the poet thereby justifies the inexpressible and himself. The poet shows *that there is* the inexpressible—by expressing it. In this way the poetic reconciles the exception and the universal. Repetition occurs as re-presentation, albeit with an unpresentable remainder.

The religious is the refusal of this reconciliation: if the young man "had had a deeper religious background, he would not have become a poet" (*FTR* 229; *SKS* 4:95). Had he developed a religious rather than poetic self-understanding, he would "have acted with an entirely different iron consistency and imperturbability, then he would have won a fact of consciousness to which he could constantly hold, one that could never become ambivalent for him but would be pure earnestness because it was established by him on the basis of a God-relationship" (*FTR* 230; *SKS* 4:96). A religious self-understanding would, in a certain sense, put an end to the dialectical torment of the young man, establish a *fact* of consciousness, but only by way of a "more painful contradiction" (*FTR* 229; *SKS* 4:95): the contradiction of a guilt identical to innocence, an originary guilt. Originary guilt: the guilt of thinking the self as the origin of itself, the occluding of originary time for time as represented, the denial of the infinite debt (*Skyld*) contracted by the very fact of being. More simply: the birth of a thinking that proceeds by way of representation (universals) rather than by way of reality (exceptions). In the poetic the distinction between the universal and the exception, the represented and the real, is still not clearly grasped. The religious "fact of consciousness" here works in the service of a radicalization: it becomes possible finally to problematize the spontaneity of self-consciousness and the regime of representation, something the poetic cannot do.

A clarity becomes possible for religious self-consciousness not found within the poetic: "It is characteristic of the young man, however, precisely as a poet, that he can never really grasp what he has done, simply because he both wants to see it and does not want to see it in the external and visible, or wants to see it in the external and visible, and therefore both wants to see it and does not want to see it" (*FTR* 230; *SKS* 4:96). The poet, as poet, wants to think the spontaneity of the will as if it were "external and visible," that is, an available present. The poet wants to represent the movement of freedom—or rather, think freedom at the limit of its representation, where it falls ambiguously between guilt and innocence. Thus the poet plays hide and seek with the act.

The religious, by contrast, grasps the guilt (denial, erasure) in every origin inaugurated by consciousness. It finds the wherewithal to interpret "consciousness raised to the second power," not as the innocence of self-positing—neither the joy of the poet nor the metaphysical joy of a Fichte —but as consciousness narcissistically involved in itself, the victim of its own representations. Thus, in the end, the religious will proclaim the undoing of the self's understanding of itself *as ground*. It coincides with a critique of innocence, a critique of the movement of self-consciousness in positing itself. It discovers and consents to a suffering that prevents its return to itself.

REPETITION DEFERRED

To conclude, it is necessary to underscore what several commentators point to: there is, in the end, no repetition in *Repetition*.[54] *Repetition* will have succeeded only in formulating the question, *whether there is repetition*. In so doing it will have exposed a possibility that is, in relation to self-consciousness, transcendent—in other words, a possibility that could arrive only, unexpected, from an absolute future. *Repetition* concludes just prior to this infinite beginning and so, in a negative or inverse way, delimits it. Just as the Socratic movement is not to depart from the idea, but always again to arrive at it, so too *Repetition* traces a movement up to the event: the breakthrough of consciousness to the real beyond its representation. But coming up to the event, inversely delimiting a future that escapes representative consciousness, makes it impossible for the reader "to say 1, 2, 3" (*FTR* 226; *SKS* 4:92). There is no dialectical movement of identity, difference, identity in difference. There is the opposite movement: one does not end by filling out an idea whose basic dimensions would already be held in anticipative foresight, but rather by creating the anticipation itself. An idea, or category, opens a possibility; it does not explain.

Deleuze, referring to both Kierkegaard and Nietzsche, states the nature of such inverse movement in relation to philosophical presentation with admirable clarity:

> They want to put metaphysics in motion, in action. They want to make it
> act, and make it carry out immediate acts. It is not enough, therefore, for

them to propose a new representation of movement; representation is already mediation. Rather, it is a question of producing within the work a movement capable of affecting the mind outside of all representation; it is a question of making movement itself a work, without interposition; of substituting direct signs for mediate representations; of inventing vibrations, rotations, whirlings, gravitations, dances or leaps which directly touch the mind. . . . They invent an incredible equivalent of theatre within philosophy.[55]

If at any moment repetition were allowed to occur, the very idea of repetition, a movement "by virtue of the absurd" (*FTR* 185; *SKS* 4:55), beyond representation, would be annihilated. Repetition is essentially deferred. To think repetition can therefore occur only by means of an ever greater thinking of its difficulty, at a limit, its impossibility. Thinking repetition takes shape as a continual stepping back from the present and self-presence to the point where freedom—whose "supreme interest" is repetition—discovers its destitution, in the ordeal. To think is to arrive ever again at the point where thought discovers an abyss (vibrations, rotations, whirlings) and freedom finds itself ungrounded. Thinking proceeds up to what cannot be thought.

Unless this inverse movement is kept in mind, it will be impossible to separate the movement of *Repetition* from the onto-theological one of retreating to foundations. This is exactly what happens, for example, in John Elrod's interpretation. He formulates the meaning of repetition in this way:

> That is to say, in the instant of repetition, the existing individual becomes eternal by virtue of his choice of the Deity in time as his eternal, divine ground. In choosing the Deity in time, the gap between his sinful self (past) and his eternal, divine ground, the Deity in time (future), is bridged in the present instant in which the self is grounded in its eternal, divine ground and, thereby returns to itself.[56]

Elrod suggests that repetition constitutes in this way the "sacralizing of time." If that is the case, and if repetition involves a movement of return to self as a return to the ground, then it will be indistinguishable from mediation. For Hegel, the return to self of absolute knowledge is a return to the ground; moreover, it is through a return to the ground that the ground temporalizes itself, that is, achieves presence or immanence, and hence "sacralizes" time. Such an interpretation, however, ignores the "inverse" character of *Repetition*. Elrod's reading does not properly measure the positive significance of the fact that a repetition does *not* occur. That is the hinge of the whole book. Aiming to clarify repetition, that is, whether and how consciousness can recover its lost immediacy, *Repetition* slowly but definitely arrives at a past that is irrecuperable and a future that is ab-solute. Time, the event, is disentangled doubly from the horizon of presence.

First, that repetition does not occur shows the distinction between the time of the event, originary time, and the time of the project (between the instant and any duration). Constantin's venture of returning to Berlin dramatizes that the movement of time exceeds the time of consciousness. Time itself, coming-into-existence, is transcendence. Consciousness cannot integrate its own temporality, that is, reduce it to a horizon of presence. Immediacy cannot be recovered precisely because it does *nothing but* return in the form of the impossibility of repetition (as project)—each moment a surprise, a slippage. Second, *Repetition* interprets the originary "untruth" of consciousness, that it will always already have suspended its immediacy, in a decisive way as guilt. To regard consciousness according to guilt would be to see it, from the beginning, as "before" or in face of an Other—an Other always already denied or repressed. In these terms, the event of repetition comes to signify forgiveness. Thus in the notes Kierkegaard says that he "could easily have worked out how repetition progresses along this path until it signifies atonement" (*FTR* 313; *Pap.* IV B 117, 294). Forgiveness, however, cannot adequately be thought in terms of a movement of sacralizing time. Even if atonement would refer to an event of the past, it would refer to a future not positable through the spontaneity of freedom. That repetition does not occur puts the emphasis on this absolute future.

What *Repetition* thematizes, then, is this: the movement of a return to self cannot be thought as a *project.* If there is return, it can be thought only vis-à-vis an enablement, a power, not identical to the spontaneity of the will —a power upon which one can only wait with an essential patience. And then, if there is repetition, it would not in all strictness be a matter of *return,* but rather departure.

FIVE

Absolute Relation to the Ab-solute
(Fear and Trembling)

❧

Fear and Trembling, perhaps Kierkegaard's most famous book, was published on the same day as *Repetition* (October 16, 1843). Probably no text is more difficult to read in Kierkegaard's corpus than *Fear and Trembling.* Subtitled a "dialectical lyric" and authored by Johannes de Silentio, the text approaches an extreme of indirection. At the center of its meditation is the binding of Isaac (Gen. 22). For Kierkegaard's author this event contains a possibility bearing upon existence itself: faith. "Faith," Johannes says, relates to "the paradox of existence" (*FTR* 47; *SKS* 4:141). *Existence,* then, is at issue; what is not at issue is a theory of ethics.[1] Yet owing to the indirection, the problematic character of the narrative of the binding of Isaac, and the canonical context of the exposition, this problematic can be missed.

Kierkegaard's author tips his hand, however, by insisting upon the possible contemporaneity of Abraham's act in the binding of Isaac. If we cannot become contemporaneous with Abraham, that is, if it cannot refer to a general possibility bearing upon existence, it is pointless to talk about him: "for what is the value of going to the trouble of remembering the past which cannot become a present" (*FTR* 30; *SKS* 4:126).

Kierkegaard's author formulates this contemporaneity by comparing Abraham's deed, where he is willing to sacrifice his own son, to the conduct of a bourgeois philistine walking home from work down a bustling street (*FTR* 38–39; *SKS* 4:133–34). The comparison, which could hardly be more dissonant, shows the need for a demythologized reading of the narrative.[2] Any reading of the text that cannot clarify its phenomenological meaning—that is, its possible contemporaneity or everydayness—cannot be adequate. At issue is existence as such, and the binding of Isaac, as Louis Mackey seems to have sensed, works as a kind of figure.[3] The key for the interpretation of *Fear and Trembling* lies in seeing its continuity not only with *Repetition,* but with the other works in the early authorship.[4] Through a series of "problemata," the book once again presents "the ordeal" in which modern metaphysics runs aground. It does so, moreover, upon the crags of temporality and finitude: "Temporality, finitude—that is what it is all about" (*FTR* 49; *SKS* 4:143). It is a question of properly weighing temporality and finitude, giving them their due in thinking. In life they take care of themselves; but to bend thinking toward life, toward temporality and finitude in excess to representation, requires unlearning a certain understanding of the subject. Toward this end *Fear and Trembling* presents a certain posture, termed "faith," capable of holding itself to what withdraws from presence: holding itself to time, the instant.

The essential conflict of *Fear and Trembling* can be summarized this way: it is between an ethical duty and an absolute duty, between a duty that can be formulated as a universal, and a duty that must remain singular, exceptional. The point is that these two cannot be "mediated," that is, thought through one another, harmonized. They express the irreducibles of the human condition, which can be formulated as a conflict between "the ethical" and "the religious." Moreover, the inversion in the "order of rank" articulated in *Repetition* pertains here as well: the absolute duty, the religious, the exceptional, is "higher than" the ethical-universal. Most generally, one could say that at issue is a conflict between the autonomy/immanence of the ethical and the heteronomy/transcendence of the religious. The subject is, on the one hand, an ethical subject: that is, in the egological terms of modern metaphysics, self-binding, self-positing, an unconditioned beginning or spontaneity. On the other hand, the subject is a religious subject, bound absolutely in its very existence to God.

But here it is necessary to be precise: what does the word "God" mean in *Fear and Trembling*? Is that so obvious? And how, in particular, is a binding to God irreconcilable with the spontaneity of the subject? Certain things are immediately clear: as in *Repetition,* God signifies the *before whom* of existence itself, transcendence as what *faces* human existence—the divine Other. In addition, though, *Fear and Trembling* adds something decisive: God is "the absolute." An "absolute duty to God" is an "absolute relation to the absolute." What is the absolute? If one attends to the logic of the text, one finds that the absolute signifies what *absolves itself,* what withdraws, what holds itself in reserve from every general order of meaning, intelligibility, presence. The God who appears in *Fear and Trembling*—God the absolute —not only faces human existence as a Thou, but withdraws in that very facing. God absolves Godself in the very drawing near. An absolute duty to God, in this sense, would signify the demand to hold oneself open to God's withdrawal; or again, a duty to *let oneself be absolved* from the sovereign, ethical order of self-consciousness (that of manifestation, meaning, universality, representation). To remain faithful to such an absolvent bond, however, would have everything to do with opening oneself to originary time (the instant). Temporality and finitude, discovered again within a "later immediacy," beyond the meaning they receive within the horizon of metaphysics—*this* is what it is all about. Faith is fidelity to time as gift, as undergoing.

I shall proceed by clarifying the "problemata" in which Kierkegaard's author presents the contradiction between the two laws claiming the subject. Then I shall consider the meaning of his term "faith," arguing that it reinscribes the Eckhartian notion of *Gelassenheit,* or releasement.

PROBLEMA I: THE SUSPENSION
OF THE ETHICAL

The problemata are controversial insofar as they present the possibility—played out in the binding-of-Isaac narrative—that murder could be made into "a holy and God-pleasing act" (*FTR* 53; *SKS* 4). Each of the problemata begins by constructing an essential conflict between ethical duty and absolute duty. This conflict constitutes "the ordeal" of Abraham, the testing of his faith. Kierkegaard's author stages this ordeal precisely: it is not a conflict between universality and particularity, but rather universality and exceptionality or singularity:

> Faith is precisely the paradox that the single individual as the single individual is higher than the universal, is justified before it, not as inferior to it but as superior—yet in such a way, please note, that it is the single individual who, after being subordinate as the single individual to the universal, now by means of the universal becomes the single individual who as the single individual is superior, that the single individual as the single individual stands in an absolute relation to the absolute. (*FTR* 56; *SKS* 4:149–50)

All of the problemata follow this same basic pattern: they stress the critical distinction between the singular capable of being subordinated to the universal, that is, the singular *as particular,* and the singular *as singular,* that is, as "higher than" and inassimilable to the universal. The singular as singular absolves itself, or rather is absolved, from the ethical-universal and so stands absolutely in relation to the absolute. The instant of ab-solution is called the "suspension" of the ethical. Nevertheless, the genuine singular can be thought only starting from the universal; the universal is what the singular presupposes.

Before coming to the suspension of the ethical and the manner in which it presupposes the ethical, let us further clarify the meaning of "the ethical" in these problemata.

The ethical signifies in each case "the universal" (or the general, *det Almene*), which the three problemata further determine as follows: it is the general as "what lies immanent in itself, has nothing outside itself that is its τέλος but is itself the τέλος for everything outside itself, and when the ethical has absorbed this into itself, it goes no further" (Problema I; *FTR* 54; *SKS* 4:148); it is the general as what is "also the divine" (Problema II; *FTR* 67; *SKS* 4:160); and finally it is the general as "the disclosed" (*det Aabenbare;* Problema III; *FTR* 82; *SKS* 4:172). Putting this together, the ethical signifies an *immanent, divine, disclosed order of universality* in terms of which "the whole existence of the human race rounds itself off as a perfect, self-contained sphere" (*FTR* 68; *SKS* 4:160). The ethical, in short, signifies totality or immanence. Its most basic meaning is that it *encompasses:* it is an all-inclusive order of intelligibility in which nothing is left out. In this sense the ethical coincides precisely with absolute knowledge. It is that in terms of which differences are sublated, the all-mediating, the very milieu of sameness, and in this sense the milieu of the universal or general (*det Almene*). Within the ethical as totality, the particular as such has no standing; it acquires real existence only as sacrificed and sublated (*ophævet*), so that it expresses the general. The general is thus the *ground* of the particular just as must as the *telos* of the particular—and only in this sense does it describe an encompassing sphere. The "ethical task" of the particular is to sacrifice its particularity in favor of ends whose realization will manifest the ultimate ground or first principle. Thus understood, ethics is the demand for the radical critique and exposure of all false interiority and any form of hiddenness.

A couple of comments are in order here. First of all, this synthetic notion of the ethical condenses the inner demand of Hegel's thought. It can well include Kantian *Moralität,* even Stoicism, but its basic trajectory rewrites Hegelian *Sittlichkeit* (which itself encompasses both Kantian and Stoic ethics). Secondly, as such, what is at stake goes beyond ethics narrowly considered. Hegel's ethics is absolutely inseparable from his conception of history as the scene in and through which absolute subjectivity (God) both manifests and realizes itself. "Realized freedom," Hegel said, "is the absolute and ultimate end of the world."[5] And freedom is realized only in the objective totality of the state. The state, however, is nothing other than "the divine Idea, insofar as it exists on earth," and "the precise object of world history in general."[6]

What becomes problematic in the problemata is this conception of immanence. Nevertheless, one should not overlook the fact that genuine singularity is thinkable only starting from totality—otherwise, one would be referring only to particularity. In that sense, only when one has an idea of totality can one have an idea of singularity. As soon as thinking begins within the horizon of self-consciousness, as Hegel does in thinking substance as subject, there is in principle no end to mediation. To be means simply to have an origin in self-consciousness; self-consciousness is in principle the whole. Only when the logic of self-positing consciousness has been thought to its end, as absolute knowledge, does it become possible to catch sight of what might be left out of total presence: the event, prior to all presence, even total presence, of coming-into-existence. It is a question of thinking, in Hegel's words, what forever "passes behind the back of consciousness."

Fear and Trembling presents the binding of Isaac as the figure through which to pursue this instant anterior to all presence. It does so, however, starting from the situation of tragic conflict. The tragic is an interruption in the field of continuous presence and so constitutes a point *from which* to think what eludes totality. Abraham's position emerges in terms of an interruption that exceeds the tragic interruption. Johannes writes:

> The difference between the tragic hero and Abraham is very obvious. The tragic hero is still within the ethical. He allows an expression of the ethical to have its τέλος in a higher expression of the ethical; he scales down the ethical relation between father and son or daughter and father to a feeling that has its dialectic in its relation to the idea of moral conduct. Here there can be no question of a teleological suspension of the ethical itself. Abraham's situation is different. By his act he transgressed the ethical altogether and had a higher τέλος outside it, in relation to which he suspended it. For I certainly would like to know how Abraham's act can be related to the universal, whether any point of contact between what Abraham did and the universal can be found other than that he transgressed it. (*FTR* 59; *SKS* 4:152)

The tragic double bind, whose meaning in the above citation is entirely derived from Hegel, involves an inner tension within the universal itself: two ethical duties oppose one another, and they cannot both be fulfilled. One will necessarily become guilty. And yet according to Johannes, who again simply rewrites Hegel, tragic conflict is capable of resolution on the same plane in which it has arisen—namely, within the universal. One duty shows itself to be a deeper expression, that is, a more universal expression, than the duty with which it conflicts. Thus the tragic sacrifice, which sacrifices a more particularized universal to a more universal universal, ushers the universal into its historical effectiveness: that is, brings it to self-consciousness, into the domain of immanence. Tragic conflict and tragic sacrifice are the very modes of the manifestation of the universal.

Thus Agamemnon and Jepthah suspend their duties to family and, acting on an "enterprise of concern to a whole nation" (*FTR* 57; *SKS* 4:151), sacrifice their children for a higher instance of universality. The tragic does not at all contest the universal; it confirms and extends it. The tragic subject acts on the basis of a firm insight into what is most originary, the principle at stake, and so knows how conflicting expressions of the universal are to be hierarchized. If Abraham is not tragic, it is because he acts without princi- ple: "it is not to save a nation, not to uphold the idea of the state that Abra- ham does it; it is not to appease the angry gods" (*FTR* 59; *SKS* 4:152). Abraham suspends the ethical *as such* vis-à-vis a telos that is outside of it, an absolute telos. He places himself in an "absolute relation to the absolute." This is the suspension of the ethical. Yet what is this? Whatever else it might be, the suspension of the ethical involves the circumstance that Abraham *cannot even be tragic.* The suspension of the ethical renders tragic sacrifice, along with the intelligibility and consolation it affords, impossible: "The tragic hero needs and demands tears, and where is the envious eye so arid that it could not weep with Agamemnon, but where is the soul so gone astray that it has the audacity to weep over Abraham" (*FTR* 61; *SKS* 4:154). Tragic sacrifice involves the logic of double negation, or sublation, which is ultimately the logic of self-positing consciousness. It is precisely this logic that is suspended in a suspension of the ethical: a divine law prevents the subject, who is otherwise an activity of self-transcending, from going be- yond. If Abraham cannot even be tragic it is not because he refuses to sacri- fice his particularity (not because he sins), but rather because he has already been set beyond the ethical as such. The inability to be tragic is itself the tragedy. Abraham cannot transcend himself in the direction of universality through his deed; he cannot appropriate to himself a universal meaning. Necessarily, then, his deed cannot be integrated into any general order of things: "Abraham cannot be mediated; in other words, he cannot speak" (*FTR* 60; *SKS* 4:153).

To think a suspension of the ethical, then, is to think the subject *inso- far as* it cannot surpass itself (i.e., sacrifice itself for the universal). In the Genesis narrative the divine law of exceptionality appears as the concrete demand to sacrifice Isaac. Given the particular narrative elements present in the Abraham story—namely, that God has promised Abraham a child, and through this child a nation—one can see how the demand to sacrifice the very promised child strikes a direct blow at Abraham's possibility for self- transcendence. Isaac, in effect, is himself Abraham qua universal. Alterity first irrupts through the divine command that destroys Abraham's possibil- ity for surpassing himself, for the moment God issues the command to sac- rifice Isaac, Abraham has been killed to the ethical. The ethical becomes in that instant precisely the temptation: "A temptation—but what does that mean? As a rule, what tempts a person is something that will hold him back from doing his duty, but here the temptation is the ethical itself, which would hold him back from doing God's will. But what is duty? Duty is simply the expression for God's will" (*FTR* 60; *SKS* 4:153).

One has to see, though, how something completely "general," a law beyond law, is named in the expression "God's will." The suspension of the ethical refers not merely to some discrete command or maxim, but to an entirely "new *category*" (*FTR* 60; *SKS* 4:153; my italics): it is not an ontic structure, we might say, but an ontological one. At stake is the subjectivity of the subject, thought beyond "Greek" and Hegelian ways: "For if the ethical—that is, social morality—is the highest and if there is in a person no residual incommensurability in some way such that this incommensurability is not evil (i.e. the single individual, who is to be expressed in the universal), then no categories are needed other than what Greek philosophy had or what can be deduced from them by consistent thought" (*FTR* 55; *SKS* 4:149).[7] The subjectivity of the subject refers not to an unconditioned spontaneity or self-positing (as in Fichte), but to an incommensurable remainder. Something remains behind (*bliver tilbage*), withdraws, from the open totality constituted by presence. The subject exists in terms of a passivity that cannot be assimilated. The domain of ethics, precisely as the domain of the self-positing taken (by Hegel) to its limit, cannot see the incommensurable otherwise than as the stubbornness of the particular. It has no eyes for singularity, for an absolute passivity. From the ethical point of view, indeed, Abraham's act can be nothing but murder, for if there is nothing incommensurable that is not evil, then "Abraham is lost" (*FTR* 56; *SKS* 4:149). The suspension of the ethical, the ordeal, brings the subject to its limit: to that point where the subject cannot appropriate itself in terms of a universal meaning—a point of silence and disappropriation.[8] The ordeal points, in its generality beyond the binding-of-Isaac narrative, to every modality of existence in which the subject suffers from itself, in which it cannot rediscover itself through its own negation. More simply, the category of a suspension of the ethical makes visible, in a way it could never be within a logic of self-positing consciousness, the precise character of suffering: suffering is always the suffering of suffering, the subject being undone without ceasing to be. It brings to light an undergoing prior to any exercise of freedom: a speechless suffering. Speechless suffering draws the subject back to what is unconditioned about a subject: its beginning as what will always already have stolen over it, as what precedes positing. It brings the subject to the anarchy of its beginning, its originary exposure to time. That beginning prior to all beginning is what "Greek" and Hegelian thought occludes. The "Problemata" are an effort at returning thought to this beginning. And "faith," I will show, is an effort to stay within this beginning.

PROBLEMA II: ABSOLUTE DUTY
(WITH LEVINAS AND DERRIDA)

The second problema is titled "Is there an Absolute Duty to God?" It begins once again by constructing a concept of the ethical:

> The ethical is the universal and as such it is also the divine. Thus it is proper to say that every duty is essentially duty to God, but if no more can be said than this, then it is also said that I actually have no duty to God. The duty becomes duty by being traced back to God, but in the duty itself I do not enter into relation to God. For example, it is a duty to love one's neighbor. It is a duty by being traced back to God, but in the duty I enter into a relation not to God but to the neighbor I love. If in this connection I then say that it is my duty to love God, I am actually pronouncing only a tautology, inasmuch as "God" in a totally abstract sense is here duty. (*FTR* 68; *SKS* 4:160)

These passages allude to Kant. As Kant says, ethics takes each command, laid upon consciousness through its own operation, *as if* it were a divine command.[9] Yet ethics needs God neither to account for the imperative nor to give a person a reason for submitting to it. To submit to the imperative is the act—the only act—through which subjectivity assumes its proper respect for itself. To posit God as the ground of the imperative would render it something merely given and thus hypothetical. A categorical imperative is necessarily one that subjectivity lays autonomously upon itself. It is to be remembered that Kant formulates these well-known theses originally by reflection upon the good will. As he argues in the *Groundwork for the Metaphysics of Morals,* the unconditional will toward the good—that is, the universal—is the one thing good without qualification. Yet Kant himself admits how strange the idea of the good will is with respect to the program of realizing happiness: it is an idea that calls upon the continual sacrifice of one's particular interests and the satisfactions of "pathological" consciousness.[10] With respect to the pleasure principle, it appears as an ontological extravagance. Thus ethics depends upon the renunciation of particularity in favor of the universal. But what accounts for moral interest in the first instance?[11] Morality would be altogether hollow if there were not a good will toward the good will. What, then, is the origin of the good will?

Kant returns to these questions in section three of the *Groundwork.* He admits that, on the question of accounting for our original interest in the good will, there is an explanatory circle:

> [We do not as yet] have any insight into why it is that we should divorce ourselves from such interest, i.e. that we should consider ourselves as free in

action and yet hold ourselves as subject to certain laws so as to find solely in our own person a worth that can compensate us for the loss of everything that gives worth to our condition. We do not see how this is possible and hence how the moral law can obligate us. One must frankly admit that there is a sort of circle from which, so it seems, there is no way to escape.[12]

This circle arises as a direct consequence of the highest principle of morality: the autonomy of the will. How can a will bind itself? Duty refers to something given or laid down—to *law*—to which the will must submit. Law demands renunciation. And yet, if a subject is itself the origin of law, if it stands present at the instant in which law is handed down, then the subject would seem to be beyond duty. How then would it bind itself? Kant resolves this problem through the distinction between two irreducible standpoints: the transcendental and the empirical. Transcendentally, the subject is itself the origin of law; it is pure spontaneity. However, empirically the subject experiences its distinction from law through its immersion in the "world of sense." Duty, though transcendentally laid down by the subject itself, nevertheless remains an infinite *demand* insofar as, for Kant, the two standpoints can never be made to coincide. And why not? Because, Kant writes, "even with regard to himself, a man cannot presume to know what he is in himself by means of the acquaintance which he has through internal sensation."[13] The "ego as constituted in itself" does not coincide with what the subject is capable of representing to itself concerning itself. In short, Kant makes a distinction between a first interiority (the empirical subject's awareness of itself) and a second interiority (transcendental interiority, the ego as it is in itself). In his *Vocation of Man* Fichte extends and rewrites this distinction as the distinction between the subject as ground or principle and the subject as ideal. In each case, however, the circle is maintained: relating to law, the subject relates to itself. Transcendence is radically excluded by being rearticulated transcendentally.

The ethical, then, involves a certain dialectic whereby the subject sacrifices itself as particular (empirical) in order to relate to itself as universal (ideal). Kant and Fichte think this circle as transcendentally closed, but empirically open. Hegel transforms this problem through the introduction of a historical dialectic. The ethical signifies the historically achieved laws and customs (*Sitten*) inscribed within the institutions of the state. The state, however, is founded upon the sacrifice of particularity. In his *Encyclopedia* (§546) Hegel writes: "the substance of the state shows itself as the power by which the particular independence of individuals (*die Einzelnen*), i.e., their absorption in the external existence of possession and the natural life, feels itself as a *nothing*; [it is also] the power which mediates the preservation of the universal substance through the *sacrifice* (*Aufopferung*), which occurs in the inward disposition [of the individual], of this natural and particular being."[14] The *Sittlichkeit* of the state is the outward manifestness of the inner sacrifice of particularity.

The common logic of these idealist texts, then, is that the ethical signifies the movement of self-transcendence toward universality through sacrifice. Sacrifice is preserved, converted into being, upheld within a universal order. Once again, Johannes attempts to strike down this circle of self-transcendence by means of an "absolute duty." He writes:

> The paradox of faith, then is this: that the single individual is higher than the universal, that the single individual . . . determines his relation to the universal by his relation to the absolute, not his relation to the absolute by his relation to the universal. The paradox may also be expressed this way: that there is an absolute duty to God, for in this relationship of duty the individual relates himself as the single individual absolutely to the absolute. In this connection, to say that it is a duty to love God means something different from the above, for if this duty is absolute, then the ethical is reduced to the relative. (*FTR* 70; *SKS* 4:162)

An absolute relation to the absolute renders the self-relation of the subject to itself on the basis of universal law into something relative, something conditioned. In addition to the law the subject is capable of assigning itself, that is, law as arising from the self-presence of transcendental spontaneity (practical reason), there is a contrary law. It is not only contrary, but in fact something logically prior, for the absolute duty is here the touchstone for the determination of the limits of ethical duty. An *ordeal* arises in the case where an absolute duty so relativizes the ethical, though without abrogating its inner logic, that it demands the very opposite of what the ethical would demand. In the present case, murder becomes a "holy and God-pleasing act."

Is there such a thing as an absolute duty? Can an imperative be conceived that would demand not the sublation of the particular through its sacrifice, but rather the sublation of the ethical order itself? How could one think this in a general, categorial way? One must remember that the ethical as Johannes has constructed it signifies the very order of sublation (the order of self-positing, self-mediating consciousness). The suspension/preservation of the ethical vis-à-vis an absolute duty would signify the delimitation of that circle whereby the subject relates, in the ethical moment, to its own transcendent/transcendental ideality. It would signify a relation to the absolute as what absolves itself from circle of self-relation, a relation that essentially could not be founded upon the self-sacrifice of natural, particular being. An absolute duty, we begin to see, will mean a duty not merely to bear up under, but indeed to achieve a free relation to, those events in which the self is stripped of its possibility for self-positing—namely, stripped of its possibility for possibility.

If it is a "duty" it is so by way of another kind of law altogether than ethical law. Ethical law can and must be formulated not only in terms of its supreme principle (for Kant, autonomy), but also in terms of maxims for the will. A principle is raised against inclinations, and in this tension duty pulls upon the will. A divine being, Kant said, cannot experience anything like duty simply because such a being, not sensuously situated, and thus never having to suffer inclinations, is already beyond particularity. A divine being would be immediately universal (hence, the analyticity of the connection between the ethical law and the divine will). One can see, then, how this way of framing the problem of duty implies that the singularity of individuals is founded upon something essentially privative: namely, the possibility for the will to be motivated by non-moral (sensuous) considerations. Singularity is understood as particularity, and particularity is precisely what must be transcended.

An absolute duty, however, could be formulated neither as a supreme principle nor as a maxim for the will, for if it could, it would by that very fact signify an ethical duty. The ethical *means* what can be formulated as a principle, what therefore has a universal sense. This would be true even if that duty were a divine command. If an absolute duty cannot be formulated as a principle or maxim, though, how could one continue to speak of a duty? Evidently, the "duty" in absolute duty signifies something other than a tension between the will as universal and the will as particular. If there is an absolute duty, it will be necessary to think of a duty that cannot in any way be formulated or constructed, that is, mediated—a duty without principle, a duty without duty. How is such a thing to be thought? Here we can note something significant. To the question, why does Abraham do it? Johannes answers: "To the question 'Why?' Abraham has no other answer than that it is an ordeal, a temptation that, as noted above, is the unity (*Eenheden*) of its being for the sake of God and for his own sake " (*FTR* 71; *SKS* 4:162–63, altered). An absolute duty cannot be traced back to a single, pure origin. Abraham just as much lays it upon himself as God lays it upon him, and vice versa. Neither God nor the pure self-presence of the will (practical reason) could serve as the origin of an absolute duty: this is exactly why it imposes an ordeal. An absolute duty remains anonymous.

In a note to the text Kierkegaard wrote: "The terrifying thing in the collision is this—that it is not a collision between God's command and man's command but between God's command and God's command" (*FTR* 248; *Pap.* IV B 67). This sentence alone should have put an end to "divine command morality" interpretations of *Fear and Trembling:* the conflict is not between autonomously derived moral maxims and heteronomously laid down, divine ones; it is not a question of Abraham respecting a maxim that, as laid down by the absolute, would "trump" every other. The pain of the ordeal is that God withdraws behind a contradiction: a duty is imposed that explodes the very idea of duty. *No one lays down an absolute duty.* In this sense, an absolute duty would emerge not *from* God, but in the withdrawal of God. God's very withdrawal imposes something absolute. To this extent, the precise character of the "divine command" for Abraham to offer up his son Isaac, what makes it absolute, is that Abraham can never be sure of its origin. The duty is absolute in that it absolves itself from any determinate origin and so cannot be formulated properly as a maxim (a why and whither). Abraham cannot speak. This is what causes the "anxiety and distress" (*Angsten og Nøden*) that characterizes the ordeal, which are "are the only justification conceivable" (*FTR* 113; *SKS* 4:203). An absolute duty to God is thus a duty conditioned by God's withdrawal from presence, a duty that arises to the extent that a creature experiences its own abandonment, its lack of consolation—a duty emergent in speechless suffering. A trial. But also, the burden of an infinite responsibility.

Yet Abraham does not just suffer. He *acts* in order to do what the ethical forbids. He binds his son and raises the knife. Moreover, he does so in the name of a purely "private relationship to the divine" (*FTR* 60; *SKS* 4:153). Isn't it a case of his acting on a purely private content—a determinate command with a determinate origin (in God), but one simply not justifiable before the universally human? How, in other words, is one to think about the specifically narrative features of the text? These questions can be addressed by reflecting on Levinas's critique of Kierkegaard—for Levinas, in a certain sense, takes *Fear and Trembling* at its word: it seems to be a text whose reflections on the binding of Isaac legitimate religious violence.

Though Levinas affirms what he understands to be Kierkegaard's justified protest against Hegelian immanence (totality), he questions whether or not Kierkegaard in fact frees himself radically enough from that horizon. Firstly, he asks whether Kierkegaard's construction of the ethical as totality is justified: "But does our relation with Others really entail our incorporation and dispersal into generality? *That is the question we must raise, against both Hegel and Kierkegaard.*"[15] According to Levinas, it is precisely the relation to the other person, and in particular in my responsibility for the Other, that I am singularized: "Being a self means not being able to hide from responsibility. This excess of being, this existential exaggeration which is called 'being a self,' this irruption of selfhood or ipseity into being, is equivalent to an explosion of responsibility."[16] Secondly, Levinas criticizes the apparently private nature, or interiority, of the absolute duty. Levinas writes: "Kierkegaardian violence begins when existence, having moved beyond the aesthetic stage, is forced to abandon the ethical stage . . . in order to embark on the religious stage."[17] If the subject is at any point thought as *absolved* from the responsibility for the other person—even vis-à-vis a divine command—the door is in principle opened to limitless violence: murder can become, in the words of Johannes, a "holy and God-pleasing act."

Levinas's objections hinge on his reading of Abraham's exceptionality, as Kierkegaard would see it, as another statement of the idealist principle that self-consciousness, according to its "for-itself" or representational structure, must be primordial. He writes: "The identification of subjectivity [in Kierkegaard] is thus prior to language, and depends simply on the way a being clings to its being. The identification of A as A is the same as A's anxiety for A. The subjectivity of the subject is an identification of the Same in its concern for the Same. It is egoism, and its subjectivity is a Self."[18] In these terms, Abraham transgresses the ethical and obeys an absolute duty out of a "sublime thirst for salvation." The Other is sacrificed for the salvation of the Same. In these terms, Kierkegaard's critique of idealism would not be opposed to its egology, but constitute precisely a radicalization of it. Levinas suggests another, non-egological reading of the binding of Isaac narrative in which the highest point of the story is found not in the act of *raising* the knife, but in that of *laying it down:*

> Kierkegaard was drawn to the biblical story of the sacrifice of Isaac. He saw in it an encounter between a subjectivity raising itself to the level of the religious, and a God elevated above the ethical order. But the story can also be taken in a very different sense. The high point in the whole drama could be the moment when Abraham lent an ear to the voice summoning him back to the ethical order.[19]

It is not insignificant that Kierkegaard, writing in his journal in 1852, proposed something similar: "Even more difficult than setting out for Moriah to offer Isaac is the capacity, when one has already drawn the knife, in unconditional obedience to be willing to understand: It is not required" (*FTR* 268; *Pap.* X 4 338). Does this constitute a later reversal of position for Kierkegaard? I would say, on the contrary, it is exactly what *Fear and Trembling* already expresses. There is room, I argue, for a more "Levinasian" reading of *Fear and Trembling* than Levinas himself allows.

Without a doubt, Levinas cuts through a host of secondary issues and comes directly to the only one that matters: salvation conceived as the fulfillment of the self. According to Levinas the subjectivity of the subject is still, for Kierkegaard, defined as its involvement with itself, its concern over itself, its aiming at itself.[20] Self-coincidence, in other words, is its fundamental project—not, perhaps, as knowledge or system, but as salvation.

This is the horizon, fundamentally ontological, that Levinas would like to break from in the name of subjectivity as "one for the other," or substitution.[21] Yet the question is whether salvation, thought as the subject's coincidence with itself, constitutes the horizon of *Fear and Trembling*. Does the subjectivity of the subject appear, in the first or last instance, as a striving to be itself? Or is there not rather the opposite: namely, a radical problematization of self-positing and unconditional spontaneity in the ordeal? Doesn't the text aim to show the truth of subjectivity as its exposure and vulnerability, its openness to the ordeal of speechless suffering—a truth denied by idealism?

The "Problemata" follow a certain Christian theological tradition— going through at least Augustine, Eckhart, and Luther—that places the love of God prior to, and the condition for, the love of the neighbor (of course without ever separating them). The priority of the God-relation opens the space for precisely interiority, thought, as Kierkegaard does, in terms of a "justified incommensurability." Levinas's great revolution is to reinscribe the thematics of transcendence within the relation to other person. Human existence is originally *before the other human being*, not before God. The ethical is absolutely primary. This would appear to leave no room for interiority. But it is not so simple. First of all, according to the logic of interiority Kierkegaard's text reproduces, the interior is not in any way identified with self-presence. On the contrary, the interior points to a relation to God that would be strictly prior to a relation to oneself.

According to this tradition of interiority the interior signifies exactly what one *cannot appropriate* or represent; it is an abyss. The interior, though constituting the subjectivity of the subject, is not in any way "one's own," a sphere of the proper. The critical thrust of Kierkegaard's texts in relation to modern metaphysics, which draws upon this understanding of interiority, involves saying that transcendental self-consciousness, originally identical to itself, is founded within the ethical as precisely a repression of the interior. Egology occludes the interior by thinking it as the subject's primordial self-presence. There is a fundamental distinction, then, between interiority as the relation to God, which is prior to the relation to self, and interiority as transcendental self-presence. Levinas does not appear to account for this distinction in his critique. He reads Kierkegaard through Fichte rather than through the Augustinian-Eckhartian tradition.

One could argue, moreover, that Levinas is himself quite capable of thinking the subjectivity of the subject in a more Kierkegaardian way: namely, in terms of the diachrony of time. In his *Otherwise than Being* Levinas suggests this: "Temporalization as lapse, the loss of time, is neither an initiative of the ego, nor a movement toward some telos of action. . . . In consciousness there is no longer a presence of self to itself, but senescence."[22] In terms of this lapse, anterior to all presence, Levinas presents an extraordinary phenomenology of aging that shows a subject involved with itself, not as a concern over itself, but in the mode of a "despite oneself." He speaks of a "subjectivity in ageing which the identification of the ego with itself could not reckon on, *one* without identity."[23] That is, without having to refer to the relation to the Other, he shows an originary relation subjectivity has to itself, an identity, defined not by possession or presence, but by dispossession and lapse.

Couldn't one speak here about a Levinasian interiority? About secrecy even? Couldn't one think about singularization, not just vis-à-vis responsibility, but in terms of temporalization? Levinas does: "Subjectivity in ageing is unique, irreplaceable, me and not another; is it despite itself in an obedience where there is no desertion, but where revolt is brewing."[24] It is possible, I suggest, in terms of such brewing revolt, to speak of an "ethical" problematic, a demand, irreducible to the responsibility for the neighbor: namely, one bearing upon the subject's relation to its own aging. One could distinguish, for example, between truthful and untruthful ways of relating to one's own temporalization. In these terms one could speak of a truth of the subject that is interior and singular—for *I am* my own aging—but without that interiority being defined by self-coincidence (since aging is precisely despite oneself).

An ethical or ethical-religious problematic of this order, I suggest, is exactly what Kierkegaard names in the "absolute duty to God." Existence presents an irreducible, singular, unavoidable demand: the demand to hold oneself open to the temporalization that dispossesses (to, we will say, the instant). Levinas points to a duty of this sort directly: "Temporality as ageing and death of the unique one signifies an obedience where there is no desertion."[25] Temporalization itself, precisely in its distinction from self-positing and mediation, works a continual absolvence of the subject from itself. The subject, as it were, hearkens to a demand that has no ideal formulation, for the temporal instant will always already have taken place behind the back of consciousness. "God's will"—what is this other than the very movement of temporalization, the time of creation? I suggest that this ethical-religious problematic, hearkening to originary time in its distinction from posited time, holding oneself open to dispossession, remains absolutely distinct from ethics conceived in terms of the general. It is a question of holding oneself open to becoming "*one* without identity," that is, singular. This "ethics" is presupposed in Levinas's account of responsibility in that what he regards as the fundamental ethical movement, that is, generosity or welcoming, must presuppose the subject holding itself open to dispossession. One can give only what one does *not* possess: preeminently, one's time, for time is what does not return. If *Fear and Trembling* contains, in this sense, a "Levinasian" moment, this may also imply a certain "Kierkegaardianism" unerasable from Levinas's account of the ethical.

The absolute duty to God present, according to Johannes's exegesis within the binding-of-Isaac narrative, is thus a duty to hearken to the dispossession that *I am,* to let everything go, to keep nothing within the orbit of my own. In the language of the theological tradition *Fear and Trembling* reinscribes, the absolute duty to God is a duty to let go of self: the demand for releasement (*Gelassenheit*), the very opposite of Spinoza's *conatus essendi.*

For Abraham, Isaac is the very meaning of what is "his own" insofar as through Isaac—the child of the promise—Abraham is able to relate to himself according to his universality: Isaac is the self-transcendence of Abraham, the truth of Abraham. God's command to let go or sacrifice Isaac intervenes to say, with harsh but unsurpassable clarity, that Isaac is not Abraham's "own." Isaac is the other. Abraham's greatness lay in the absolute promptitude by which he releases everything and bypasses the moment of consolation.

If Levinas suspects any absolute duty not tied to responsibility for the Other, Derrida's *The Gift of Death,* by contrast, seeks to uphold the distinction. "[Kierkegaard's] account of Isaac's sacrifice," he writes, "can be read as a narrative development of the paradox of the concept of duty and absolute responsibility."[26] Derrida reads *Fear and Trembling* for its deconstructive power vis-à-vis ethics—namely, insofar as it articulates a certain "aporia of responsibility." Derrida says:

> I cannot respond to the call, the request, the obligation, or even the love of another without sacrificing the other other, the other others. Every other (one) is every (bit) other [*tout autre est tout autre*], every one else is completely or wholly other. The simple concepts of alterity and singularity constitute the concept of duty as much as that of responsibility. As a result, the concepts of responsibility, of decision, or of duty, are condemned a priori to paradox, scandal, and aporia. . . . As soon as I enter into a relation with the other, with the gaze, look, request, love, command, or call of the other, I know that I can respond only by sacrificing ethics, that is by sacrificing whatever obliges me to also respond, in the same way, in the same instant, to all the others.[27]

On Derrida's reading, then, the suspension of the ethical in the name of an absolute duty is an ineffaceable moment of the ethical itself: it is nothing other than an expression of the *temporality and finitude* of every response before an absolute responsibility. It is an expression of the immeasurable dissymmetry between what obligates us, the responsibility for the Other, for every other who is wholly other, who can be responded to only by letting go what is "my own," and our need to respond to *each* Other. To respond at all to one other is to sacrifice every other other and thus suspend the ethical obligation to that person. Derrida finds a sharp double bind at the center of *Fear and Trembling:* the responsible subject—that is, the *Levinasian* subject—is caught between two irreducible duties, two Others, without being able legitimately to subordinate one to the other in such a way as to render the decision justifiable. Nothing could *justify* giving one's time and resources to one and not to the other. To exist at all within an order of responsibility for the Other is, in this sense, absolutely or irreparably tragic. Abraham stands before a responsibility to which he is essentially incapable of measuring up. Responsibility turns to infinite guilt. The absolute tragedy is that there is no way around this double bind; a good conscience is impossible. The integrity of the autonomous, ethical subject founders in responsibility.

The ingeniousness of Derrida's reading of *Fear and Trembling* and Genesis 22 is that it tries to grasp its phenomenological content (its possible contemporaneity). Derrida is able to generalize the binding-of-Isaac narrative by displacing the lines of transcendence, in a basically Levinasian way, toward the other person.[28] This displacement is captured in his formula "every other (one) is every (bit) other" (*tout autre est tout autre*). Every Other binds me just as absolutely as each Other and so double binds me. God has no priority and neither, by implication, does the goal of "salvation." One could say Derrida shows the simultaneous suspension of the ethical *and* the religious.[29] It would appear that, by a strange kind of anachronism, Derrida reads *Fear and Trembling* as a deconstruction not only of the Kantian "good conscience," but also of Levinasian ethics—for the aporia of responsibility arises, strictly speaking, only where the responsibility for the Other is absolute and unlimited. The suspension of the ethical in Derrida's account is a suspension of what Levinas calls "the ethical." Thus Derrida deconstructs Levinasian responsibility by resituating its primarily transcendental meaning within the context of facticity or finitude. The effect of this reading—which cuts against both Kierkegaard and Levinas—is to render the suspension of the ethical into precisely the "most common thing."[30] Indeed, everything one does—feeding one's cat, speaking a particular language, going to work—counts as a suspension of one's absolute duty to the Other. Any form of positing is violence. The suspension of the ethical, one can say without exaggeration, is for Derrida what makes the world go around: the irreparably tragic law of history.

Derrida frankly admits the displacement he effects on the meaning of the suspension of the ethical: "But what seems thus to universalize or disseminate the exception or the extraordinary by imposing a supplementary complication upon ethical generality, that very thing ensures that Kierke-gaard's text gains added force. It speaks to us of the paradoxical truth of our responsibility."[31] Nevertheless, one may wonder whether, given the factical and universal meaning of the suspension of the ethical, an absolute duty could have any ethical meaning at all—that is, could still be conceived as something to hearken to. We could imagine Hegel, for example, asking whether or not Derrida's "knight of responsibility" is a beautiful soul whose inner life is consumed by an artificial sense of its inability to be pure. And couldn't one imagine the dialectical possibility of a knight of responsibility, exhausted by tragic knowledge, embracing the war of all against all as sim-ply the way of things?[32]

On the other hand, Derrida upholds something essential to both Kierke-gaard and Levinas: "the gift of death," a generosity that is forgetful of itself, the capability for letting-go. The gift of death is a gift conditioned by death: that is, by the readiness to hold oneself open to what dispossesses. Here it is a question of a certain sacrifice of self toward the wholly Other, a "giving oneself death." Derrida writes: "One has to *give [death] to oneself by taking it upon oneself,* for it can only be mine alone, irreplaceably. That is so even if, as we just said, *death can neither be taken nor given.*"[33] Derrida thematizes here the structure of a paradoxical act, which Kierkegaard will name "faith." It is one that never quite appears in Levinas (though may be presupposed): giving and taking what can be neither given nor taken—death, but also time. No doubt Levinas would fear that the expression "giving oneself death" or "giving oneself time" is still too egological, too close to *positing* time or *representing* death. Nevertheless, it is not a question of positing, but of releasement—a question of relating to the absolute as the absolute.

What Derrida's "gift of death" seems to see is that, under the thematics of sacrificial violence, *Fear and Trembling* problematizes the metaphysics of sacrifice—at least, that is, to the extent that sacrifice involves a logic of self-surpassing (salvation). On the one hand, Abraham's act is clearly sacrificial: "[Abraham] must love God with his whole soul. Since God claims Isaac, he must, if possible, love him [Isaac] even more, and only then can he *sacrifice* (*offre*) him, for it is indeed this love for Isaac that makes his act a sacrifice by its paradoxical contrast to his love for God" (*FTR* 74; *SKS* 4:165). On the other hand, however, sacrifice is not the task: "[Abraham] knew," Johannes writes, "that it is kingly to sacrifice a son like this to the universal; he himself would have found rest therein, and everybody would have rested approv-ingly in his deed, as the vowel rests in its quiescent letter. But that is not the task—he is being tested" (*FTR* 77; *SKS* 4:168). The test or ordeal is that God asks Abraham to show that he respects Isaac's alterity—and how could he possibly do this without taking up the knife, in the face of God, *with his own hand*? To raise the knife with one's own hand, to give the gift of death, if one can translate this into existential-phenomenological terms, would be to hold oneself open to a dispossession of everything that is "one's own"— to a future beyond one's own project, beyond the possibility of self-tran-scendence. It would be to accept one's exposure to time in all its radicality, without reservation, to dwell a temporalization not identical to the present consciousness posits. And such would be the condition of generosity, a wel-coming of the other without reserve.

It is in these terms that Johannes counterinterprets the binding of Isaac, not ultimately as a sacrifice of Isaac, nor even as Abraham's sacrifice of him-self, but as the *receiving back* of Isaac: "By faith Abraham did not renounce Isaac, but by faith Abraham received Isaac" (*FTR* 49; *SKS* 4:143). With re-spect to the Other, the giving up *is* the receiving back: one possesses only to the extent one does *not* possess. But not to possess will mean finally learn-ing that one does not possess *oneself;* it will mean consenting to the dispos-session at work in temporalization; it will mean receiving time *where it dis-possesses.* Thus, looking at faith one cannot avoid being seized by a "*horror religiousus*" (*FTR* 61; *SKS* 4:154), both appalled and attracted at the same time.

PROBLEMA III: THE INTER-ESTING

The third problema in a certain way begins all over again. It returns to the same problematic, the ordeal of exceptionality, yet does so "purely esthetic-cally" (*FTR* 82; *SKS* 4:172). The philosophical issue concerns "disclosure" (*Aabenbarelse*) and "hiddenness" (*Skjulthed*), which is to say the problem of essence and manifestation, and again the question is whether there is "justi-fied hiddenness." "The ethical," Johannes writes, "is the universal; as the uni-versal it is in turn the disclosed" (*FTR* 82; *SKS* 4:172). And again the possi-bility of an essential nondisclosure or secrecy is contrasting with the inner demand of Hegel's thought: "The Hegelian philosophy assumes no justi-fied hiddenness, no justified incommensurability" (*FTR* 82; *SKS* 4:172).

The "aesthetic" plan of the third problema involves sketching various scenarios through which to approach the notion of an essential secrecy that would coincide with what is most singular. What is particular always falls within a horizon of representation, disclosure, or intelligibility. The singu-lar, however, cannot be drawn out in language: it would refer to a "subject" without predicates. Yet, as becomes clear in the third problema, this docs not refer a subject present to itself and dwelling on its own ineffable con-tent. Singularity arises through an ordeal in which it lies *stripped* of predi-cates. The subject undergoes a kind of apophasis, or stripping bare. "Abra-ham lies silent" Johannes writes, "but he cannot speak . . . [and] therein lies the distress and the anxiety" (*FTR* 113; *SKS* 4:201). It is not so much that

Abraham holds a secret, but that a secret holds him. He is bound over to secrecy in anxiety and distress. It is by way of such secrecy that, once again, "the single individual as the single individual is higher than the universal, whereas the universal is in fact mediation" (*FTR* 82; *SKS* 4:172). This secrecy plays out in that Abraham bypasses three "ethical authorities": "So Abraham did not speak, he did not speak to Sarah, or to Eliezer, or to Isaac; he bypassed these three ethical authorities, since for Abraham the ethical had no higher expression than family life" (*FTR* 112; *SKS* 4:200).

In the third problema, however, Johannes approaches such silence purely aesthetically, by way of the category of the "interesting." The interesting, which is also the category of the "turning point," signifies what falls between being (*inter-esse*) as categorially determined. It refers to the incommensurable, the exceptional, and the like. Thus structurally the interesting repeats the primary problematic of the problemata: the ordeal of the rule. Yet, as an aesthetic category, the interesting will in the end remain in "absolute dissimilarity" (*FTR* 85; *SKS* 4:173) to the exceptionality of existence. The self itself, as existing, falls beyond or prior to categorial determination and the total field of presence; the self remains, in this sense, indeterminate or "immediate." Here, however, Kierkegaard's poet makes an essential distinction between a first immediacy and a later immediacy: "Faith [i.e., justified singularity] is not a first immediacy but a later immediacy" (*FTR* 82; *SKS* 4:172). The difference between these two immediacies is this: the first immediacy refers to the immediacy of what is in fact already mediated, the immediacy of what has not yet come to explication. It is the immediacy that appears in Hegel's discussion of "sense certainty" and in *Johannes Climacus*. First immediacy is, in and for consciousness, always already suspended. A "later" immediacy would signify what *remains* in and beyond the movement of mediation. The universal is mediation, the integration of differences or exceptions on the plane of presence, within the unity of self-consciousness. That this immediacy comes "later," however, is somewhat misleading: it is a later immediacy only in that it manifests itself in a failure of mediation. It is "later" on the phenomenological order, but not on the order of existence itself. What remains incommensurable to mediation, what cannot be re-presented, is the event of coming-into-existence itself (the instant). This prior immediacy "shows itself" only in the interruption of mediation. Now the interesting presents, initially, some singularity or interruption in what is expected. Something appears that resists categorial determination and cannot be thought on the basis of a principle; the principle is exactly what one looks for, what is in play. To this extent it remains concealed. Concealment is the "tension creating factor" (*FTR* 83; *SKS* 4:173) in the phenomenon, yet it provokes and demands recognition, which is "the resolving, relaxing element" (*FTR* 83; *SKS* 4:173). One can see then how, initially at least, aesthetic concealment (presupposed in the interesting) overlaps with the problem of negation in Hegel. Concealment creates tension that is then resolved. Negation is negated; disclosure happens.[34]

Johannes presents Abraham, if he is justified, as an instance of some essential concealment, a tension that cannot be relaxed through recognition. Such concealment will remain absolutely unique and, in its own way, categorial: namely, it will refer to the category of a-categoriality. Here one should bear in mind that existence itself signifies this category that interrupts all categoriality. Abraham's situation signifies "the paradox of existence" itself. Necessarily, then, Abraham cannot be approached directly. Johannes says: "It was also pointed out that none of the stages described contains an analogy to Abraham; they were explained, while being demonstrated within its own sphere, only in order that in their moment of deviation they could, as it were, indicate the boundary of an unknown territory" (*FTR* 112; *SKS* 4:200). Thus Johannes's strategy for presenting Abraham's position takes shape in the following way: he presents Abraham's singularity as a point of convergence, never given, to which a series of interesting cases or "stages" all point. The unknown territory is the space, fundamentally indeterminate, that precedes and conditions every particular "stage." It is the space of existence itself, existence in its "pure" givenness prior to and after any determination.

I shall not run through all of the "stages" presented in the third problema. Instead, I will concentrate upon two scenarios, both of them involving a failed effort to marry. Quite obviously, these scenarios bear closely upon Kierkegaard's own break with Regina Olsen. My interest, though, is not biography, but rather the (transcendental) problematic of existence Johannes formulates through reflection upon these scenes. Marriage constitutes for Kierkegaard's pseudonyms an exemplary expression of ethical self-transcendence. Hence these two cases will allow us to draw out the structure of singularity in its divergence from ethical universality.

The first story is from Aristotle's *Politics:* the augurs in Delphi prophesy a calamity if the bridegroom goes through with the marriage, and so, at the crucial moment, he does not marry. The decisive point Johannes concentrates upon is the bridegroom's relation to the augur's pronouncement: "Everything depends upon the relation in which the bridegroom stands to the augur's pronouncement, which in one way or other will be decisive for his life" (*FTR* 92; *SKS* 4:182). The augur's pronouncement is enigmatic. Some indeterminate calamity is alluded to; it is decisive for his life, yet remains in concealment. The augurs thus disclose what Johannes calls the "epic remnant" at work in Greek tragedies—namely fate, in which "the dramatic action vanishes and in which it has its dark, mysterious source" (*FTR*

84; *SKS* 4:174). The law of indetermination or singularization thus appears, in the Greek context, as the "blindness" of fate: it crushes whom it crushes. The acts of subjects are reversed in their basic meaning and so are annihilated as acts of a subject: "A son murders his father, but not until later does he learn that it was his father" (*FTR* 84; *SKS* 4:174), and so on. Fate, in other words, works according to *a law contrary to self-positing*. It interrupts the self-transcending movements of subjects. Fate cannot be thought on the horizon of presence (e.g., it cannot be anticipated). Nevertheless, Johannes suggests, with respect to the situation at Delphi, this indeterminate factor is still basically contained within the intelligibility of the ethical: "an augur's pronouncement is understandable by all. . . . Thus the augur's pronouncement is intelligible not only to the hero but also to all and does not eventuate in any private relation to the divine" (*FTR* 92; *SKS* 4:182–83). The situation of the bridegroom is that of the tragic figure: he must give up one form of self-transcendence for another. In this context, he is able to speak. To conceal the pronouncement from others, first of all from the bride, would be to transgress the ethical illegitimately.

At this point Johannes intervenes with a permutation on the story designed to shed light on Abraham's situation. Suppose, he suggests, that the bridegroom had heard the pronouncement against marriage through some purely private, purely interior medium—in that case the analogy to Abraham becomes relevant. In such a case he could not speak any intelligible speech. "Then," Johannes says, "his silence would not be due to his wanting to place himself as the single individual in an absolute relation to the universal but to his having been placed as the single individual in an absolute relation to the absolute" (*FTR* 93; *SKS* 4:183). Johannes does not say what sort of purely private medium that he imagines as replacing the augurs. One thing, however, is clear: the Greeks never conceived any purely private relation to the divine (it would always have to be mediated, however enigmatically, by the public medium of the oracle). Nor, for the same reason, did the Greeks have a conception of self-consciousness as what posits itself. Only in the metaphysics of modernity does that concept emerge. Hence, in modernity, the blindness of fate is cancelled by reflection: "modern drama has abandoned destiny, has dramatically emancipated itself, is sighted, gazes inward into itself, absorbs destiny in its dramatic consciousness" (*FTR* 84; *SKS* 4:174). Modernity eliminates the notion of fate insofar as it thinks self-consciousness, consciousness "gazing inward into itself," as the ground of the real. Reducing reality to its being-for-consciousness, modernity traces all events to the spontaneity of the will. Nothing remains fundamentally opaque or ambiguous.

The question, then, by which one draws nearer to Abraham's position, is whether one can think the tragic dispossession that fate brings *once again*, in a modern context. More simply: can one recover a purely interior notion of fate? Kierkegaard's author leaves this question hanging and proceeds to the next examples. We can interject, however, to suggest that a purely interior fate is already thought in the notion of originary time. That time cannot be interiorized or represented, even though it is precisely what is most interior, signifies an immediacy that remains the condition of all mediation, and hence unmediated and unsayable.

The second scenario Johannes considers, which comes very near to Abraham, is the story of Sarah and Tobias, taken from the apocryphal book of *Tobit.* "Sarah," he writes, "has a tragic background. She has been given to seven men, all of whom perished in the bridal chamber" (*FTR* 102; *SKS* 4:191). It is this "tragic background" that fixes Johannes's attention. The tragic background is that "[Sarah] knows that an evil demon who loves her will kill her bridegroom on the wedding night" (*FTR* 102; *SKS* 4:191). Here, then, is the tragedy: "Many a girl has become unhappy in love, but she nevertheless did become that; Sarah *was* that before she became that. It is grievous not to find the person to whom one can give oneself, but it is *unspeakably* grievous not to be able to give oneself" (*FTR* 103; *SKS* 4: 192). The speechless pain of Sarah draws her near to Abraham. Her "tragic background" makes her unable to give herself to her beloved; it renders her exceptional to the satisfactions of morality. This example reflects explicitly upon the temporality involved in becoming an exception: the event whereby one is excepted occurs *always in a temporality prior to the present.* There is a becoming, an event, prior to any becoming the subject herself could author. Sarah does not become unhappy in an event that has duration, but prior to any present. She is always already unhappy, or comes into being in unhappiness. She is herself unhappiness coming into being, the very figure of unhappiness. As with the "Unhappiest One," the temporal present is not an ecstatic thrust toward future possibility, but a being-bonded to a prior instant that cannot be mastered. She is thrust into the double bind of two contradictory temporalities: one which she posits, the other in which she is herself de-posited. This is the situation of the "paradox."

The bridegroom, however, knows full well of her tragedy and is willing to marry anyway. He is heroic. And hence "if a poet read this story," Johannes assures us, "I wager a hundred to one that he would make everything center on the young Tobias [the bridegroom]" (*FTR* 103; *SKS* 4:192). Poets as poets are interested in acts of self-renunciation, that is, self-transcendence. The poetic maximum is the sublime. Yet for a poet such as Johannes who takes a special interest in *dialectic*—which is to say in double binds—Sarah is the main interest. She is the figure of response, of acting on an absolute duty. Given her tragic background, Sarah cannot express any direct relation to the ethical. She can only enter the ethical (marry) by rupturing the ethical—that is the double bind—for she must take the "responsibility of permitting the beloved to do something so hazardous" (*FTR* 104; *SKS* 4:193). Yet does she have the *right* to let the other person sacrifice himself for her? Imagine her saying: I love you enough to let yourself be destroyed by me. Ethics will balk. Out of respect and indeed love for the other, should she not forbid his undertaking? Isn't her love for the other most fully expressed in the renunciation of her love? Wouldn't the consent to marriage be precisely irresponsible? These are *ethical* questions. And if she expresses her love by renouncing her desire to marry, she is a tragic hero.

One can see the parallels between Sarah and Abraham: both, apparently, are willing to "sacrifice" the beloved. The only difference, which is not a significant one for ethics, is that Abraham himself is ready actively to put Isaac to death, whereas Sarah is ready passively to allow Tobias to martyr himself for her sake. In each case the very condition for receiving the other is to become irresponsible with respect to the other (and, hence, to ethics). For how could Sarah justify her consent? Sarah, like Abraham, has been rendered exceptional. And in her case the suspension of the ethical is even clearer: it will always already have taken place. She must express the ethical, but she cannot, for she is herself—"from the very beginning"—the exception. If she returns to the ethical by way of a renunciation of her love, she will have negated the negation (that is tragic). Yet if she returns to the ethical by way of an affirmation of her love under an unjustifiable responsibility, then—whether Tobias lives or is killed—she will have intensified her exceptionality.

For Johannes, her act is an expression of "the great mystery that it is far more difficult to receive than to give" (*FTR* 104; *SKS* 4:193). To receive is to give the very possibility of giving. Evidently what is at stake is the ethically problematic character of this gift of death. Does she have a right to let the other make a gift of *himself*? Not only this, but does she have the courage to withstand the essential asymmetry that would open up through this gift, for how could she be sure that "she would not in the very next moment hate the man to whom she owed everything!" (*FTR* 104; *SKS* 4:193). To owe one's commensurability, that is, one's ethically conceived personhood, to the other—would this not constitute a rupture in the foundation of the self, a deadly blow against self-positing, and thus an ongoing source of torment? The gift, then, simultaneously redeems and condemns, binds and looses, kills and enlivens. And if Sarah is great, for Johannes, it is because she responds to the gift of himself Tobias makes, for that means she is ready to affirm her singularity and all its ensuing torments.

As already indicated, however, Johannes has considered the position of Sarah only to throw indirect light on Abraham's position. Strictly speaking, neither Sarah nor any other example constitutes an analogy to Abraham. Although Johannes is able to think Sarah's case as involving an absolute relation to the absolute, he deflects this similarity by claiming that "everything said here about Sarah . . . has its full meaning when with a psychological interest one explores the meaning of the old saying: *Nullum unquam exstitit magnum ingenium sine aliqua dementia*" (*FTR* 106; *SKS* 4:195). No genius has ever existed without a touch of madness. Sarah's case, then, is made emblematic not of a suspension of the ethical or absolute duty, but of the situation of the genius. Sarah is the poet.

At this point, however, we may wonder about the necessity to insist upon the absolute uniqueness of Abraham. Why make Abraham the *paradigmatic* exception?[35] Undoubtedly it is because Abraham, like the "Unhappiest One," is less a person than a *category*. Abraham is everyone and no one; his ordeal is the ordeal of existence itself. Abraham is the name for the subjectivity of the subject. Not only this, but Abraham's act—faith—must in a certain sense remain impossible, that is, retain its ideality; it must remain an absolute *duty*. That no one is Abraham means that he presents a task impossible to finish: the task of releasing oneself to reality, giving oneself death, welcoming the other, holding oneself open to the anarchy of time.[36]

What Johannes presents in the figure of Abraham, then, is the very structure of exceptionality, the subjectivity of the subject. The subjectivity of the subject is an act—not of self-positing—but of releasing, of giving. This is an act different from all re-presenting, all mediation, and so different from the work of bringing reality to presence and manifestness. If consciousness is, as in idealism, a work of apophansis or speech, Abraham's position coincides with an essential silence: Abraham *cannot* speak. Nevertheless, that he cannot speak does not mean that he holds some ineffable content; ineffable content would not constitute a later immediacy, but rather a first immediacy. If his silence were his communion with ineffable content, or if he had simply nothing to say, then something essential would be missing: one has to perceive "the necessity for Abraham to consummate himself in the final moment, not to draw the knife silently but to have a word to say, since as the father of faith he has absolute significance in the direction of spirit" (*FTR* 117; *SKS* 4:205).

Abraham *does* speak and so consummates himself as a subject. Yet his speech *consummates silence:* "First and foremost, [Abraham] does not say anything, and in that form he says what he has to say. His response to Isaac is in the form of irony, for it is always irony when I say something and still do not say anything" (*FTR* 118; *SKS* 4:205). Abraham speaks without speaking. When Isaac asks him where is the lamb for the sacrifice Abraham replies, "God himself will provide (*see sig om*) the lamb for the burnt offering my son" (*FTR* 119; *SKS* 4:206). God will, more literally, *see to it*. In this discourse Abraham "is not speaking an untruth, but neither does he say anything, for he is speaking in a strange tongue (*et fremmed Tungemaal*)" (*FTR* 119; *SKS* 4:206). In his speech Abraham appropriates for himself, makes his own, what *precisely cannot be made one's own:* the future. He gives himself time insofar as he cannot give it to himself, for the future belongs entirely to God. In saying "God will see to it" he holds himself open to the absolute future, the future insofar as it exceeds an anticipative experience of it in the present—the future beyond representation. In speaking, and only in speaking, he gives himself to that future. His saying is an absolute relation to the absolute, a releasement.

FAITH AS RELEASEMENT

In various ways the "Problemata" expose a demand upon the subject, an absolute duty, which cannot be formulated as an ethical demand. It is a duty that violates the ethical in that it violates the presupposition of the ethical: preeminently, the notion that the subject is, originally, in possession of itself. Through its temporality the subject is not identical to what posits itself; it is first of all an undergoing of itself, an exposure, one *without* identity. Yet in Abraham we have a picture of a consummate subject. This is the subject whose existence is constituted through the movement of "faith." Faith here signifies the opposite of self-positing or re-presenting: as alluded to above, it involves a giving oneself what cannot be given or taken. Faith is a letting-be, or releasement. The structure of this act has to be considered more closely.

Kierkegaard's author details the meaning of faith in the "Eulogy on Abraham" and "Preliminary Expectoration." The structural features of faith, to sketch them briefly, are the following: it is a "double movement," a return to temporality and finitude, an "absolute relation to the absolute," and an absolute beginning. To these elements must also be added something decisive: the one who has faith, Johannes says, "gives birth to his own father" (*FTR* 27; *SKS* 4:123). Though it may appear as an oddity, a strong and embarrassing paradox—and no doubt for this reason the phrase has been almost universally ignored by commentators[37]—this proposition articulates the operative logic of the whole text: the logic of an event. Faith gives birth to that from which it is supposed to derive. One could speak here of a "supplement of origin."[38] The origin, the beginning, the principle—that which is supposed to precede the event as its ground—is itself produced in the event. The event (of birth) does not unfold continuously in, or as, time; rather, time itself, as continuity or presence, is itself produced. What precedes time does not fall in a prior present, for at issue is the original arrival of presence (whether as past present, present present, or future presence). Now, it cannot escape our notice that the trope of "giving birth to one's own father" derives from the Eckhartian tradition. In his sermon 22, for example, Eckhart refers directly to giving birth to one's own father: "Out of the purity he everlastingly bore me, his only-born Son, into that same image of his eternal Fatherhood, that I may be Father and *give birth to him of whom I am born*" (my emphasis).[39] Eckhart aims at thinking the event whereby presence is first given—an origin, but not a principle (or, sometimes, a principle without principle). He articulates a movement, called *Gelassenheit* (releasement, letting be), of entering into time as event, time as birth or becoming, rather than as presence.[40]

I suggest, then, that "faith" be interpreted along the lines of Eckhartian apophaticism, that is, vis-à-vis the metaphysics of birth and the movement of *Gelassenheit*.[41] To give birth to one's own father is to give to oneself what cannot be given, that is, re-presented or posited: the origin, the beginning. As the movement through which the subject consummates its very subjectivity, faith constitutes time without, however, making it its "own." Faith constitutes time as what cannot be constituted, by letting it be. An act of this order, however, can only be thought in terms of a certain *double* movement.

FAITH AS DOUBLE MOVEMENT

What captures the attention of Johannes de Silentio is the temporal posture of Abraham: he "arrived neither too *early* nor too late" (*FTR* 35; *SKS* 4:130–311). He responds with an exactness and promptitude that is the inversion of the Unhappiest One, who, founding time on representation, arrives essentially too soon to his own temporal instant, and is therefore also always too late. Faith arrives in each instant into its own temporal instant; it leaps into its *own instant*. The image is that of the ballet dancer leaping into place:

> It is supposed to be the most difficult feat for a ballet dancer to leap into a specific posture in such a way that he never once strains for the posture but in the very leap assumes the posture. Perhaps there is no ballet dancer who can do it—but this knight does it . . . to be able to come down in such a way that instantaneously one seems to stand and to walk, to change the leap into life into walking, absolutely to express the sublime in the pedestrian—only [the knight of faith] can do it, and this is the one and only marvel. (*FTR* 41; *SKS* 4:135–36)

At stake in faith is an approach to temporality: both an infinite distance taking and an infinite return, a double movement. The point, however, would be to think the distance taking as the return and the return as the distance taking. One leaps into the present, into place, yet in such a way that the leap is already a position-taking. Walking signifies the *continuous* transition from one present to the next, that is, time in its character as continuous presence or duration. In this image, however, what is to be thought is the eventful character of time. The leap here figures the event in which presence arrives; it is the beginning of the present, and not something that either precedes the present or takes place in presence. The leap is always *already* a taking position (*Stillingen*). No time at all is required for an assuming of position, for in the taking position the temporal present itself has its inception. Time begins in the leap; the leap is originary time, or the time of origination. Each present, then, is a departure, an inception, a beginning. In this sense, the leap signifies the discontinuous character of the present: in every present "all things are made new."

Faith means: I begin with time *again*, with time as leap, as event; I orient my relation to time, not in terms of the pedestrian structure of the project, but in terms of the *marvel* that continuity exists. The pedestrian is the greatest marvel. Faith grasps the absolute discontinuity presupposed in all continuity: the shock that time is given at all. Faith is that whereby I *receive* temporality: not that I receive it in terms of some a priori intuition (whereby I receive it in representing it), but that I receive it by giving myself to it.

Kierkegaard's author formulates the structure of this receptivity as a "double movement" (*Dobbelt-Bevægelse*): first "infinite resignation," then "faith" proper. He writes: "Infinite resignation is the last stage before faith, so that anyone who has not made this movement does not have faith, for only in infinite resignation do I become conscious of my eternal validity, and only then can one speak of grasping existence by faith" (*FTR* 46; *SKS* 4:140). The distinction between infinite resignation and faith is an essential one; everything turns on it. Faith *presupposes* infinite resignation. That means: at every moment faith is always also infinite resignation. Faith is never less than infinite resignation, but more than it. If faith is not *always also* infinite resignation, it is not faith. The distinction between the two, however, will turn on the relation to temporality: resignation absolves itself to the eternity of self-consciousness, that is, to its capability of keeping itself constantly present to itself. It signifies the maximization of self-positing consciousness, and it annihilates time as event by absolving itself to eternity. Faith, by contrast, moves from time as re-presentable—that is, time in its character as pure presence, or eternal—into time as eventful. It "returns" to temporality and finitude. Commenting on their relation, Johannes de Silentio writes:

> The act of resignation does not require faith, for what I gain in resignation is my eternal consciousness. This is a *purely philosophical movement* that I

venture to make when it is demanded and can discipline myself to make, because every time finitude will take power over me, I starve myself into submission until I make the movement, for my eternal consciousness is my love for God, and for me that is the highest of all. (*FTR* 48, my italics; *SKS* 4:42)

Infinite resignation is, quite precisely, "a purely philosophical movement" (*reen philosophisk Bevægelse*) and an "act of consciousness" (*Bevistheds-Akt*). It inscribes the movement of every egology: the movement whereby self-consciousness grasps its sovereignty over all external phenomena, the sovereignty whereby it constitutes phenomena. Through its knowledge of itself in its "eternal validity," the absolute certainty of its presence to itself, it discovers an absolutely immovable point amidst the eventfulness of time. This absolvence to self, through which it establishes its priority to any givens (any beings), it should be pointed out, coincides with the beginning of philosophy—whether in Socrates (as understood by Plato), Stoicism, Kant, Fichte, or Hegel. Philosophy begins where the consciousness of an absolute presence, that is, an eternal consciousness, is achieved beyond the temporal flux. As infinite differentiation, the movement of infinite resignation is simply a *passing beyond* temporality and finitude. As soon as consciousness knows itself, it becomes impossible to posit any other origin for itself than itself—for what could it possibly mean for self-consciousness to think a moment in which it was *not?* Self-consciousness, thought in its purity, posits itself as original, *eternal.*

The secret of infinite resignation is thus that, for it, self-consciousness, the identity of the ego with itself in reflection, is the highest—indeed absolute—principle. Convinced inwardly of the unconditional validity of self-consciousness, the knight of infinite resignation infinitely negates all forms of consciousness in which it becomes bound to an object *outside itself*: "he who loves God without faith reflects upon himself [that is, reflects infinitely upon himself]; he who loves God in faith reflects upon God" (*FTR* 37; *SKS* 4:132). Infinite resignation resigns itself to God as the "highest of all," the constantly present (eternal) being of beings. But "God" here, Johannes suggests, is simply another name for the self—the self qua eternal, qua absolute. The act of infinite resignation, however, is occasioned existentially by the experience of the impossible; it "looks impossibility in the eye" (*FTR* 47; *SKS* 4:141). The "impossible" signifies an event that reveals the reality of the world as a resistance to human desire, the character of the world as necessity. The impossible arises wherever a desire is rendered an ontological embarrassment by the machinations of the world, where a desire stands without any horizon of fulfillment in terms of given reality. The impossible blocks the movement of self-transcendence and stalls out the temporality of projects. Facing the impossible the self may save itself by giving up its desire and submitting to the necessity of the world. And in this there is reconciliation with being: "In infinite resignation there is peace and rest; every person who wills it, who has not debased himself by self-disdain . . . can discipline himself to make the movement, which in its pain reconciles one to existence" (*FTR* 45; *SKS* 4:140).

To learn the meaning of infinite resignation, Johannes suggests, may be task enough for a person's whole life. Yet it is not the task of faith and therefore not the "highest task." Nevertheless, if one has not sighted the profound reconciliation offered within philosophical (i.e., "Greek") experience, then to speak of faith would be pointless. If it occurs at all, faith emerges not as a substitute for philosophical experience, but in excess to it. Thus, presupposing infinite resignation, faith is not a form of consolation. It does not open up as a mere supplement or wish-fulfillment, filling a lack that the world has brought about. Faith is always superfluous, an ontological "luxury," but purchased at a high price. But what then is faith in contrast to, but also as presupposing, infinite resignation? The doubleness of faith involves the fact that it simultaneously enacts and violates infinite resignation; it is and is not a movement of self-positing. Kierkegaard's poet writes:

> The act of resignation does not require faith, but to get the *least little bit more* than my eternal consciousness requires faith, for this is the paradox. The movements are often confused. It is said that faith is needed to renounce everything . . . [but] by faith I do not renounce anything; on the contrary, by faith I receive everything exactly in the sense in which it is said that one who has faith like a mustard seed can move mountains. It takes purely human courage to renounce the whole temporal realm in order to gain eternity, but this I do gain and in all eternity can never renounce—it is a self-contradiction. But it takes a paradoxical and humble courage to grasp the whole temporal realm now by virtue of the absurd, and this is the courage of faith. (*FTR* 48–49, my italics; *SKS* 4:143)

Faith grasps what exceeds eternal, self-positing consciousness—that is, temporality! Having abandoned time, it returns to time. Or again, insofar as faith presupposes infinite resignation—that is, includes infinite resignation within itself—one has to think the simultaneity (the paradox) of leaving time by entering into it and entering into it by leaving it. The doubleness of this act is essential: faith neither flees time toward its eternal ground nor takes it up by inaugurating a project. Johannes writes: "it is great to lay hold of the eternal, but it is greater to hold fast to the temporal after having given it up" (*FTR* 18; *SKS* 4:115). To flee time toward the eternal is a philosophical, metaphysical act; yet so is entering time through the project, that is, through remaking time in terms of spontaneous freedom. Faith enters time without taking it up or positing it. In other words, faith enters time, refusing the metaphysical move, but not first of all by relating time to its thetic power; it refuses to understand itself as the constitutive ground of temporality. The act of faith, then, is not an act of freedom as spontaneity or positing, but an act done "in the power of the absurd." Faith relates to temporality as such and as a whole starting from the fact that it did not posit it. Johannes writes: "the whole earthly figure [the knight of faith] presents is a new creation by the power of the absurd. He resigned everything infinitely, and then he grasped everything again in the power of the absurd" (*FTR* 40; *SKS* 4:135). "At every instant," Johannes says, "the knight of faith buys the opportune time at the highest price, for he does not do even the slightest thing except in the power of the absurd" (*FTR* 40; *SKS* 4:135).

The infinite resignation presupposed in faith, then, is not a resignation of temporality, but a *resignation of itself*. Faith is the renunciation of renunciation. Yet the "dialectic" here is not that of double negation in Hegel's sense; rather, in Eckhart's sense. Faith renounces even its conception of itself as capable of infinite resignation. It renounces that final gesture, the most basic gesture, of philosophical mastery: the power to renounce as *my own* power, that final power whereby I preserve my autarchy. In this sense faith is what Eckhart calls *Gelassenheit,* or "true obedience," the renunciation of oneself or going out of oneself. Yet here, as in Eckhart, the renunciation of oneself is identical to a receiving of everything: receiving everything back, namely as "on loan" (Eckhart) or "in the power of the absurd." Faith receives everything without ever possessing anything; it receives on condition that its very act of receiving is grasped as on loan, in the power of the absurd. Thus faith is an essential humility that keeps nothing in reserve; it is a giving oneself to time with no conditions: a humble *courage*.

SERIOUS PLAY

The double movement of faith returns to temporality and finitude, discovering them, letting them be for the first time. In so doing, according to the "Epilogue," faith begins with temporality and finitude "primitively" (*primitivt*), from the beginning. If the "unhappiest one" describes the absolute limit of discord between self-consciousness and temporality—he is simultaneously too early and too late—the knight of faith describes an absolute promptitude in which self-consciousness remains perfectly in sync with each instant, though only by grasping it in the power of the absurd, as non-posited or gift. In that sense, faith begins at the beginning. This remaining in the beginning, positing it as what cannot be posited, is the absolute relation to the absolute. In the epilogue this absolute beginning is separated from the ideal or represented beginning of speculative thought.

Johannes's comments in the epilogue are of a historical nature; they bear upon the contours of "the present generation" (*den nærværende Slægt*). "Are we so sure," he asks, "that we have achieved the highest, so that there is nothing left for us to do except piously to delude ourselves into thinking that we have not come that far, simply in order to have something to oc-cupy our time?" (*FTR* 121; *SKS* 4:208). The "present generation" under-stands itself as the one in which the absolute understands itself, in which the absolute has achieved itself. It thinks reality in terms of the presence that arises through positing. What reality will have meant, the "highest," can anticipatively be enjoyed. The present generation is thus defined by the sense of return, completion, satisfaction, closure—in other words, by ab-solute knowledge—and, hence, not by passion (*Lidenskaben*). The very meaning of passion is to be pulled beyond closure and exposed to what is endless: to "tasks" that are "authentically human."

It is a question in the epilogue, then, of articulating the difference be-tween absolute closings and absolute openings, between recuperable ori-gins and anarchic origins. What is striking is that Johannes claims that only a "pious self-deception" could prevent us from seeing that the present moment—where we are now—is indeed defined by absolute knowledge. Hegel is the name for where we are. For Hegel, the human being is the being in whom and for whom closure happens. If spirit begins at the be-ginning—which, for Hegel, it does in the moment of absolute knowl-edge—this is then only to say that it recollects and retraces the movement of its own genesis. To begin is to recollect and re-present what to spirit re-mains eternally present. In the introduction to his *Philosophy of History* Hegel writes:

> Because we are concerned only with the idea of Spirit—and we regard the whole of world history as nothing more than the manifestation of Spirit—when we go over the past, however extensive it may be, we are really con-cerned only with the present. This is because philosophy, which occupies it-self with the True, is concerned with what is eternally *present*. Nothing in the past is lost to philosophy: the Idea is ever present, Spirit is immortal, i.e., Spirit is not the past, nor the non-existent future, but is an essential *now*.[42]

Absolute knowledge, that is, that knowledge which grasps history as pre-cisely the progressive manifestation of "the Idea," relates to history primi-tively—yet it does so recollectively. To begin primitively is to return to the foundation of constant presence. Then, from this knowledge of the essen-tial, spirit is capable of assimilating into itself the entire spiritual content of the past. The alienation between spirit and itself that is a result of its historicity can be overcome. Striving is not endless; it is, rather, bounded by the "Idea," the ground. This closure defines the presence of the present.

At the very heart of this experience, and conditioned by it, however, lies a profound alienation: for the present generation, "all existence seems wrong to it" (*FTR* 122; *SKS* 4:209). As soon as existence measures itself by the experience of infinitude, that is, becoming self-coincident or self-present (becoming "free" in Hegel's terms), and as soon as this identity of presence is taken as the ground of temporality, a certain relation toward temporality as such and as a whole will have been adopted. Time will have been regarded in its reality only in terms of a continuous unfolding of presence. The "present generation" is the one unable to acknowledge time as gift, that is, the temporality in which the self is dispossessed of its identity without ceasing to be. For this very reason it will have no sense for *absolute tasks*— which is to say, for tasks in which the self is unable to transcend itself, tasks that never get beyond the beginning. The repeated affirmation of the epilogue, however, is that the discovery of the authentically human is an endless task:

> Whatever one generation learns from another, no generation learns the essentially human from a previous one. . . . Each generation begins all over again; the next generation advances no further than the previous one, that is if that one was faithful to the task and did not leave it high and dry. That it should be fatiguing is, of course, something that one generation cannot say, for the generation does indeed have the task and has nothing to do with the fact that the previous generation had the same task. (*FTR* 122; *SKS* 4:208)

The human task is in itself an absolute opening, a matter of essential passion. The absolute task is for the finite to receive its own finitude, to turn toward itself as always already offered up to itself, dispossessed, and let be. Human life is an endless repetition of this same beginning, for the temporal instant itself constitutes a departure without finality: each instant is a beginning all over again, primitively. The task is thus to let this beginning be as beginning (as non-possessable, non-positable). Thus the human being is not the being in whom closure takes place, but rather the one in whom opening never ceases to take place. The essentially human task, which a human being will never get beyond, is to open oneself to that exposure or opening: to temporalization.

But is this not a case of the "bad infinite?" Johannes alludes to a Hegelian-type objection: would not the incessance of beginning, never progressing past the beginning, constitute the hollow circularity of endless, truly Sisyphean labor? Does not the authentically human lie rather in way spirit inherits and appropriates the riches of the past? Does it not lie in the power to gather the past recollectively into the interiority of the self by means of anticipative insight into the end-goal? Does it not lie precisely in the thrust to the future, the project? In freedom as overcoming?

In a certain way, after Hegel, Johannes reinscribes the Fichtean understanding of faith as "infinite striving."[43] In his *Vocation of Man,* a religious text as much as an ethical one, Fichte too raises the specter of the hollow, unending circularity of time, a spell broken only by the "resolution" of faith: "What is the purpose of this circle ever returning into itself, of this game ever beginning anew in the same way, a game in which everything comes to be only to pass away, and passes away only to become again as it already was?"[44] Such temporality, ever beginning at the beginning, is a horrific "monster that ceaselessly devours itself." For Fichte, however, faith breaks the spell where subjectivity takes itself as the radical ground and end-goal of the temporal process: "I become for myself the sole source of all my being and my appearances; and from now on I have life in myself unconditioned by anything outside myself."[45] Temporality acquires reality only as the movement in which the subject comes to coincide with itself—that is, time is understood entirely within the horizon of presence and self-presence. Thus for both Fichte and Hegel the decisive movement is the *labor* of the subject realizing itself across, and as, temporality. Something different emerges in Johannes' estimation:

> As long as the generation is concerned only about its task, which is the highest, it cannot become weary, for the task is always adequate for a person's lifetime. When children on vacation have already played all the games before twelve o'clock and impatiently ask: Can't somebody think up a new game—does this show that these children are more developed and more advanced than the children in the contemporary or previous generation who make the well-known games last all day long? Or does it show instead that the first children lack what I would call the endearing seriousness that belongs to play (*den elskelige Alvor, der hører til at lege*)? (*FTR* 122, slightly altered; *SKS* 4:209)

More than a metaphor or example, this passage brings us to the heart of faith as releasement. The child on vacation is given the day and given over to the day. The day is just as much gift as task because there is *nothing* to be done, nothing that must be done, within it. The day stands open. But now suppose that there is too much of the day—what would this reveal? For Johannes, it would show a lack of the kind of seriousness that belongs to play. That kind of seriousness is the kind capable of sustaining itself in the openness of the time offered—which is to say in openness as such, in time as openness—a seriousness (*Alvor*) not identical to that of projects. If seriousness generally takes root where a span of time opens between a projecting and a projected subject, so that it signifies the subject staying identical to itself across a span of time and, hence, a labor, here, by contrast, there is a relation to time beyond time as represented, that is posited. Play is a simple capacity for absorption, for sinking, for letting-go oneself. Faith as play would then signify sinking into finitude, into the time offered, as well as the time in which one is offered up, the time to which one is exposed. It would mean radical consent to the exposure of one's own temporality. Such consent would underlie every authentically human task.

SIX

The Instant
(The Concept of Anxiety)

*T*he Concept of Anxiety, subtitled *A Simple Psychological Deliberation on
the Dogmatic Issue of Hereditary Sin* and written by Kierkegaard under
the pseudonym Vigilius Haufniensis ("Watchman of Copenhagen"), was
published in 1844, four days after *Philosophical Fragments*. The text, one of
Kierkegaard's most straightforwardly philosophical, in a certain sense completes the arc of thinking opened up in *The Concept of Irony*. The main argument of this book has been that Kierkegaard's early authorship as a whole
concentrates upon the problem of beginning. Rigorously to stay with the
paradoxes of beginning is to problematize the egological interpretation of
subjectivity by pointing to what is pre-originary—that is, what cannot be
converted into a principle or serve as a foundation. Beginnings are anarchic.
This thought serves Kierkegaard as a critical tool that allows him to stay
with phenomena suppressed by idealism, in particular, and more broadly
by the metaphysical tradition of the West. Kierkegaard's path of thought
has been to draw thinking back to the instant prior to presence, the granting or opening of presence. The clarification of the instant reaches its pitch
in 1844 with the dual publication of *Philosophical Fragments*[1] and *The Concept of Anxiety*.

"In the individual life," Vigilius says, "anxiety is the instant" (*CA* 81;
SKS 4:384). Anxiety is a phenomenon whose analysis demands explicit reflection upon the instant. The instant is the caesura or event through which
presence opens. It signifies the birth of presence: not only the temporal present as the "now" of self-consciousness in its distinction from past and future, but presence also as parousia, presence as salvation. In the end it will
be precisely anxiety, a relation to nonbeing working an absolution from
presence, which is "saving." But this will not be a case of double negation
or dialectics, as if the *Afgrund* of nonbeing were in the end to function as a

ground. Salvation will signify releasement, sinking into nothing. The logic will be Eckhartian, not Hegelian.

If the phenomenon of anxiety is the condition for releasement, it is also, simultaneously, the condition for grasping. An intense ambiguity surrounds Kierkegaard's account of the instant: it is at once the granting of presence and the seizing of presence, that is, it is inseparable from the onto-logically defining act in which the subject posits itself. The transition from innocence to guilt happens "in" the instant. Positing itself, the subject re-lates to itself as ground. It inaugurates an interiority that is constituted thoroughly as representation and a temporality that occludes originary time. Yet the self-positing subject remains anxious. Thus the project of self-constitution becomes hyperbolic, abyssal, *demonic.* In this sense *The Concept of Anxiety* shows what is at stake in the critique of egology: the clarification of the conditions of evil or "sin." It will be no surprise, then, that Kierkegaard's text is informed by a reading of Schelling's *Philosophical Investigations into the Essence of Human Freedom* and, in particular, its Boehmean horizon.

ANXIETY AS PHENOMENON: THE UN-GROUNDING OF SUBJECTIVITY

The concept of anxiety is supposed to explain the irruption of sin both "retrogressively in terms of its origin," and "progressively" in terms of its continual rebirth. In either case, to explain sin will not mean to show its on-tological necessity. It will mean, rather, to show how subjectivity is potenti-ated toward sin, how the possibility of sin amasses itself at the center of the subject. However, in the first case—explaining sin in terms of its origin—what is at issue is a transcendental problem of genesis: in other words, what are the conditions through which singular subjectivity originally posits itself in distinction from the totality of being?

It is crucial to keep sight of this transcendental problematic in order to clarify the meaning of sin and the critique of egological consciousness. Sin signifies the originary act of the subject in positing itself. It is, strictly speak-ing, the act through which the subject first comes to be as subject. What Kierkegaard's author analyzes under the problem of sin, in other words, covers the same territory as Fichte's *Thathandlung:* the ego as self-positing, self-presupposing, an absolute beginning explainable by nothing other than itself. He writes: "[S]in presupposes itself . . . it comes into the world in such a way that by the fact that it is, it is presupposed. Thus sin comes into the world as the sudden, i.e., by a leap; but this leap also posits the quality, and since the quality is posited, the leap in that very moment is turned into the quality and is presupposed by the quality and the quality by the leap"

(*CA* 32; *SKS* 4:338). Sin is a leap as an act that has no precursor or precedent—an unconditioned act. Or again, it is an act that institutes a condition. Fichte's circle operates here: one must speak of an act that precedes any substantive, any "one" who acts, for the one who acts only emerges simultaneously with the act itself. Sin, as self-positing, is an act without a departure point in being. It presupposes itself.

What should be noted here is that the problem of the originary act of self-consciousness in Fichte emerges in the effort to clarify the ultimate "explanatory ground" of consciousness and of the world of phenomena. Fichte seeks the "first principle of knowledge" on the basis of which the entire system of presentations can be grasped: it is a question of grasping the ego in terms of its radical origin. For Fichte the movement of self-positing is already the ground, beyond which one cannot go. *The Concept of Anxiety* departs from this problematic in two ways: first, the suggestion that the movement of self-positing coincides with sin sets it within an entirely different context than one that clarifies the ultimate explanatory ground of *knowledge;* it acquires an irreducibly ethical context. Second, because anxiety constitutes the conditions for the possibility of the act of self-positing, it refers back to what comes prior to the "first principle" of knowledge—it refers to what comes *prior to the concept.* This brings us straight back to the opening move of the authorship outlined in the discussion of *The Concept of Irony,* that is, the articulation of the standpoint of Socrates. In both cases, whether for Socratic irony or anxiety, what lies prior to the first principle of knowledge is the relation to nothing or nonbeing.

Hence, it should be clear what is at stake in the phenomenological analysis of anxiety: the relation to nonbeing as what falls prior to, and not in dialectical opposition to, being. Subjectivity never has sovereignty over nonbeing in any of its "shapes": as time, as possibility, as the future; or, in terms of its historical representations, as fate (Greeks), or law (Judaism), or forgiveness (Christianity). Nonbeing remains, to use an appropriate phrase from Levinas, "otherwise than being." Once a subject posits itself, installs itself in being as present to itself, it proclaims itself sovereign over being *and* nonbeing. For Kierkegaard's author this is precisely "sin." Yet, what is sin? He refuses to define it as either pride or concupiscence. Rather, the meaning of sin in his analysis follows the Eckhartian tradition of interpreting it as *Eigenwille*—the will to the possession of self. In this sense sin signifies positing oneself as a center or ground of reality, or rather taking reality as reducible to the sphere of one's ownmost possibility. It is the reduction of the abyss of possibility—or nonbeing, which we shall see is an un-ground —to the ground of one's own projects, as "room to maneuver." *Eigenwille* reduces nonbeing to the dialectical opposite of being. It is to take the ego as an innocent spontaneity. The sinful ego is the Fichtean I (egology). This is to say that a discourse on the ego must, in Kierkegaard's terms, surpass a discourse on the ultimate conditions of knowledge and begin to question, according to a problematic that becomes radical, the right of the "I" to be.

This is the trajectory of the text. For the moment, however, we may bracket the question of sin and look more specifically to its conditions, that is, the phenomenon of anxiety. Anxiety first of all explains sin "retrogressively in terms of its origin." Yet because the origin of sin is at the same time the origin of the ego as self-positing, and therefore because the question concerning the origin already departs from the position of self-consciousness (or "spirit"), the analysis has to move transcendentally back to originary conditions. The originary conditions of knowledge, according to both Kant and Fichte, lie in an irreducible unity of self-consciousness, its presence to itself. Here, it is a question of accounting for the conditions of the unity of self-consciousness itself. In other words, Kierkegaard's author takes one more step transcendentally back and asks concerning how self-consciousness comes to posit itself in the first place. He goes beneath the first principle of Fichte and discovers anxiety, the relation to nonbeing, as what conditions the movement of self-positing. How so?

Anxiety conditions the sudden breakthrough of self-consciousness—though without in the end explaining it—by *seducing* or soliciting it. Between the state of innocence, which signifies the lack of differentiation between self and other, and the state of self-awareness, there occurs the unaccountable and groundless leap. But between innocence and sin there is a solicitation of self. The dynamics of this solicitation are the dynamics of anxiety. The question is an ancient one: what accounts for the movement from non-differentiation to differentiation? Here, where the entire analysis holds in reserve the problem of sin, it is not a question of asking, as in Plotinus, concerning the transition from the One to multiplicity; rather, it is a question of accounting for the movement from innocence to sin—the "fall." Sin signifies a departure from not only an original innocence that cannot be retraced, but one for which the very effort of retracing constitutes another modality of sin: "It would never occur to the innocent person to ask such a question [concerning sin], and when the guilty asks it, he sins, for in his aesthetic curiosity he ignores that he himself brought guiltiness into the world and that he himself lost innocence by guilt" (*CA* 36; *SKS* 4:343). There is an entanglement or deadlock here: to think about sin at all in terms of its "why," to trace back to its original ground, is to reproduce it. An investigation into its possibility has to think it without thinking it—a released thinking is required.

Sin does not become a metaphysical problem in other words. The sign of this is Vigilius's refusal to assimilate the originary condition of innocence with the immediacy of *being*. He clearly has Hegel in mind: "That the im-

mediate must be sublated, we do not need Hegel to tell us, nor does he deserve immortal merit for having said it, since it is not even logically correct,
for the immediate is not to be sublated, because it at no time exists. The
concept of immediacy belongs in logic; the concept of innocence, on the
other hand, belongs in ethics" (*CA* 35; *SKS* 4:341). Immediacy, he says—
directly following Hegel—signifies either "pure being" or "nothing" (*CA*
36; *SKS* 4:342); it signifies the element in which science begins absolutely.
The relation between immediacy and mediacy, between non-differentiation
and differentiation, is for logic (i.e., metaphysics) an immanent, self-sublating one. Vigilius summarizes: "The sublation of immediacy is therefore
an immanent movement within immediacy, or it is an immanent movement in the opposite direction within mediacy, by which mediacy presupposes immediacy" (*CA* 37; *SKS* 4:343). If innocence signified non-differentiation as the immediacy of being, then according to the entire trajectory
of Hegelian logic the movement of differentiation would be immanently
necessary, that is, coincide with the self-movement of being.[2] This dialectical reading of differentiation is what Vigilius seeks to avoid: "It is indeed
unethical to say that innocence must be sublated" (*CA* 35; *SKS* 4:341).

Innocence, then, signifies something other than either (1) the pure
plenitude of being reposing upon itself in a non-differentiated way, as in
Plotinus's One, or (2) the simple immediacy of being, as in Hegel, where it
signifies a fundamental lack of being, a need to be. The "fall" from immediacy is consequently neither the Neoplatonic fall downward into multiplicity nor the Hegelian fall "upward" into self-presence—though it comes
as close to the Hegelian position as is possible to come. Though the movement into differentiation, into self-possessiveness, is not grasped strictly
speaking as a necessary moment, as in Hegel—which would destroy its
character as illegitimate—it is presented as universal and inevitable. One
may say that "universal and inevitable" is no different from "necessary," but
this would be to overlook the fundamental demand Vigilius wants to enunciate: the whole framework of the discussion of differentiation, of sin and
evil, has to be broken open. What has to change is that nonbeing must be
understood, no longer as mere privation in being (Plotinus), nor as the dialectical opposite of being (Hegel), but rather as a *solicitation* into being.
Anxiety is the voice of its appeal.

The self is seduced into being, into self-positing—that is the most crucial thing. It consents to a solicitation from an ambiguous and "foreign
power" (*CA* 43; *SKS* 4:349). Before considering the nature of this foreign
power and its manner of solicitation, however, it is necessary to consider
more exactly the meaning of innocence. Innocence is neither the plenitude
nor the lack of being, neither a perfection nor an imperfection. Kierkegaard's author writes:

Innocence is a quality, it is a *state* that may very well endure, and therefore the logical haste to have it sublated is meaningless. . . . Innocence is not a perfection that one should wish to regain. . . . Innocence is not an imperfection in which one cannot remain, for it is always sufficient unto itself. . . . The narrative of Genesis also gives the correct explanation of innocence. Innocence is ignorance. It is by no means the pure being of the immediate, but it *is* ignorance. The fact that ignorance when viewed from without is regarded in the direction of knowledge is of no concern whatever to ignorance. (*CA* 37; *SKS* 4:343)

Innocence is a state that hovers between being and nonbeing—a pre-differentiated, virtual or dreamlike state: "Dreamily the spirit projects its own actuality, but this actuality is nothing, and innocence always sees this nothing outside itself" (*CA* 41; *SKS* 4:347). Spirit (the self) is implicit, but not yet posited as such; it hovers within a certain potentiality to be. In innocence spirit accesses its own potential to be in a non-thematic way. Thus, following the Genesis narrative, Vigilius characterizes innocence as *ignorance*. Yet ignorance here signifies not a state defined by what it lacks (knowledge), but rather an ignorance of self, an ignorance of ignorance, or naiveté. Thus he says that innocence is "always sufficient to itself" and may "very well endure." That it may very well endure and is sufficient to itself signifies that innocence is not intrinsically ordered toward self-surpassing, toward a telos, but abides with positive reality. This is a decisive notation: it suggests that the potentiality resonant within innocence overflows dialectical or archeo-teleological ordering. In innocence (qualified as anxious) the excess of nonbeing resonates. To recapitulate for a moment: what has to be clarified are the conditions for the movement of self-positing. This is indeed a speculative problematic concerning how to evaluate and analyze the movement from ignorance (of self) to knowledge (of self). It is speculative (or, better, transcendental) as opposed to mythical or historical, concerning every human being, and the conditions of self-consciousness as such. Adam cannot essentially be any different than any other human being. If this happens, the history of the human race acquires a "fantastic beginning" (*CA* 25; *SKS* 4:332). What is decisive, however, is to secure the correct beginning in thought. The phenomenon of anxiety guides thought to this beginning by presenting the last state before the beginning, where the self posits itself. As to the beginning itself (sin), it is and remains groundless. Yet this last state is a state of disclosure in which freedom (the self) shows itself to itself. Yet nothing becomes manifest in this showing. No object appears. This is the basis of the distinction between anxiety and fear, for fear always has a determinate object (*CA* 42; *SKS* 4:347).

The potentiality that characterizes the state of innocence is, one may say, anarchic possibility—that is to say, possibility that stands in excess to any path of realization, any telos. In innocence, spirit or freedom relates to itself not merely as potential to be or possibility, but as the "possibility of possibility" (*CA* 42; *SKS* 4:348). Innocence is spirit's relation to itself as to an abyss of possibility: namely, as a capability, a sheer "being able" (*at kunne*), that has no implicit path, a capability that is not *for* anything. Innocence is groundless and whyless. The secret, however, is that groundlessness is the very engine of anxiety, for innocence is also anxious: "This is the profound secret of innocence, that it is at the same time anxiety" (*CA* 41; *SKS* 4:347). And again: "In this state [innocence] there is peace and repose, but there is simultaneously something else that is not contention and strife, for there is indeed nothing against which to strive. What, then, is it? Nothing. What effect does it have? It begets anxiety" (*CA* 41; *SKS* 4:347). Nothing as the possibility of possibility, possibility anarchically in excess to any determinate ends, begins to weigh upon and agitate innocence. More exactly, innocence comes to weigh upon itself because it has to bear the immense and intolerable burden of its own whylessness—its own freedom from being. Innocence will prefer anything, anything at all, to the vertigo it faces in gazing into the *Afgrund* of its own possibility. Vigilius thus compares anxiety to dizziness:

> Anxiety may be compared with dizziness. He whose eye happens to look down into the yawning abyss becomes dizzy. But what is the reason for this? It is just as much in his own eye as in the abyss, for suppose he had not looked down. Hence anxiety is the dizziness of freedom, which emerges when the spirit wants to posit the synthesis and freedom looks down into its own possibility, laying hold of finiteness to support itself (*at holde sig ved*). Freedom succumbs in this dizziness. Further than this, psychology cannot and will not go. In that very moment everything is changed, and freedom, when it again rises, sees that it is guilty. Between these two moments is the leap, which no science has explained and which no science can explain. (*CA* 61; *SKS* 4:365–66)

In innocence, the self relates to itself according to its potential to be, the possibility of its possibility. The excess of possibility beyond all determinable ends leads to anxiety insofar as it prevents mere repose, mere identity. Its excess signifies that identity is not at the origin. There is a certain dynamic, which involves freedom "showing itself for itself" (*CA* 76; *SKS* 4:380), where anxiety draws nearer and nearer to itself, where the self, still innocent, finally *cannot but* gaze into the *Afgrund* of its own possibility. Its groundlessness paralyzes it, simultaneously attracting and repelling it in a state of "sympathetic antipathy" and "antipathetic sympathy" (*CA* 42; *SKS* 4:348). Here freedom is entangled in its own groundlessness: "Do away with itself, the spirit cannot; lay hold of itself, it cannot, as long as it has itself outside of itself. Nor can man sink down into the vegetative, for he is qualified as spirit; flee away from anxiety, he cannot, for he loves it; really love it, he cannot, for he flees from it. Innocence has now reached its uttermost point" (*CA* 44; *SKS* 4:349).

At the outermost point, facing the *Afgrund* of whylessness—of not having any determinate reason to be, or ground—the self posits itself by making *itself* into its own ground. Everything turns on the correct understanding of freedom's relation to itself as to the possibility of possibility, an abyssal ground that remains non-appropriatable to self-consciousness—for which reason it is precisely as alluring as it is threatening. In the face of this, innocence posits itself by contracting itself into a ground, enters into self, and takes on *Eigenwille*. In this instant it wills its sovereignty over the *Afgrund* by reducing the possibility of possibility to *possibility-for-x,* some calculable possibility. The self supports itself by substituting a finite possibility-for-x, what it can project and control, for the immeasurable possibility of freedom. It can't bear not having a reason to be, so it posits one through itself, or rather itself as one. *Eigenwille* means the self relates to itself as its own reason to be, as ground.

THE *AFGRUND* OF FREEDOM

The characteristic move of Hegelian onto-theology is to force nonbeing (the beginning, the possibility of possibility) to signify the potential-to-be within an archeo-teleological structure, to transform the *Afgrund* into a *Grund*. Already Kierkegaard's reading of Socrates in *The Concept of Irony* showed an effort to reverse this trajectory: Socrates does not *begin* with nothing, he *ends* with nothing. He brings thinking to the abyssal or withdrawn ground. Something similar happens in *The Concept of Anxiety.* Possibility, it will turn out, is the "weightiest of all categories" (*CA* 156; *SKS* 4:455). It cannot adequately be thought as *determinate potential* awaiting its actualization.[3] The possibility of possibility is possibility beyond a horizon of realization, a beginning in excess to any telos (thus an anarchic beginning). Hegel would likely interpret such indeterminate potential as an abstraction. But for Kierkegaard's author the phenomenon of anxiety simply cannot be explained without such excess. It is precisely the excess that generates the non-identity at the heart of innocence.

Kierkegaard's most immediate model for this conception of possibility is Schelling. Scholarly consensus has been building concerning the deep and substantial links between *The Concept of Anxiety* and Schelling's thought.[4] Most important in this regard, as Axel Hutter has recently argued, is Schelling's notion of the "ground" (*Grund*), in his *Philosophical Investigations into the Essence of Human Freedom* and—a related notion—the "un-pre-thinkable" (*das Unvordenkliche*) of later works (including the lectures Kierkegaard attended in Berlin in 1841–42).[5] Both of these notions register Schelling's break from idealism—its egology, if not necessarily its onto-theology—by way of an irreducible remainder or indeterminate potential falling outside presence and representation. The Schellingian ground constitutes a beginning that is in dissension with principles, beginning as anarchy.[6]

Significant for the relation between *The Concept of Anxiety* and Schelling's text is that he first introduces the idea of the ground in order to account for the real possibility of evil. Schelling accounts for the possibility of autonomous, self-positing being—and thus for the possibility of evil—through a fundamental reconfiguring of onto-theology[7] that draws heavily on the apophatic tradition, especially the thought of Jacob Boehme.[8] As both Alexander Koyré and Miklos Vetö argue,[9] Boehme is one of the first thinkers in the West to raise the positive reality of evil—evil as position and not merely privation—as a fundamental and guiding problematic. To grasp evil in its positivity, according to Schelling, requires allowing ontological space in relation to the absolute for an act that is both singular and radically self-determining. An irremediable gap in being, or presence, is necessary that extends all the way into the absolute—hence, the notion of the indeterminate *Grund* as what lies "beyond absolute identity."

Yet for Schelling (as for Boehme, whom he is rewriting here[10]), God *exists* absolutely, that is, as an eternal resolution to subordinate the will of the ground—an open, indeterminate will—to the will of existence, that is, an expansive will to self-communication and self-revealing. God definitively and eternally ejects *Eigenwille* in favor of self-communication (love). God creates. The creature remains, however, ontologically indeterminate because it draws its singularity from that *in God* which is *not* God (i.e., from the ground). This is true for every creature—hence, the fragmentary nature of all things—but true in an exemplary way for the human being, who is the true "counter-stroke" (Boehme's *Gegenwurf*) to God. The human being is a "being of the Center," in whom resides "the whole power of the dark principle [the ground], and . . . the whole force of light [the will to self-communication]."[11] What is eternally resolved in God—the tension in the forces of indetermination and determination—remains unresolved in the human being: "The unity that is indivisible in God must therefore be divisible in [the human being]—and this is the possibility of good and evil."[12] Incumbent upon the human being is therefore the task of positing or determining *itself,* for the divine act of creation, operative only vis-à-vis the ground, does not fully determine the creature. One can even say, more precisely, that the ontic particularity of the human being rests in having a radically undetermined center: which means, in being free, absolved from being. God creates, but creates a creature that is forced, as it were, to create itself. The nothing, the abyss of possibility, resides at the heart of the creature as its radical possibility: for good *and* for evil.

Schelling's *Grund,* then, constitutes that gap, that event, in which singularity is "un-pre-thinkably" absolved from the horizon of being (presence, determination, actuality, unity). In fact, Schelling's account of the ground of existence is anything but a ground; it would be preferable to call it an un-ground.[13] The ground is "the incomprehensible basis of reality in things, the indivisible remainder, that which with the greatest exertion cannot be resolved in the understanding, but rather remains eternally in the ground"[14] Schelling's ground is, in all strictness, *between* being and nonbeing, God and human being, determination and indetermination, identity and nonidentity. The ground signifies nonbeing beyond dialectical interplay with being.

The counterpart in *The Concept of Anxiety* is nothing, for nothing "begets anxiety" (*CA* 41; *SKS* 4:347). To clarify anxiety is to clarify nothing in its positive sense, apart from the classical consideration of nothing as a privation in being and the Hegelian sense of nothing as the incipience of being. What Kierkegaard's author learned from Schelling's text is that the dynamics of anxiety—that is, how it troubles and arouses innocence—cannot be understood unless the experience of nothing (or possibility) is an experience of an abyss. He even appropriates the details of Schelling's account in the metaphor of dizziness: for Kierkegaard's author anxiety is the "dizziness of freedom," whereas Schelling had described anxiety "as [when] a mysterious voice seemingly calls a man seized by dizziness on a high and precipitous pinnacle to plunge down."[15] Dizziness generates grasping, holding onto, the opposite of releasing. But there is no dizziness apart from a peering into the abyss. The possibility of possibility, then, must not be thought as a possibility proper to human beings. It is not the human being's *own* possibility, for it is precisely what undoes the domain of what is "one's own"; it prevents innocence from simply being, giving birth to anxiety.

However, Jochem Hennigfeld is right to point to the differences between Schelling's text and Kierkegaard's. Schelling's discourse remains ontological or onto-theological, whereas Kierkegaard's, as he says, is existential or psychological.[16] Kierkegaard's text does not attempt any systematic theological exposition even if, as Vincent McCarthy suggests, what his account presupposes "cannot be radically different from Schelling's."[17] The primary difference between Kierkegaard and Schelling emerges at that point where Schelling attempts systematically (onto-theologically) to draw the relation between God as ground and God as existence. In other words, the difference emerges decisively at the point where Schelling engages the task of *theogony*. The theogonic impulse becomes extremely ambiguous on the

question of evil: in spite of every warning against conceiving evil dialectically, in the end Schelling seems to regard evil, according to its actuality, as
the *element of resistance* necessary for divine subjectivity to become manifest
to itself. Following certain moments in the thought of Boehme[18] Schelling
writes: "Since [evil] is undeniably actual, at least as a general opposite, already there can be no doubt that it was necessary for the revelation of God.
. . . For every being can only be revealed in its opposite: love only in hate,
unity only in conflict."[19] Evil, in short, becomes assimilated back into being
and understood dialectically. Hegel, we have seen, is even clearer: evil is the
necessary other to being—the fall is a fall upward.[20]

In a footnote, Kierkegaard's author himself draws attention to Schelling
and Hegel on this point: "Schelling himself has often spoken of anxiety,
anger, anguish, suffering etc. But one ought always to be a little suspicious
of such expressions, so as not to confuse the consequence of sin in creation
with what Schelling also characterizes as states and moods in God. By these
expressions, he characterizes, if I may say so, the creative birth pangs of the
deity. By such figurative expressions he signifies what in some cases he has
called the negative and what in Hegel became: the negative more strictly
defined as the dialectical" (*CA* 59; *SKS* 4:363–64). These sentences refer to
Schelling's characterization of the *Grund* as longing or desire in God: "If
we wish to speak of this being (*Wesen*) in terms more accessible to [the
human], then we can say it is the longing (*Sehnsucht*) felt by the eternal one
to give birth to itself. This longing is not the one itself, but is eternal with
it."[21] Now the ambiguity of Kierkegaard's relation to Schelling is that, on
the one hand, he denounces the distortion of "treating dogmatics meta-
physically and metaphysics dogmatically" (*FTR* 59; *SKS* 4:363–64). That is
to say, he denounces Schelling's anthropomorphism. Nevertheless, he adds
that "a full-blooded anthropomorphism has considerable merit" (ibid.)—
namely, to the extent that it clarifies the situation of existence.[22] In contrast
to Schelling, Kierkegaard's author, then, insists upon the "anthropological"
or "psychological" coordinates of his consideration of the *Afgrund* of possibility. He does so, however, not because (as Heidegger might suggest) he
stays fixated upon an ontic as opposed to an ontological problematic, but
rather through a refusal of any discourse on evil that would involve its legitimation. He treats the abyss of possibility even more abyssally than, in
the end, Schelling does.[23]

DELIMITATIONS

In the introduction to the text Vigilius argues that sin cannot be treated
within any of the philosophical sciences. It cannot be treated in logic,
where it is reduced to the dialectical and necessary counterpart to being; in

anthropology, where it is turned into an empirical state or disposition of the subject; in ethics, which necessarily rejects it in order to insist upon ideality; and finally in metaphysics or "first philosophy," where it is reduced to illusion or ignorance (interpreted as privation). According to Kierkegaard's author sin is essentially *placeless:* "Sin has its specific place, or more correctly, it has no place, and this is its specific nature" (*CA* 14; *SKS* 4:322): that is to say, it is non-localizable in terms of any particular "region" of being or even in terms of being as such. It therefore introduces a rupture that cannot be sutured back into any larger framework, whether narrative or conceptual.

The Concept of Anxiety, then, approaches the problem of sin only in terms of a radical displacement of that problem from its metaphysical or systematic inscription. As Kierkegaard's author says: "sin does not properly belong in any science, but it is the subject of the sermon, in which the single individual speaks as the single individual to the single individual" (*CA* 16; *SKS* 4:323). A discourse on being, or one that finally situates itself within the horizon of being, cannot achieve the proper *mood* necessary for the concept of sin: seriousness (*Alvor*), that sin is "to be overcome" (*CA* 15; *SKS* 4:322) rather than observed, explained, understood. Vigilius writes: "When sin is treated in a place other than its own [which is no place], it is altered by being subjected to a nonessential refraction of reflection. The concept is altered, and thereby the mood that properly corresponds to the concept is also disturbed" (*CA* 14; *SKS* 4:321). To treat sin in any context other than the sermon, it is necessary precisely not to treat it. One has to leave a gaping hole in one's discourse. Yet at the same time it is necessary to allow this hole to organize the discourse in its totality.

This is exactly what *The Concept of Anxiety* does insofar as it never explains sin, nor even sets out the *sufficient* conditions of its possibility. Sin remains a surd. As essentially placeless, sin cannot be arranged or organized as an element or moment within an articulated whole. The latter happens, for example, wherever sin is turned into a narrative element, a stage in some development, or grasped as a state of things, for example, as a sickness or abnormality. As soon as sin is made to fit or cohere with *what is,* with being in its presence, with the whole, as soon as it is graphed on a continuum, its essential specificity is lost: that it fits nowhere. Sin is the limit of any system. It "is" what cannot be incorporated into being. Maintaining the otherwise-than-being character of sin leads Kierkegaard's author to posit a distinction between *proté philosophia* (first philosophy or metaphysics) and *secunda philosophia* (second philosophy). He writes:

> It is common knowledge that Aristotle used the term πρώτη φιλοσοφιά primarily to designate metaphysics, though he included within it a part that according to our conception belongs to theology. In paganism it is quite in

order for theology to be treated there. It is related to the same lack of infinite penetrating reflection (*Gjennemreflekterethed*) that endowed the theater in paganism with reality as a kind of divine worship. If we now abstract from this ambiguity, we could retain the designation and by πρώτη φιλοσοφιά understand the totality of science which we might call "ethnical," whose essence is immanence and is expressed in Greek thought by "recollection," and by *secuda philosophia* understand that totality of science whose essence is transcendence or repetition. The concept of sin does not belong in any science; only the second ethics can deal with its manifestation, but not with its coming into existence. (*CA* 21; *SKS* 4:328–29)

Within Greek thought—and here the allusion is to Aristotle's *Metaphysics* —God is treated in the context of the reflection on the being of beings. The ambiguity, or "lack of infinite penetrating reflectedness" pointed to, is not exactly the same as the ambiguity that Heidegger identifies as the origin of onto-theological confusion: namely, the conflation of the being of beings with a highest being. As becomes clear later in the text, according to Vigilius the Greeks lacked the concept of *spirit* and God as spirit. By this he means they had no proper concept of subjectivity and so could not see the absolute as absolute subjectivity, that is, an infinitely (self-)penetrating reflectedness. Pure or absolute subjectivity, however, precisely as infinite *reflectedness,* is no longer as such being, but an absolute distance from being. Reflection relates to being only as what is suspended, presupposed.

Thus, as spirit or infinite subjectivity God cannot properly be treated in terms of being. By placing God within the context of a consideration of being, the Greeks placed God implicitly within the horizon of available presence. Hence, the representation that takes place in the theater always takes place within a divine milieu, the space of objectivity and vision—ultimately, the milieu of recollection or immanence. What Kierkegaard's author calls for in the above is a second philosophy and a second ethics, both of whose essence is "transcendence or repetition." God and sin belong to this *philosophia secunda*—though in this text God's distance from being does not become, as such, an explicit problematic.[24] The secondary status of this "science," however, does not signify that it stands subordinately in relation to first philosophy or metaphysics. It is not a question of adding another science while leaving first philosophy in place as first philosophy. What "second" refers to is a thinking that cannot coincide with a principle, that does not attain to the origin. The science of repetition thinks an *event as an event,* as what thought cannot coincide with. Thought is always either too early or too late for an event because an event does not take place in the present; it is rather what gives or qualifies the present.

The instant of sin, just as the instant of redemption, are events—interruptions—and hence fall outside the milieu of presence. This is the primary critical delimitation Kierkegaard's author insists upon at the outset of *The Concept of Anxiety.* The task of the introduction is to show "the sense in which the subject of our deliberation [i.e., sin] is a task of psychological interest and the sense in which, after having been the task and interest of psychology, it points directly to dogmatics" (*CA* 9; *SKS* 4:317)—the former explains the "real possibility of sin" and the latter its "ideal possibility" (*CA* 23; *SKS* 4:330). Only second philosophy, therefore, can deal with sin—not, however, in terms of its genesis, but only in terms of its manifestness. An event cannot be thought conceptually. The specific nature of an event is that it *presupposes itself.* That is to say, an event becomes possible only in the moment it becomes actual; its possibility for happening arrives in the very moment of happening. An event is always and essentially "the sudden" (*det Pludselige*). It breaks discontinuously upon the present as an interruption. An event is not in the present or an unfolding of possibilities coiled up in the present, but the qualification of the present in terms of its actuality *and* possibility. As an event or leap, sin becomes possible only in the moment it is actual—not "before." To think sin is therefore to confront a diachrony: the concept is either too early or too late. Thinking stands either prior to its possibility, in which case an anticipative insight is impossible; or after its irruption, in which case the thought of sin finds itself entangled in an abyss of origin: to approach it is to find oneself already determined by it.

As event, there is no concept of sin. Vigilius writes: "Its [sin's] idea is that its concept is continually annulled (*bestandig ophævet*)" (*CA* 15; *SKS* 4:323). A concept here signifies nothing more than an *approach* to phenomena, an anticipatory insight into what the phenomena are phenomena of, a way of gathering and relating diverse phenomena around a central principle. It coincides with what Schelling calls intellectual intuition: the faculty of seeing the whole within the parts and the parts within the whole. With the concept of sin, however, the possibility of the concept is continually, at each moment, suspended. In terms of the delimitation already made, one can say this: dogmatic theology thinks sin in the absence of intuition, while "psychology" intuits sin in the absence of thought, that is, thought that *determines* and places its object. Hence, dogmatic theology explains sin, but explains it only by presupposing it, "like that vortex about which Greek speculation concerning nature had so much to say, a moving something that no science can grasp" (*CA* 20; *SKS* 4:327). It explains sin not by setting forth its inner possibility and actuality, that is, its principle—for like the whirlwind it is a principle without principle—but rather by explaining *everything else* on its basis. The one thing dogmatic theology does not explain is sin; but presupposing sin, it explains everything else. Psychology, on the other hand, formulates concepts—but its concepts are only ways of drawing near to the event.

A concept, in this sense, always involves something twofold: on the one hand, its "object" is nonbeing, nothing; on the other hand, in letting the nothing resonate, it articulates its various modulations across a series of aggravating factors. Thus every concept, to the extent it brings nonbeing into focus, halts before the event of a qualitative leap. Yet its halting at this limit is no mere breaking off of thinking, but a turning of thinking toward the phenomena that bear upon the subject. The latter, as we shall see below, are subject to a historical and cultural process and capable of a quantitative piling up (more and less). Hence a concept captures the distinction between a qualitative event and its quantitative "before" and "after"—between an event and a state.

LANGUAGE

The event of sin, remaining irreducible to any scientific (explanatory) or even mythical discourse, signifies the movement from innocence to (self) differentiation. Anxiety, it has been said, is the engine that potentiates innocence toward self-differentiation—though without determining it. Anxiety is the secret of innocence. Something remains obscure here, however. Since innocence is a plenitude that can "very well endure," what brings about movement in the state of innocence? That is to say, what accounts for the *rising pitch* of anxiety, the movement toward freedom's disclosure of itself that, nevertheless, never occurs—that is, not until the crisis of self-positing? Through what conduit is innocence drawn into self? What medium catalyzes self-disclosure?

Vigilius Haufniensis, following the biblical narrative, places *language* into the role as what draws innocence into self. Both in the form of the prohibition against eating from the tree of good and evil and in the serpent's speech, language solicits selfhood by seeming to give content to the abyss of nonbeing (of freedom) disclosed in anxiety. Language is therefore the medium of self-disclosure, the agent of seduction, that operates within innocence to draw latent spirit into self. Prior to self-consciousness explicitly positing itself, language must already have been operative. Vigilius writes:

> Innocence still is, but only a word is required and then ignorance is concentrated. Innocence naturally cannot understand this word, but at that moment anxiety has, as it were, caught its first prey. Instead of nothing, it now has an enigmatic word. When it is stated in Genesis that God said to Adam, "Only from the tree of the knowledge of good and evil you must not eat," it follows as a matter of course that Adam really has not understood this word, for how could he understand the difference between good and evil when this distinction would follow as a consequence of the enjoyment of the fruit? (*CA* 44; *SKS* 4:350)

Prior to its positing of itself, and as the catalyst for this, seduction is always already operative: seduction, in the form of a *voice,* an appeal, a solicitation to be. As is clear in the above quotation, it is not language as the communication of any determinate content, any *said,* but rather *saying* as such that solicits presence, for Adam "has not understood what was spoken" (*CA* 45; *SKS* 4:350), and thus relates to the mere saying of it. Nor is it language as the speaking of someone definite, but rather language itself that speaks: "The imperfection in the narrative—how it could have occurred to anyone to say to Adam what he essentially could not understand—is eliminated if we bear in mind that the speaker is language, and also that it is Adam himself who speaks" (*CA* 47; *SKS* 4:353). In the state of innocence then, Adam speaks, but he says nothing. He speaks, but it is really language that speaks, without intentionality and without determining anything—in a way "similar to that of children who learn by identifying animals on an A B C board" (*CA* 46; *SKS* 4:352). Language as such speaks prior to any judgment or apophansis, without any determinate concepts. Vigilius's account thus focuses upon the way, in the state of innocence, language *seems* to disclose something determinate, but does not. Through the word of prohibition, the word of the serpent, and then finally the sentence "you shall surely die," there is a progressive disclosure of the possibility of freedom—and yet it is only nothing, the *Afgrund* of freedom, that is "disclosed." Language does not reveal being, but nonbeing. And in the revelation of nonbeing freedom begins to resonate with an affection of itself. It becomes anxious for itself: "The infinite possibility of being able that was awakened by the prohibition now draws closer, because [in the sentence of death] this possibility points to a possibility as its sequence. In this way, innocence is brought to its uttermost. . . . Innocence is not guilty, yet there is anxiety as though it were lost" (*CA* 45; *SKS* 4:351).

Language, in short, precedes and conditions the movement of self-positing.[25] And if language (as saying outside of any determinate said) operates prior to and as the soliciting condition of self-consciousness, then self-presence cannot be taken as originary. Vigilius continues:

> If one were to say further that it then becomes a question of how the first man learned to speak, I would answer that this is very true, but also that the question lies beyond the scope of the present investigation. However, this must not be understood in the manner of modern philosophy as though my reply were evasive, suggesting that I could answer the question in another place. But this much is certain, that it will not do to represent man himself as the inventor of language." (*CA* 47; *SKS* 4:353)

One cannot say, as in idealism, that the human being—nor self-consciousness, nor intellectual intuition—stands at the origin of language. Presence does not sovereignly control language. The speaking of language is the condition of the human. In fact, deferring the issue in principle rather than merely as a matter of fact, the text pointedly refuses to assign any origin to language at all. The human being is neither its inventor nor its real subject. Is God then? This is not said. Language remains without determinate origin. Perhaps this is why the serpent, who is *always already* in the garden, a strange and placeless "third" to God and human beings, functions for Vigilius not only as a seducer but as the very emblem of language: "I freely admit my inability to connect any definite thought with the serpent" (*CA* 48; *SKS* 4:353). The serpent is language as indeterminate, prior to intentionality, apophansis, the determining of something as something—language with no telos.

Language seduces: it mediates the self's relation to itself, but it does not disclose *what the self is*. And if language has, in this regard, no apophantic or disclosive power—other than the negative one of conditioning the self's auto-affection—then a concept of the self, or absolute knowledge, will be impossible to formulate. Determinate language will always be "fallen," without the power to unveil the self to itself according to determinate predicates and in such a way that it could achieve self-presence and self-transparency. Perhaps it would not be off the mark to see in this conception of language a reinscription of the Schellingian ground (or Boehmian Un-ground): to see language, in other words, as what is neither divine nor human, as an abyss of possibility lying beyond the sphere of absolute identity, but also as a desire that seeks to constitute itself, the restless hunger for being. Innocent spirit bites; it eats. But in so doing it nourishes itself only with nonbeing; thus will open the craven, addictive cycle of the demonic, whose hunger only grows—without end—in the very eating.

THE DEMONIC

Through the solicitation of language, spirit comes to feel itself, though only as a sheer being-able that is not an ability-for-x. Anxiety is this affection that freedom has of its own abyssal nature; it is the last state before the qualitative leap in which spirit posits itself, or sins. Sin, I have suggested, signifies *Eigenwille,* the will toward ownness or possession of self; or better, it is the will that seizes the abyss of possibility as the domain of the free and sovereign play of the "I." *Eigenwille* is the will toward totalization. Yet, owing to the nature of the self, Kierkegaard's author points to two distinctive formations that arise once spirit posits itself: anxiety about evil and anxiety about the good, or the demonic. Anxiety about evil still preserves a living association with the good; anxiety about the good, however, signifies spirit monologically closed off within itself, trapped in the "living annihilation" of the addiction to being. This latter formation (the demonic) bears close attention, for it expresses the really positive significance of evil.

In order to grasp the demonic, however, it is necessary first to set up its place in the text. Kierkegaard analyzes the demonic in chapter four. The groundlessness disclosed in anxiety signifies that spirit is a site in which contradictory principles—specifically, the animate (*det Sjelelige*) and the bodily (*det Legemlige*)—enter indeterminately into a tensile and unstable proximity with one another. Spirit signifies something double: both the *site* of this relation and the active structuring of the relation, that is, the *syn-thesis,* or positing-as-together, of the principles. Kierkegaard's author writes:

> That anxiety makes its appearance [in innocence] is the pivot upon which everything turns. [The human being] is a synthesis of the psychical and the physical; however, a synthesis is unthinkable if the two are not united in a third. This third is spirit. In innocence, [the human being] is not merely an animal, for if he were at any moment of his life merely animal, he would never become [a human being]. So spirit is present, but as immediate, as dreaming. Inasmuch as it is now present, it is in a sense a hostile, for it constantly disturbs the relation between body and soul, a relation that indeed has persistence (*Bestaaen*) and yet does not have endurance (*Bestaaen*), inasmuch as it first receives the latter by spirit. On the other hand, spirit is a friendly power, since it is precisely that which constitutes the relation. What, then, is [the human being's] relation to this ambiguous power? How does spirit relate itself to itself and to its conditionality? It relates itself as anxiety. (*CA* 43–44; *SKS* 4:349)

Spirit is, ambiguously, a synthesis and the site of a synthesis. It is a relation to its own condition—that is, to itself—but in the first instance this is not a positing of itself. Spirit has to achieve a relation to itself by setting into relation two aspects, the bodily and the animate, that in *it*—though not in animals—have no determinate or intrinsically ordered relation to one another. Spirit is under the duress of having to resolve two principles in the absence of a principle of resolution. Hence, the synthesis that spirit enacts in positing itself is accomplished groundlessly, without principle.

Spirit's positing of itself is the originary act of the self—it is actuality (*Virkelighed*) in the strict sense. In this regard Kierkegaard's author is in full agreement with Fichte. The act of the self is not an effecting of anything determinate, any "this" or "that," but an effecting of itself. Remaining outside of being, spirit makes itself be. Its capability to do so finally resides, as already indicated, in that its freedom is without ground: "Freedom is infinite and arises out of nothing" (*CA* 112; *SKS* 4:414–15). The act through which it posits itself, however, would seem to eradicate anxiety, since anxiety is the mode of the disclosure of the self's possibility. Yet this does not happen: "The qualitative leap is clearly actuality, and so it would seem that possibility is annulled along with anxiety. However, this is not the case. First of all, actuality is not one factor (*ikke eet Moment*); second, the actuality posited is unwarranted actuality" (*CA* 111; *SKS* 4:413). Anxiety is suspended in the act, yet it returns. The act of freedom, in positing itself, draws its possibility from nothing (the *Afgrund* of freedom), but precisely because it is possibility in excess to any realizable end, its annulment or sublation (*Ophævelse*) in the act is never more than an instantaneous suspension that keeps it in reserve. Spirit determines itself, but it does not succeed in what it aims at—namely, emptying the abyss of possibility. Spirit differentiates itself, achieves itself, breaks from undifferentiated innocence, but then it stands nakedly as a self before the same abyss—though now, post-differentiation, the abyss of possibility becomes contoured in different ways: either as the possibility of an unending project of establishing and securing the differentiated ego (the demonic), or as the frightful possibility of an endless fall into guilt.

Anxiety over a further descent into evil, which at bottom is anxiety over the future, is a position that, in its totality, stands within the good. The recovering gambling addict will not pass a casino without anxiety, and that very anxiety expresses a good will. The demonic formation, on the other hand, embraces the *Afgrund* of possibility as if it were a mere extension of the self—as if the possibility of possibility were *its* possibility. In the phrase of Jacob Boehme (who again stands in the background here), it "probes difference" (*die Schiedlichkeit probiren*), that is, it searches and tests itself in order to possess itself. It desires to find and exploit the basis of its power. Yet it does so on the way toward taking itself as ground, toward constituting itself, and so toward ruling over nonbeing.

Kierkegaard's author defines the demonic in the following ways: as "unfreedom that wants to close itself off" (*CA* 123; *SKS* 4:424); as "in-closedness" (*Indesluttedheden*); as "anxiety about the good" (*CA* 118; *SKS* 4:420); as the sudden (*det Pludselige*) (*CA* 130; *SKS* 4:430), as the "unfreely disclosed" (*CA* 129; *SKS* 4:425); and as monological, contentless consciousness, or "the boring" (*CA* 128; *SKS* 4:433). The nerve that connects all of these determinations concerns the relation to the good: the demonic is *closure* to the good. Hence arises the question, what is the good? Kierkegaard's author raises and answers this question: "The good cannot be defined at all. The good is freedom" (*CA* 111; *SKS* 4:413). The good, hence, is freedom as what is indefinable. Yet a more exact categorial determination of the good is that "which comes to its boundary [viz., the self's] from the *outside*" (*CA* 119, my italics; *SKS* 4:421). The good is outside, transcendence, *alterity*. It is what arrives of itself to preempt the self-enclosure of the self. The demonic "wants to close itself off (*vil afslutte sig*). This, however, is and remains an impossibility" (*CA* 123; *SKS* 4:421). The truth of the demonic, which, however, it cannot acknowledge, is the other as what undermines all self-enclosure, all totalization. The other prevents one from consummating the will toward self-coincidence, and this interruption in the circuit of the self is nothing merely negative, but rather the very good of the self. It is a good, however, that is abyssal and makes one anxious. Thus the extraordinary profundity of the demonic—which does not signify its legitimacy—lies in the fact that its anxiety reveals, *against its will,* the reality of the other as the good. The mystery of the good and the mystery of evil are the same: both reveal alterity.

The phenomenon of the demonic shows, albeit inversely, the impossibility of eliminating the other from the identity of the self. The other is the possibility of possibility, the origin of anxiety. This is why Kierkegaard's author understands freedom, not as the power of self-positing, but rather as "disclosure" (*Aabenbarelse*), the "expansive" (*det Udvidende*), "transparency" (*Gjennemsigtigheden*), the communicating ("freedom is always *communicerende*" (*CA* 124; *SKS* 4:425). Proximity to the other, rather than the self's presence to itself, is the possibility of freedom; and freedom is a becoming transparent, not to oneself as in absolute knowledge, but to the other. Freedom is the welcome of the other simply. If it is expansive, it is not because it expands itself to include the other within *its* orbit, but because it makes room for the other and so allows itself to be expanded. If it is communicating—and Vigilius suggests that "it does no harm even to take into account the religious significance of the term" (*CA* 124; *SKS* 4:424)—it is not because it communicates any definite content, but rather because it orients itself in a *receptive* way toward the other so that discourse becomes possible. If it is disclosive, it is because it opens itself to the other by not trying to control disclosure.

In terms of the demonic, evil, made possible by the abyssal nature of freedom, signifies *closure to the other.* Because freedom is already a relation to the other—a relation that is indeed prior to the self's relation to itself, for otherwise the other could not make one anxious—the opposite of freedom, which is guilt, can only involve an impossible and contradictory will toward a self-presence "unburdened by otherness" (Hegel). The demonic is the struggle to rule over nonbeing (the other); or better, to rule over the nonbeing at its very heart, as the condition of its possibility, the nonbeing it can never separate itself from. In this analysis, it should be clear, the demonic acquires "a much larger field than is commonly assumed" (*CA* 123; *SKS* 4:425): its possibility lies coiled up in every particle of anxiety about the other, no matter how small. The demonic wills separation and self-enclosure *in the face of* the other. Its will strikes against the originary standing open of the self to the other, and thus takes shape as non-disclosure, non-communication, non-transparency. The demonic is essentially mute: not, perhaps, that it says nothing, but rather that its saying is only another mode of self-enclosure. It involves saying as dissimulation, saying as the very modality of one's withdrawal from the other, as the excusing of oneself before the other.

At a limit, the demonic locks itself up within its own phantasmagoric picture-show, becoming unable to distinguish between the real and the semblance of the real. Kierkegaard's author writes: "The demonic does not close itself up with something, but it closes itself up within itself, and in this lies what is profound about existence (*Tilværelse*), precisely that unfreedom makes itself a prisoner. Freedom is always *communicerende*... unfreedom becomes more and more enclosed and does not want communication" (*CA* 124; *SKS* 4:425). The demonic withdraws from its disclosure to the other and seeks itself. It probes difference, seeking its ground in itself. Yet this is an essentially bottomless activity, for its ground is an *Afgrund*—it doesn't lie within itself, but within the other.

The demonic formation, conceiving the other dialectically in terms of its *own* possibility, shows itself as hyperbolic. The gesture of self-founding, and thus all of the discourses that thematize it as ultimate (idealist discourses), finds itself ever exposed to a remainder that cannot be integrated. True freedom is not to be found in self-positing, but in the receptive turn toward what remains transcendent. Freedom is not positing but receptivity, a becoming open to what interrupts self-positing and ungrounds the self. That is the decisive turn: the Good interrupts. Hence, strictly speaking, the good cannot be willed; or rather, it can be willed only where to will has become identical with to suffer, where willing has become a letting happen. To let happen, to turn toward, to welcome: these are the gestures of the self where it is thought according to its freedom, which is always communicating.

At bottom, however, the demonic can be understood as a certain refusal of time, a refusal of the instant, for the instant—the event of coming into existence itself—is always sudden and thus interruptive. Temporality itself faces as an other in the shape of the absolute future. In order further to specify the opposite of the demonic (faith) it will therefore be necessary further to clarify the structure of temporality.

THE INSTANT:
TIME AND ETERNITY

Chapter three of *The Concept of Anxiety* begins all over again in its consideration of the phenomenon of anxiety. The first two chapters are dominated by the notion of anxiety as freedom's showing itself to itself, that is, of the disclosure of the *Afgrund* of possibility as what enables freedom. In chapter four, which analyzes the demonic, the *Afgrund* signifies the good as the other. In chapter three a third understanding of the *Afgrund* is given: "In the individual life, anxiety is the instant (*Øieblikket*)[26]—to use a new expression that says the same as was said in the previous discussion, but that also points toward that which follows" (*CA* 81; *SKS* 4:384). The instant is the abyss of possibility before which freedom is anxious. Anxiety about time is another mode of disclosure of the abyss.

The analysis of the instant is more than merely another moment in the dialectic of the book; rather, it is the hinge of the book on which everything turns. Indeed, it is the hinge on which the whole of the early authorship turns. Louis Dupré is no doubt correct in observing that "the instant is perhaps Kierkegaard's most original category."[27] The analysis of the temporal instant is extremely compact and multi-layered. First and foremost it is an effort, "transcendentally," to account for the conditions of the possibility of anxiety (which are, again, the conditions for the possibility of sin). Anxiety is essentially a relation to the future just as much as it is always a relation to nonbeing; it is a relation to the future as nonbeing. Yet what has to be clarified transcendentally and phenomenologically is how the nothing of the future *gives rise to the present* in its character as anxious. At issue here will be a definite "synthesis" of time and eternity.

As I will argue, it is of utmost necessity to see the instant in its extreme ambiguity: it is not merely a synthesis carried through transcendentally by the subject, as in Kant's unity of apperception or Fichte's intellectual intuition, but, exploding the egological horizon, the event through which a subject is first *enabled* to posit itself as a subject, to differentiate itself, and so to be. The instant, I will say, does not refer, as a synthesis, to the present—nor to what takes place on the basis of the present—but to what originally allows the present at all. And anxiety is the phenomenological clue that allows one to catch sight of this event, an event for which the present always and essentially lags behind. Not only that, but anxiety becomes the authentic teacher that puts freedom into contact with the originary and irrecuperable instant of its enabling.

A crucial part of the break from the transcendental analysis of temporality enacted here is the retrieval of the Platonic cipher of "the sudden" (το εχαιφνης): "What we call the instant, Plato calls το εχαιφνης" (*CA* 87–88; *SKS* 4:391). The Platonic sudden suggests the guiding thought that leads to a non-dialectical interpretation of nonbeing and a post-transcendental interpretation of the temporal instant. Yet Plato's analysis, however much it surpasses Hegel's, itself requires extensive revision and supplementation. The direction of this revision is already sketched, though not completed, in the Neoplatonic use of the sudden—for it is within Neoplatonism that the sudden first comes to signify the instant of contact between the temporal and the eternal. This is definitely the case with Eckhart, but also with the entire apophatic tradition that depends upon Eckhart.[28] The analysis here has to be understood as standing firmly within that tradition.[29]

THE TEMPORAL SYNTHESIS

In the individual life, anxiety is the instant. To account for anxiety in terms of its condition is to clarify the temporal instant. As already shown, Hegel's account of the temporal instant (the "Now") relies upon the notion of mediation. The Now is the *result* of the originary movement of consciousness as self-othering and self-returning. Temporal diachrony is therefore reducible to consciousness's own domain: consciousness controls the transformations of time. Already in *De omnibus dubitandum est* and, more indirectly, in *Repetition* Kierkegaard presents temporalization, the originary event of coming-into-existence, as transcendence. *The Concept of Anxiety* deepens these analyses by a relatively straightforward account of what must be presupposed in our experience of time.

The phenomenon of anxiety is the key. In what sense, one could ask, could the instant (the Now) be qualified as *anxious* within a self-sublating dialectic? How could a self-mediated present be basically anxious? Insofar as anxiety is always a relation to nothing, there must be a relation to nothing—maybe covered over—within each present. There must be a relation to the *Afgrund* of possibility. At the same time, however, unless there were a synthesis at work—an act of unifying, of making identical or rendering present—consciousness would be impossible. This is the great lesson of transcendental idealism. To account for the general possibility of anxiety, therefore, the task is to think a dual synthesis: one that relates consciousness to itself and this self-consciousness (or spirit) to nothing. The instant signifies, ambiguously, both of these—namely, spirit as what posits itself *and* spirit as what relates itself to nothing (here, the eternal).

There arises, then, an ambiguity at the heart of the synthesis of spirit: it signifies simultaneously the movement of spirit positing or differentiating itself (in relation to soul and body) and spirit as a synthesis of the temporal and the eternal. Commenting on this ambiguity, Vigilius writes:

> As for [the synthesis of the bodily and the psychical], it is immediately striking that it is formed differently from the [synthesis of time and eternity]. In the former, the two factors are psyche and body, and spirit is the third, yet in such a way that one can speak of a synthesis only when spirit is posited. The latter synthesis has only two factors, the temporal and the eternal. Where is the third factor? And if there is no third factor, there really is no synthesis,

for a synthesis that is a contradiction cannot be completed as a synthesis without a third factor, because the fact that the synthesis is a contradiction asserts that it is not. (*CA* 85; *SKS* 4:388)

Ultimately, the synthesis of body and psyche sustained by spirit is the "same" as the synthesis of time and eternity: "The synthesis of the temporal and the eternal is not another synthesis but is the expression for the first synthesis [of psyche and body]" (*CA* 88; *SKS* 4:392). There are not two syntheses, which would then require a third to synthesize these two, but a single synthesis. That spirit posits itself by explicitly relating to its animate body—where it thereby incurs the fundamental possibilities of shame and modesty—is its singularizing act. Yet already the sense of modesty (a form of anxiety) indicates the horizon of alterity inseparable from self-positing. One is modest or ashamed only before the gaze of the other. In other words the synthesis of self-positing originally also implicates a relation to something that can never be brought into presence. This is true also in the present case: self-positing takes place in the context of another synthesis that is not really a synthesis at all—not at least in the transcendental sense—because it involves a relation between two things (time and eternity) that can never be brought into a single present. The synthesis of the temporal and the eternal is a synthesis without synthesis (for how could there be a synthesis with nothing?) This is exactly why the "third factor" is missing. The third factor—that is, that which unites time and eternity and thus renders the present possible—has always already withdrawn or disappeared.

Let us leave aside, then, the synthesis that spirit accomplishes between body and soul, and consider more carefully this strange synthesis where two incommensurables are united by a missing third, whereby they are united without a criterion, measure, or principle. What is at stake here, to underscore the point, is the very possibility of the present: what is that event whereby there is a present at all? The name of this event is "the instant." Moreover, since there is a past and a future only once there is a present, the instant emerges as that whereby there is a consciousness of time at all, and hence the possibility of historical consciousness: "Only with the instant does history begin" (*CA* 89; *SKS* 4:392). What is at stake in the analysis of the instant, then, is the problem of beginning in the strictest sense as the birth of the temporal present. The temporal instant is the beginning presupposed in any beginning.

To get underneath the present in order to clarify the beginning (or originary) possibility of presence, an act of thought (*Tanken*) is required. It is necessary to bracket representation (*Forestillingen*). Generally, Kierkegaard's author suggests, time is not thought, but merely represented. For representation time is spatialized—as in a timeline—and the present is reduced to a point discriminating a "before" and "after." But this procedure is surreptitious: the representation of time already proceeds on the basis of the present. Time spatialized is the present rendered into an object and set before intuition. What needs to be thought, however, is the condition of any present, the capability of representation in the first place. One has to bracket representation in order to excavate the conditions prior to the present that render it possible. For thought time is simply "infinite succession" (*CA* 85; *SKS* 4:388), pure process or "passing by" (*Gaaen forbi*). It is without presence and without any distinctions: there "is in time neither present, nor past, nor future" (*CA* 85; *SKS* 4:388). Thus Kierkegaard's author writes: "The present, however, is not a concept of time, except precisely as something infinitely contentless, which again is infinitely vanishing. If this is not kept in mind, not matter how quickly it may disappear, the present is posited, and being posited it again appears in the categories: the past and the future" (*CA* 86; *SKS* 4:390). The point is to think how presence arises at all.

To remain with thought and bracket representation is to ask, transcendentally, concerning that whereby there is presence at all. The condition of the present, however, as thought recognizes, lies in a *negation* applied to time as pure passing-by. That is, unless there is a moment whereby the infinite succession of time is retained—a moment whereby time is prevented from being pure self-difference and forced, so to speak, to be *identical* to itself—there could be nothing like a present and so nothing like the phenomena of past, present, and future (i.e., time consciousness). The only thing that could negate, stop, or hold time, precisely because the latter is infinite succession, would be the infinite annulment of succession. Yet this is precisely the idea of the eternal: "For thought, the eternal is the present in terms of a sublated (*ophævet*) succession (time is the succession that passes by)" (*CA* 86; *SKS* 4:389; my translation). The use of *ophæve* here, which coincides with the German *Aufheben,* points to the dual operation of canceling and preserving: succession is not *annihilated,* which would render the present impossible, but *held back.* The instant therefore signifies the sublation in which time as succession is held back by "the eternal" enough so that the present may open up.

The eternal sublates succession insofar as it confers presence, for "The present is the eternal, or rather, the eternal is the present, and the present is full" (*CA* 86; *SKS* 4:389). We are surprised. Is it a question, then, of grounding the presence of the present upon the eternal, conceived as pleromatic presence? Does the instant, which we shall see signifies exactly the "glance of the eye," name the subject's intuition of the eternal as what constantly abides amidst all temporal flux? The great innovation of idealism vis-à-vis the classical onto-theological tradition was to locate the milieu

of pleromatic presence within self-consciousness itself, in its eternal identity with itself. If there is a critique of idealism here, does it proceed by way
of a return to classical onto-theology? It would seem we are close to Heidegger's charge that Kierkegaard's metaphysics, still structured in terms of
the grounding opposition of time and eternity, allows no radical conception of temporality.

Essential, however, is to recall the context of this exposition: the analysis of the phenomenon of anxiety. In anxiety the subject finds itself unable
to remain identical to itself; the subject finds itself exposed to the excess of
possibility, the excess of the future. Anxiety is a displacement of the subject
from its position in being, an ungrounding. Even if eternity is conceived as
pleromatic presence, such presence does not ground, but ungrounds. What
the analysis subverts finally is the notion of the *glance*: the glance into eternity is what makes one anxious. To speak of a temporal synthesis, then, between time and eternity—to speak of the instant—will be to speak of the
subject losing a hold on itself and its world. Temporal consciousness arises
only where the subject loses itself, where an absolute loss has taken place. It
arises, precisely, in the withdrawal of presence. Aiming to make good the
absolute difference, the subject posits a synthesis—a presence and an identity—that remains utterly exposed and precarious.

Vigilius presents an image to grasp the structure of the instant, an
image of *parting*:

> Thus when Ingeborg looks out over the sea after Frithiof, this is a picture of
> what is expressed in the figurative word [the instant]. An outburst of her
> emotion, a sigh or a word, already has as a sound more of the determination
> of time and is more present as something that is vanishing and does not
> have in it so much of the presence of the eternal. For this reason a sigh, a
> word, etc. have power to relieve the soul of the burdensome weight, pre-
> cisely because the burden, when merely expressed, already begins to be
> something of the past. (*CA* 87; *SKS* 4:390)

This refers to the moment in *Frithiof's Saga* where Ingeborg watches her
lover disappear over the horizon—a parting that turns out to be irrevocable.
Vigilius could hardly have selected a better image to capture the ambiguity
of the instant: time and eternity part, like two lovers, whose only connection then becomes that of desire. The desire, inseparable from a "burden-
some weight," arises in the parting—desire as a relation without relation, a
synthesis that does not *syn*-thesize. Desire is concentrated in the *glance of
the eye*. This is the basis for the link, pointed to explicitly by Vigilius, between the instant (*Øieblikket*) and the glance of the eye (*Øiets-blikk*): "'The
instant' is a figurative expression, and therefore not easy to deal with. How-

ever, it is a beautiful word to consider. Nothing is as swift as the glance of the eye, and yet it is commensurable with the content of the eternal. . . . A glance is a designation of time, but mark well, of time in the fateful conflict when it is touched by eternity" (*CA* 87; *SKS* 4:390).[30] Frithiof's glance becomes commensurate with the eternal only in the irreparable loss of its object: irreparability is the eternal cut into the present, the fateful conflict.

The instant constitutes a synthesis that operates as an *interruption*. Kierkegaard's author suggests this when he writes:

> In the New Testament there is a poetic paraphrase of the instant. Paul says the world will pass away in an instant. . . . By this he also expresses that the instant is commensurable with eternity, precisely *because the instant of destruction expresses eternity at the same instant.* Permit me to illustrate what I mean, and forgive me if anyone should find the analogy offensive. Once here in Copenhagen there were two actors who probably never thought that their performance could have a deeper significance. They stepped forth onto the stage, placed themselves opposite each other, and then began the mimical representation of one or another passionate conflict. When the mimical act was in full swing and the spectators' eyes followed the story with expectation of what was to follow, they suddenly stopped and remained motionless as though petrified in the mimical expression of the instant. The effect of this can be exceedingly comical, for the instant in an accidental way becomes commensurable with the eternal. (*CA* 88, my italics; *SKS* 4:391)

The eternal "appears" only in the destruction of the present; or, as the illustration of the two mimes makes clear, in the sudden failure of the structure of temporal representation. The eye follows the movements of the two mimes within a horizon of expectation founded upon the present as it is retained in immediate memory. The present, held in consciousness, suggests the next moment. Time unfolds continuously as duration. Yet the sudden stop, precisely as sudden (unexpected), produces a failure in the structure of temporal representation. It is the failure itself that makes it (comically) commensurate the eternal. In the instant, then, the eternal grants presence through the interruption of presence. In other words, time and eternity are never, strictly speaking, synthesized, that is, if by synthesis one means an integration of the diverse into a unity in the present. One cannot even, in all strictness, speak of a coincidence of opposites, if by that one means the integration of contradictions within a single, unpresentable present.[31] Nor, of course, can one say that time and eternity are mediated, that is, appear as the abstract poles or moments of a single concrete reality. Time and eternity are not integrated or structurally conjoined. In the instant they "touch" one another: exteriority is maintained. Yet this is also not the touch of a tangent line on a circle, which intersects at a single point. These models of synthesis all operate, implicitly at least, under the idea that a synthesis refers to a structure of *being*. They neglect the interruptive or anarchic character of the instant—the instant as precisely *event*. Eternity touches time in the eventfulness of time, in the sudden.

The critique of idealist temporality, then, does not return to onto-theology. If there is a "classical" reference for the understanding of the instant as the sudden irruption of eternity into time, it is the Neoplatonic understanding. In Neoplatonic texts (e.g., Plotinus) the sudden signifies the inbreaking of the absolute into time, the instant of salvation.[32] The Eckhartian tradition, moreover, overtly exploits the etymological link between the sudden, which in German as in Danish translates as the "glance of the eye" (*Augen-blick*), and the metaphorics of vision: salvation is linked to the vision of the absolute—a vision, however, that is sudden, nondiscursive, immediate, and ultimately objectless. The vision of the absolute is a vision of nothing.[33] In this way, the metaphorical link between vision and knowledge, so central for Plato, is ultimately subverted: *nothing* becomes visible. Vision is a cipher, not for knowing, but for non-knowing. What is striking about Eckhartian anthropology is that it places the spiritual reality of the self in the glance, yet it interprets the glance according to a *twofold* eye: an eye that gazes into eternity and an eye that gazes into temporality. Inaugurating a tradition that runs through Tauler, the *Theologia Germanica*, Boehme, and the pietists, Eckhart writes: "The soul has two eyes, one inward and one outward. The inward eye of the soul is the one that sees into being and takes its being from God without anything else mediating. This is its proper function. The outward eye of the soul is the one that is turned toward all creatures, taking note of them by means of images in the manner of a faculty."[34] The outer eye signifies the power to represent objects within a temporal horizon. The inner eye, however, represents nothing: "seeing" rather becomes a conceptual cipher for the reception or gift of the present itself.[35] Seeing is not representing, but receiving—and receiving what cannot finally be received. This is the direction according to which Kierkegaard's author interprets the glance of the eye.

Moreover, if the instant is the synthesis of time and eternity, such a synthesis has to be carefully distinguished from the model of synthesis operative in idealist texts. In these terms synthesis means that two elements are set into some stable relation to each other in terms of some third factor. The third, the milieu of identity or principle, organizes the economy between the two. Kierkegaard's author already pointed to the synthesis of the animate and bodily vis-à-vis self-consciousness, or spirit. With respect to the synthesis of time and eternity, however, there was a problem: no third factor could be enunciated. Now it is possible to see why: time and eternity, in fact, are not synthesized, that is, are not organized vis-à-vis one another within some milieu of identity or deeper economy. At the same time, however, there can be no question of a dualistic ontology, as if time and eternity constituted different regions of being. Time and eternity are neither identical nor different. They touch each other, not in the present, but rather as the condition of any present. The instant is not the present moment; it is not a synthesis grounded in self-consciousness; it is not a structure of being. Kierkegaard's author clarifies this by a fuller reflection upon the Platonic notion of the "sudden."

RETRIEVAL OF PLATO'S SUDDEN

In Plato's *Parmenides* the sudden signifies the "category of transition" that falls essentially *between* being and nonbeing—something that is neither being nor nonbeing—that is necessary to account for movement between, for example, motion and rest. In a footnote Vigilius summarizes Plato's dialectic: "the instant appears to be this strange entity (ατοπον, the Greek word is especially appropriate) that lies between motion and rest without occupying any time, and into this and out from this that which is in motion changes into rest, and that which is at rest changes into motion. Thus the instant becomes the category of transition (μεταβολη), for Plato shows in the same way that the instant is related to the transition of the one to the many, of the many to the one . . . etc." (*CA* 83, slightly altered; *SKS* 4:386).[36] Vigilius takes the Platonic sudden as the guiding coordinate for his own analysis of the instant: "What we call the instant, Plato calls το εχαιφνης" (*CA* 87–88; *SKS* 4:391). Two factors here are essential: first, that the sudden is essentially a category of the *between* and thus constitutes a kind of synthesis, a holding of contraries together as one; and yet, precisely as between, the sudden is essentially placeless (ατοπος), that is, neither here nor there, neither in being nor outside of being. The instant, precisely as sudden, must therefore be thought as placeless, irreducible to being and nonbeing. The instant remains outside of or at the limit of being.

Though Vigilius aligns himself with Plato in this way in order to point, against Parmenides and Hegel,[37] to the necessity of a category that is not a category of being—and thus, in effect, not a category at all—the alliance is only provisional. Plato's dialectic, against Hegel, shows the impossibility of elevating transition or movement into logic, that is, the doctrine of being. Transition requires what is neither being nor nonbeing. Yet, according to Vigilius, Plato did not yet draw the radical conclusions from his analysis for temporality. Vigilius writes:

> Greek culture did not comprehend the instant, and even if it had comprehended the atom of eternity [i.e., that the instant "occupies no time at all"],

it did not comprehend that it was the instant, did not define it with a forward direction but with a backward direction. Because for Greek culture the atom of eternity was essentially eternity, neither time nor eternity received what was properly its due. (*CA* 88, altered; *SKS* 4:392)

In Plato's dialectic the instant appears as an essential placelessness, the rupture of continuity that informs any new beginning. Plato's clarity on the irreducibility of the instant either to being or to (dialectically conceived) nonbeing, according to Vigilius, surpasses Hegelian dialectic. Yet what marks the limit of Plato's account is that he defined the eternal with a "backward" rather than "forward" direction. Herein, Vigilius notes, lies the significance of Platonic recollection wherein "the eternal lies behind as the past that can only be entered backwards" (*CA* 90; *SKS* 4:393). What is at stake here is not so much recollection (versus its opposite, i.e., repetition), as the conception of temporality that makes recollection appear as the authentic relation to the eternal. What, then, does it mean to define eternity with a backward direction? It means positing the eternal in terms of the immutability of closure. Only the past has real being because it remains eternally self-identical, and it remains *eternally* self-identical only because it has *already* passed through differentiation.[38] The time of differentiation is past, and so identity reigns absolutely unchallenged. The silent presupposition of Plato's analysis is thus that eternity constitutes the real, and that the reality of the real lies in its unalterable presence to itself. Yet if the eternal lies in the past, then temporality (the moment of differentiation) is at bottom unreal or merely abstract (as Hegel also finally argues). Hence, on Greek presuppositions, the instant of eternity is identical to eternity insofar as the instant is finally unreal or reducible. The Platonic text effects a reduction of the instant to eternity: what is real of the instant is reducible to the eternal or to presence; eternity and the instant are, at bottom, the same.

By contrast, for Vigilius the instant of eternity has to be thought as the "extreme opposite" (*CA* 84; *SKS* 4:388) of eternity. The instant, in other words, is not allowed to be reduced to mere evanescence or illusion; rather, it is precisely the real. The event is not a *passage to* reality, but reality itself. Or more simply: passage as such is real, identity is illusion. This evaluation of what remains between being and nonbeing is conditioned on defining eternity with a *forward* direction. Eternity is not what remains eternally self-present, or what can be reduced to that, but what never ceases to beckon and threaten from the future. The eternal cannot as such be integrated into the present but remains essentially futural: the present and the eternal are thus extreme opposites. This essential gap, the excessive futurity of the eternal, awakens precisely *anxiety*. And anxiety imposes the most strenuous demand upon the subject.

THE ABSOLUTE FUTURE

By means of the instant the horizon of temporality opens as past, present, and future. The instant, eternity's destruction of presence, opens the present to time *consciousness*. Yet here we have to return to an ambiguity. There is an ambiguity insofar as the instant signifies both the initiatory moment of self-consciousness in its positing itself (the leap of sin), hence as a synthesis founded within self-consciousness, and the touching of eternity and time, which is strictly speaking not a synthesis since there is no third factor. As the inbreaking of the eternal into time, the instant is not a synthesis *of* self-consciousness, it is first of all the synthesis *whereby* there is self-consciousness, *whereby* there is a consciousness of future and past. As arising through self-positing, however, the instant signifies the synthesis of future and past on the basis of the present, that is, the present moment itself in its full sense. These two syntheses, though inseparable, are nevertheless essentially distinct. How then is one to think through the transcendental fact of self-positing, and thus the subject's power to posit time, and the always prior event in which time and eternity touch? What is the relation between the *instant* and the *present*?

That relation is, precisely, *anxiety*. Anxiety is the sense that the present, though constituted through self-consciousness, remains exposed to instantaneous time. Anxiety means that the synthesis of self-positing, though originary, nevertheless does not constitute a radical origin. The instant is not the present or integratable into presence, but *everything turns on it.* There is the anxiety. Anxiety is the phenomenon that unveils the absolute future. The absolute future, in other words, must be distinguished from the future as anticipated or projected. Yet the future signifies, ambiguously, both the *future present,* what one represents to oneself as to-come in the form of projects or expectations (i.e., posits), and the *absolute future,* that is, the future as what *comes of itself,* as the sudden burst of presence that cannot be posited. The absolute inability to synthesize these two, continuum and disruption, manifests itself as anxiety. Broaching the distinction between the two, Kierkegaard's author writes:

> [T]he future in a certain sense signifies more than the present and the past, because in a certain sense the future is the whole of which the past is a part, and the future can in a certain sense signify the whole. This is because the eternal first signifies the future or because the future is the incognito in which the eternal, even though it is incommensurable with time, nevertheless preserves its association with time. (*CA* 89; *SKS* 4:392)

The absolute future is the incognito of the eternal, the place where it appears without appearing. The future in this sense is "the whole," is "more," in the precise sense that it holds open what everything will have meant. The future as incognito of the eternal is also more than the future itself as represented. The sense of this excessive futurity, rendering all closure relative, is the most radical, most fateful engagement with time. The engagement with time reveals an engagement with nonbeing, nonbeing as the abyss of possibility, for "the possible corresponds exactly to the future" (*CA* 91; *SKS* 4:394). The absolute future, holding the abyss of possibility in excess to all calculation or expectation, is the gap that separates the present from its own reality as posited. In this separation of the present from its own reality lies the origin of anxiety. To possess oneself is impossible, and yet to flee oneself is equally impossible. One is bound over to oneself, and in being bound to oneself one is bound inexorably to what comes of itself, the absolute future. How to face it?

ABSOLUTE SINKING: *GELASSENHEIT*

The final chapter of *The Concept of Anxiety,* "Anxiety as Saving through Faith," begins an entirely new dialectic: one that leads to salvation. Anxiety has been discussed as a relation to the possibility of possibility (the *Afgrund* of freedom), to the other (the good), and to the instant (the absolute future). In each case anxiety constitutes a disclosure of nonbeing; and in each case it is vis-à-vis this disclosure that freedom is simultaneously enabled toward its positing of itself and disabled from constituting an origin. In general, Vigilius's analyses have focused upon the way in which the disclosure of nonbeing conditions the move toward *Eigenwille,* or sin. That is only one side of it, however. Section five presents the dialectic through which anxiety consumes itself and leads not to evil, but to "salvation." The conditions of sin are identical to those of salvation. Salvation, however, means what here? Minimally it signifies being able to "praise actuality . . . even when it rests heavily upon [one]" (*CA* 156; *SKS* 4:455). Salvation is reconciliation with actuality, unreserved affirmation, the finite entering into its finitude. According to the dialectic Vigilius presents, if one is "honest toward possibility" (*CA* 157; *SKS* 4:455), anxiety becomes a "serving spirit" that leads one back to reconciliation with actuality, no matter how heavy. Salvation hangs on a certain "dialectic" that should not be confused with the process of double negation; it is an Eckhartian rather than Hegelian dialectic. Nonbeing is not negated, but allowed to "be."

What is necessary is to let oneself sink absolutely into the *Afgrund* of indeterminate possibility. Vigilius Haufniensis writes:

> Now if [a person] did not defraud the possibility that wanted to teach him and did not wheedle the anxiety that wanted to save him, then he would re-

ceive everything back, as no one in actuality ever did, even though he received all things tenfold, for the disciple of possibility received infinity. . . .
In actuality, no one ever sank so deep that he could not sink deeper. . . . But
he who sank in possibility . . . He sank absolutely (*sank absolut*), but then in
turn emerged from the depth of the abyss (*Afgrund*) lighter than all the
troublesome and terrible things in life. (*CA* 158; *SKS* 4:457)

The "dialectic" of this passage becomes intelligible as soon as one recognizes that "sinking" is the very cipher for letting-go, releasement, or *Gelassenheit* (or sometimes *abegescheidenheit*) as it is articulated in Eckhartian
apophaticism.[39] To sink absolutely means to let go of being, the root of at-
tachment, the ego as ground or origin. It signifies a released relation to self,
which at bottom will involve a released relation to possibility, the opposite
of which would be "shrewdness" (*Klogskabet*)—or, as is better translated,
"calculative thinking." Hence the final section involves a critical separation
between releasement, or faith, and calculative thinking: the former alone remains honest toward possibility, whereas the latter deludes itself. Moreover,
only releasement involves reconciliation with actuality and thus true affirmation.

The argument Vigilius makes for releasement hinges on the radical conception of possibility already articulated: namely, possibility as what falls
outside any dialectical recuperation within being, possibility as in excess to
all ends. It is only in this sense that possibility is "weightiest of all categories" (*CA* 156; *SKS* 4:455)—a category, it should be noted, that is beyond category. Generally speaking, Vigilius notes, possibility is reduced to
something light, to the "possibility of happiness, fortune etc.," in terms of
which actuality appears as what has weight. Yet such a conception of possibility, nourishing wish-fulfillment, is merely a "mendacious invention of
human depravity" (*CA* 156; *SKS* 4:455). Possibility is the weightiest of all
categories only on condition of a critical distinction between represented
possibility, that is, possibility that has been taken under the sovereignty of
human intentionality, and absolute possibility. The latter signifies possibility wherein "all things are equally possible . . . the terrible as well as the
joyful" (*CA* 156; *SKS* 4:455). In absolute possibility all oppositions—for
example, between joy and misery, salvation and damnation, sanity and insanity—are held in equilibrium. Everything is equally possible; the fate of
anyone is the fate of everyone; everything that has been done can just as
well be undone. What everything will have meant remains unresolved.
Here then is an *Afgrund,* articulated historically as fate (the Greeks), Law
(Judaism), and forgiveness (Christianity), in which any calculable order of
things is suspended. Anxiety discovers this abyss and therefore holds out the
possibility of a relation to reality beyond the subject's representation of it
(in terms of which it is rendered calculable).

Thought strictly the abyss of possibility presents itself as an *impossibility*. This is clear already in the Greeks' relation to fate. Fate points to the future as what arrives suddenly and undoes the whole human order of intentionality. It is the nothing of the future enigmatically disclosed through the oracle. Yet the oracle, which here concentrates the weight of possibility, is just as enigmatic as fate itself: "Whoever wants to explain fate must be just as ambiguous as fate. And this the oracle was. However, the oracle in turn might signify the exact opposite. So the pagan's relation to the oracle is again anxiety. Herein lies the profound and inexplicable tragicalness of paganism" (*CA* 97; *SKS* 4:400). To act on the basis of an oracular utterance is to have resolved its meaning, that is, to have reduced it to a calculable meaning. But it is always the case that its meaning may have been the very opposite. The either/or of decision necessarily remains open, and so acting on principle remains without a basis. Yet the groundlessness of decision as such is not what is tragic—rather, it lies in "the pagan's not daring to forbear taking counsel with [the oracle]" (*CA* 97; *SKS* 4:400). The tragedy lay in the double-bind that one could not forbear, on the one hand, to consult the oracle—for the need to consult the oracle is identical to the need to act on the basis of some knowledge, that is, on principle—and yet, on the other hand, that consultation would not produce any determinate relation to fate. Knowledge is necessary but impossible; the impossible is necessary.

The fundamental trait of calculative thinking is its impermeability to all critique. That is to say, it is convinced of its own infinite extendability: all of its failures to anticipate reality, and thus to reduce the real to the domain of its sovereign control, act for it only as a stimulus toward redoubling its calculative efforts. Calculative thinking "always explains in parts, never totally" (*CA* 161; *SKS* 4:459). Reality simply cannot defeat calculative thinking, no more than "a man will lose faith in the lottery if he does not lose it by himself but is supposed to lose it by continually losing it when he gambles" (*CA* 160; *SKS* 4:458). Wish-fulfillment is mighty, stubborn, ineradicable. What is upheld in the calculative attitude, for Vigilius, is the illusion of control over the (absolute) future—in other words, the denial of the absolute future. At bottom this is a metaphysical will that denies the fundamentally anarchic character of the temporal instant, a denial whose insignia would be the suppression of anxiety (for it is precisely in anxiety that the anarchy of time is disclosed).

In contrast to calculative thinking, Vigilius presents a released attitude toward possibility termed "faith." Faith is simply to "be honest toward possibility" (*CA* 157; *SKS* 4:455). Facing the abyss of possibility it does not turn from it, clinging to what it can calculate, but rather "bids it welcome" and "greets it festively" (*CA* 159; *SKS* 4:457–58) like a friend. Faith "remains with anxiety" (*bliver hos Angesten*) in order to heed its disclosure: namely, that every *calculable order of things* through which the ego can assure and console itself—and this applies par excellence to metaphysical consolations —constitutes a projection of that same ego. Discovering what cannot be interiorized or calculated, anxiety discovers reality beyond the ultimates, whether moral or onto-theological, the ego posits as the fulfillment of *its* hopes and dreams.

To sink absolutely into the abyss of possibility is to let go of any self-understanding that allows, however secretly, the gesture of mastery; it is to become "absolutely educated" concerning one's non-ultimacy, one's nothingness. Anxiety becomes a serving spirit insofar as it effects a detachment of the subject from its own understanding of itself as originally capable. Here Kierkegaard's text supplies perhaps an element missing from Eckhartian discourses on detachment (*abegescheidenheit*) and releasement (*gelassenheit*): the phenomenon of anxiety as the "middle term," the solvent, through which the subject *finds itself* detached from its usual understanding of itself as capable. Releasement cannot be thought as the act or project of a subject without sacrificing its essential character. In and through anxiety the subject is *offered* nonbeing—not as what it posits or can be shown to have posited, but as what prevents it from coinciding with itself. The risks are great, for Kierkegaard's author notes the essential "danger of a fall, namely, suicide" (*CA* 159; *SKS* 4:457). Yet faith releases itself to this offering and in so doing "receives everything back" (*CA* 159; *SKS* 4:457), emerging "from the depths of the abyss lighter than all the troublesome and terrible things in life" (ibid.).

Being led by anxiety, faith lets go of its own will absolutely. It is an infinite task. Ever since Eckhart it has been said that this is quietism, nihilism, or hatred of life. It is not. It is a relation to actuality, fundamentally affirmative, on a different condition than one finds within metaphysical discourses. It is in fact the discovery of the actual as it really is, beyond its being enframed by ultimate, posited grounds (which render the real calculable). The discovery or disclosure of the actual is not its being given for knowledge or representation, but its being given simply. Faith finds reason for affirmation—if we can still say this—precisely in this groundlessness. Losing everything, it receives everything: not in a dialectical sense, but in the sense that its losing everything *is* its receiving everything. If faith discovers consolation, it is the one Eckhart articulated: "But you must know that God's friends are never without consolation, for whatever God wills is for them the greatest consolation of all, whether it be consolation or desolation."[40]

Conclusion:
The Exteriority of Interiority

The philosophies of German idealism constitute an extraordinary theoretical elaboration and defense of the priority of the problematic of self-consciousness to any other problematic. Self-consciousness finds its legitimation as ground. The values associated with self-consciousness become preeminent: (self)-presence, identity, unity, freedom, and (self)-possession. Nothing can be more intimate to the ego than itself. Such self-intimacy or self-possession, raised to the point where the subject is conceived as positing itself, is what transcendental idealism would call "interiority." The trajectory of idealism from Kant to Hegel discovers the illusory or provisional quality of everything exterior. In Kant's terms, the conditions of any object are the conditions of the possibility of the object lying in transcendental interiority; in Hegel's terms, self-consciousness as reason discovers itself to be "all reality." What I hope to have shown is that, for Kierkegaard, such egological interiority constitutes an effacement of the genuinely interior. His path of thinking in the early works is the critical one of recalling the originary conditions of the ego's involvement with itself: its link to a beginning prior to presence.

Thus if idealism involves thinking the ground of reality according to a logic of self-positing consciousness, and thus on the horizon of its representability, Kierkegaard's texts return, in a very qualified sense, to the critical distinction Kant drew between reality *in-itself* and reality *for-consciousness*, between the real and its representation. The thrust of Hegel's dialectic in particular is to suggest that this distinction is one *consciousness itself draws* and so, on the basis of this insight, he could denounce Kant's "thing-in-itself" as a pre-critical throwback. Hegel knows how reality withdraws into itself and holds itself apart from its becoming present to consciousness. He sees with complete clarity that something always passes "behind the back of consciousness."[1] Nevertheless the distinctive mark of Hegel's idealism is to grasp this dark background of consciousness against the horizon of its total presentability. The presence of consciousness to itself is implicit in reality. The distinctive mark of Kierkegaard's thought, on the contrary, is to show ineradicable difference and nonidentity at the heart of self-consciousness.

Given that, for Kant, temporality constitutes the most basic horizon of interiority (the "form of inner sense"), it is no surprise that Kierkegaard's critique focuses on time. Hegel's analysis of sense certainty, which proclaims the thoroughly mediated character of the temporal now, only makes the basic thrust of idealism explicit. Yet I have shown that for Kierkegaard temporality cannot adequately be analyzed in terms of self-consciousness or within the horizon of presence. The past, the present, and the future, always still thought in terms of their *being for* self-consciousness, or in terms of its synthetic work of re-presenting, are not adequate for the analysis of time. Thus Kierkegaard refers to what remains "outside" time: the eternal. Nevertheless, the emphasis of Kierkegaard's analysis is not to show how the eternal grounds the temporal present (a thoroughly classical move), but rather to focus on the *granting* of presence. Presence is granted through an event—the instant—that is not itself analyzable on the horizon of presence. The instant, what Plato's *Parmenides* called "the sudden," will always already have taken place; and the instant is to-come prior to any expectation one can form. Self-consciousness in all of its modalities is thus shown to have a condition it cannot interiorize, something it meets in the encounter with nonbeing (disclosed in phenomena such as melancholy and anxiety).

Kierkegaard's notion of interiority thus emerges in a paradoxical way: the interior is constituted precisely as what *self-consciousness cannot interiorize.* The interior is not constituted as representation or self-presence, but as exposure to temporalization: to temporality insofar as it *cannot* be recollected, anticipated, or brought to presence, and thus to an absolute beginning that can never be converted into an ideal or representable origin (a principle) and to an absolute future that is not already contained in the present. The interior has no place or time; it neither is nor is not. One should speak of the *event* of interiority, for the interior is incessant opening of self-consciousness to its outside, is the fact that self-consciousness can never coincide with its own conditions and so achieve a knowledge that is absolute. By means of its interiority self-consciousness is never finished and never in full possession of itself.

The critical force of such interiority vis-à-vis idealism is to insist upon the essential and irrepressible distinction between the real and its re-presentation within self-consciousness. In one sense, Kierkegaard grants idealism its essential point: we never have to do with reality unmediated by the synthetic work of self-consciousness. Every object or determination must find its ultimate and legitimating ground in the spontaneity of self-consciousness. Anything asserted beyond the terms of such legitimation is dogmatism. Agreed. Nevertheless, Kierkegaard would add the following qualification: it may be that in *knowledge* or representation we never have to do with unmediated reality, but the self bears a relation to reality that cannot be formulated as knowledge. There is a relation to reality that falls *prior to* the total horizon of presence, prior even to the self's presence to itself, a relation that conditions presence and makes knowledge initially possible. The prior relation is that whereby the self is given time and given to itself. The theoretical accomplishment of the early works is to have made this originary temporality a problematic. The fundamental falsity of idealism is to have covered over this prior "secret of existence"—in other words, to have exchanged reality *as it is* for reality insofar as it can be given *for-consciousness.* The really real or actual is not what can be given in presence or represented, but what allows presence. The really real is movement, event, coming-into-existence. Idealism, Hegel in particular, only *represents* movement. That is the essential critique.

Prior to spontaneity, the unconditioned beginning posited by a free subject, there is the suffering of coming-into-existence or temporalization. To exist is already to have been dispossessed of the unity, command, and self-possession of the egological subject. The trajectory of idealism, and perhaps the destiny of the West, is to have expelled any essential vulnerability from the conception of the subject. Fichte's self-positing ego, the very author of its own being, is most emblematic in this regard. Kierkegaard's texts aim at showing a relation of the subject to itself more originary (more interior) than one constituted as positing, representing, or knowing. The most interior is what is not possessed, but rather what dispossesses. Interiority, then, is not a foundation for the constitution of the real, but non-foundation, groundlessness. The preeminent—most originary and singular—tasks of the subject arise in the relation to its own groundlessness. Following the Eckhartian tradition, I have suggested that Kierkegaard's texts counsel faith as releasement: that is, becoming one's own groundlessness, becoming nothing, letting go of one's self-understanding as foundation, letting go of the conception of being (and of God) as what grounds and secures the self's being. One has to sink absolutely into nonbeing and accept dispossession (or the self mutilates itself in demonic closure). Concretely, this means accepting suffering in terms of its general possibility, for the very subjectivity of the subject lies in its suffering temporalization.

Hegel famously warns against a thinking that is "merely edifying." Indeed, he opposes philosophical insight to precisely the edifying: "Whoever seeks mere edification, and whoever wants to shroud in a mist the manifold variety of his earthly existence and of thought, in order to pursue the inde-terminate enjoyment of this indeterminate divinity, may look where he likes to find all this. He will find ample opportunity to dream up something for himself. But philosophy must beware of the wish to be edifying."[2] This warning against edification flows from the very center of Hegel's thought: the critique of indetermination, of nonbeing, as merely abstract, a critique that goes hand in hand with the prioritization of the values of self-con-sciousness. For his part, Kierkegaard wrote a series of edifying discourses at the same time as the theoretical texts considered in this book. From the per-spective developed in this book it can now be seen that these works, which Heidegger judged to be Kierkegaard's most philosophical,[3] are anything but adventitious. In particular, they have nothing to do with the consoling dreams of a thought that refuses the hard work of science. Rather, they fol-low from a precisely *more critical* sense of what is originary to the human condition: not the spontaneity of a consciousness that begins through and with itself (absolutely), but the event through which the horizon of pres-ence first opens, the gift of presence.

The edifying writings, which deserve but have never received equal con-sideration with the theoretical writings,[4] address the human condition in terms of this irremissible exposure, this suffering, its inability to posit time. They dare to speak of the gift of suffering in the conviction that a thinking that cannot address suffering *where it is and is conceived as irremissible* can-not claim to address what is originary to the human condition.

NOTES

INTRODUCTION

1. See his article "Philosophy after Kierkegaard," in *Kierkegaard: A Critical Reader,* ed. Jonathon Reé and Jane Chamberlain (Oxford: Blackwell, 1998), p. 15.

2. This is true in an exemplary sense for Hegel. See especially Jean-Luc Nancy's radically non-idealist reading of Hegel in his *Hegel: The Restlessness of the Negative,* trans. Jason Smith and Steven Miller (Minneapolis: University of Minnesota Press, 2002).

3. *Critique of Pure Reason,* trans. Werner Pluhar (Indianapolis: Hackett, 1996), p. 161 (A 111).

4. *J. G. Fichte Science of Knowledge,* trans. Peter Heath and John Lachs (Cambridge: Cambridge University Press, 1982), p. 93 (*Fichte* 1:91). In Kant's thought the constitutive power of the ego refers to an order of *phenomena*. Through its sensibility the ego still remains passively receptive to reality, a "thing in itself," beyond the phenomenal order. Fichte's notion of the apperceptive function of consciousness involves dismissing the distinction between phenomena and a thing in itself as a vestige of pre-critical dogmatism. Thus Fichte fully interprets the transcendental subject as a radical origin of the real. Cf. especially Fichte's discussion of his relation to Kant's thought in the second introduction to his 1794 *Wissenschaftslehre* or *Science of Knowledge*, pp. 29–84.

5. *The Vocation of Man,* trans. Peter Preuss (Indianapolis: Hackett, 1987), p. 73 (*Fichte* 2:256). There is a difference between the Fichte of the 1794 *Wissenschaftslehre* and the 1800 *Die Bestimmung des Menschen*. In the latter Fichte has already begun his turn toward religious philosophy in which the transcendentally constitutive function of self-consciousness operates vis-à-vis an absolute ego. This turn receives even sharper articulation in the later *Die Anweisung zum seligen Leben* (1806).

6. *System of Transcendental Idealism,* trans. Peter Heath (Charlottesville: University of Virginia Press, 1997), p. 27. In his later *Philosophical Investigations into the Essence of Human Freedom,* however, Schelling breaks with this egological understanding of subjectivity in a way, we shall see, of essential importance for Kierkegaard (cf. chapter 6).

7. *Phenomenology of Spirit,* trans. A. V. Miller (Oxford: Oxford University Press, 1977), p. 10 (*Hegel* 2:22).

8. Ibid.

9. Ibid., p. 140 (*Hegel* 2:183).

10. *Hegel's Science of Logic,* trans. A. V. Miller (Amherst, N.Y.: Humanity Books, 1999), pp. 67–78 (*Hegel* 4:69–84).

11. Ibid., p. 71 (*Hegel* 4:75).

12. Hegel's *Phenomenology of Spirit,* p. 11 (*Hegel* 2:24).

13. Very much depends upon how one reads Hegel: is absolute knowing the moment of completion or closure, the full recuperation of the beginning? Or is it, on the contrary, the very opening up of reality beyond every closure? Kierkegaard's Hegel, in any event, is guided by the thought of closure. Nothing is more uncertain in the interpretation of Hegel than

this question. For readings that stress the moment of closure, see Jacques Derrida's article "From a Restricted to a General Economy: A Hegelianism without Reserve," in *Writing and Difference,* trans. Alan Bass (Chicago: University of Chicago Press, 1978). For more open-ended readings, see above all Jean-Luc Nancy's *The Restlessness of the Negative.*

14. It has become more customary to translate *Øieblikket,* which means literally the glance of the eye, as "the moment." I prefer "the instant" in order to underscore the central conceptual meaning of the term: it points to a discontinuity, a suddenness. The term "moment" more suggests continuity and duration, a span of time. An instant passes before one even knows it as there; a moment, though ephemeral, lasts.

15. *What is Called Thinking?* trans. Glenn Gray (New York: Harper, 1968), p. 213. Both Adorno and Levinas have a version of this criticism. Adorno argues that Kierkegaard reprises a contentless version of idealist interiority capable of criticizing idealism only at the cost of losing touch with historical actuality. See his *Kierkegaard: The Construction of the Aesthetic,* trans. Robert Hullor-Kentor (Minneapolis: University of Minnesota Press, 1989), ch. 2. In his essay "Existence and Ethics" Levinas credits Kierkegaard for the defense of singularity as over against all totalizing systems of thought, yet criticizes him for reinscribing the metaphysical egoism of the German idealists. Levinas writes: "The subjectivity of the subject is [for Kierkegaard] an identification of the Same in its concern for the Same. It is egoism, and is subjectivity is a Self." Cf. *Kierkegaard: A Critical Reader,* ed. Jonathon Rée and Jane Chamberlain (Oxford: Blackwell, 1998), p. 28.

16. The very notion that "truth is subjectivity," presented in *The Concluding Unscientific Postscript,* would seem, for example, to suggest that *being's truth* becomes available in and for subjectivity. Heinrich Schmidinger observes: "For both [Fichte and Kierkegaard] it remains fundamentally the case that neither actuality nor truth may be determined or conceived apart from the human being's act of self-constitution. . . . For both the human being's free act is, following Kant, the ground for the manifestation of actuality and truth as such." See his article "Kierkegaard und Fichte" in *Gregorianum* 52 (1971), pp. 526–27. In these terms Heidegger's judgment would appear to be validated. However, this overlooks the way critique happens in and through appropriation.

17. Heidegger's critique speaks, perhaps, more of the reception of Kierkegaard's texts within existentialism and neoorthodox theology than of the texts themselves. Interpreters such as Emmanuel Hirsch, Jean Wahl, Lev Shestov, and Jean-Paul Sartre as well as Heidegger enlisted Kierkegaard in the effort to think existence in its difference from the great philosophical rationalisms; and on the theological side, people such as Martin Buber, Karl Barth, and Paul Tillich found in Kierkegaard an advance beyond the ethical humanism of nineteenth-century theology. In either case, though, Kierkegaard's thought was interpreted as offering a new kind of philosophical or theological *anthropology.* See Emmanuel Hirsch, *Kierkegaard-Studien* (Gutersloh: C. Bertelsmann, 1933); Jean Wahl, *Ètudes Kierkegaardienne* (Paris: J. Vrin, 1949); Lev Shestov, *Kierkegaard and the Existential Philosophy,* trans. Elinor Hewitt (Athens: Ohio University Press, 1969).

18. This is the mark of onto-theology Heidegger puts particular emphasis upon in his essay "The Onto-Theo-Logical Constitution of Metaphysics." He writes: "Metaphysics thinks of beings as such, that is, in general. Metaphysics thinks of beings as such, as a whole. Metaphysics thinks of the Being of beings both in the ground-giving unity of what is most general, what is indifferently valid everywhere, and also in the unity of the all that accounts for the ground, that is, of the All-Highest. The Being of beings is thought thought in advance as the grounding ground." See *Identity and Difference,* trans. Joan Stambaugh (Chicago: University of Chicago Press, 2002), p. 58.

19. For John Elrod, they comprise the "systematic foundation" of Kierkegaard's thought, an "ontological structure . . . that is present in his writings and essential to his total project." See his *Being and Existence in Kierkegaard's Pseudonymous Works* (Princeton: Princeton Uni-

versity Press, 1975), p. 17. For James Collins, it is his theory of the stages of existence that earns Kierkegaard a place in the history of philosophy. See his *The Mind of Kierkegaard* (Princeton: Princeton University Press, 1983), p. 42. Cf. also: Mark C. Taylor, *Kierkegaard's Pseudonymous Authorship: A Study of Time and the Self* (Princeton: Princeton University Press, 1975); Stephen Dunning, *Kierkegaard's Dialectic of Inwardness: A Structural Analysis of the Theory of the Stages* (Princeton: Princeton University Press, 1985).

20. Stephen Dunning's *Kierkegaard's Dialectic of Inwardness* presents perhaps the most comprehensive effort to draw forth the basically Hegelian structure of the stages. Dunning convincingly demonstrates the pervasive presence of Hegelian dialectical structures, in particular related to the dialectic between inner and outer, throughout Kierkegaard's authorship. Likewise, Jon Stewart points to the profoundly Hegelian nature of the stages: "Hegel's dialectic runs through the movement of what he calls immediacy, mediation and then mediated immediacy, which is a return to immediacy at a higher level. Thus, Kierkegaard's conception of faith [or the religious] on this point in fact follows a Hegelian scheme and could very well be derived from it." See his *Kierkegaard's Relations to Hegel Reconsidered* (Cambridge: Cambridge University Press, 2003), p. 387. In both cases, we may agree that the stages received a dialectical-teleological—and thus basically Hegelian—ordering. However, what each misses, or at least underplays, is the way the dialectical-teleological scheme is appropriated in order to be undone. The problematic of existence exceeds that of the stages.

21. Cf. *Lectures on the History of Philosophy,* trans. E. S. Haldane and Frances Simson, 3 vols. (Lincoln: University of Nebraska Press, 1995), vol. 1, p. 22.

22. Adorno, for example, argues that the existential subject is for Kierkegaard what the absolute subject of world history is for Hegel: namely, a "total image" that draws existence systematically together within consciousness. Thus he agrees with Heidegger that the stages merely repeat the egology of German idealism. See his *Kierkegaard: The Construction of the Aesthetic,* p. 86.

23. Adorno is one of the few readers of Kierkegaard who has thematized the conflict between the phenomenological content of Kierkegaard's texts, which resists reduction into stages, and the teleological movement from inauthentic to authentic existence, which the stages are supposed to describe. In his *The Construction of the Aesthetic,* Adorno finds a basic and irreconcilable conflict between the dialectic of the stages, or "spheres"—which he regards as entirely idealist and even Hegelian in origin—and what he calls Kierkegaard's notion of "objectless inwardness." According to Adorno the construction of the stages is an effort to build (an illusory) determination and content back into an ultimately vacuous interiority that Kierkegaard felt he had to posit in the face of a world overrun by commodification. In effect, the stages operate as an ideology—in Marx's sense—of self-constitution; or perhaps simply as an ideology of the self, full stop. Nevertheless Adorno thinks he finds, in the *phenomenological* content of Kierkegaard's metaphors, rather than in his teleologically constructed dialectic, a historical and material truth that overflows the idealist and teleological schema of the stages. Leaning upon Walter Benjamin, Adorno finds a truth in various figures in which Kierkegaard condenses a melancholic, quasi-messianic hope: "For the true desire of melancholy is nourished on the idea of an eternal happiness without sacrifice, which it still could never adequately indicate as its object," p. 126.

24. "Socrates had the absolute in the form of nothing. By way of the absolute, reality became nothing, but in turn the absolute was nothing" (CI, 236; *SKS* 1:277).

25. *CA* 158; *SKS* 4:457. See my analysis in chapter 6, pp. 191–194.

26. Eckhart's writings were difficult to find as such in the 19th century. An important source seems to have been the 1522 "Basel Ausdruck" of *Tauler's Predigten*—a volume that includes a number of Eckhart's sermons. Quotations from Eckhart, however, could also be

found in the pietistic literature. For example Valentin Weigel's treatise *Von Gelassenheit* includes extensive quotations from Eckhart; Johann Arndt's influential *Vom wahres Christentum,* book three (which has been unfortunately excised from the English translation), constitutes essentially of a series of excerpts from Tauler's and Eckhart's writings. Kierkegaard was quite familiar with Arndt's book.

27. In his *Three Upbuilding Discourses* from 1843 Kierkegaard cites a passage from chapter 11 of the *Theologia Germanica*. See *Eighteen Upbuilding Discourses,* trans. Edna and Howard Hong (Princeton: Princeton University Press, 1990), p. 98. Oddly enough, the passage Kierkegaard cites is a passage the anonymous author has himself cited—from Eckhart!

28. Cf. *Pap.* III A 125. *Der Weg zu Christo* contains a number of important treatises, including one titled *Von wahrer Gelassenheit*. Rohdes' *Auktionsprotokol* also indicates Kierkegaard owned a number of other works by Boehme, including *Mysterium Magnum* and *Christosophia.*

29. For an excellent short study of Kierkegaard's relations to the pietists, see Marie Thulstrup's *Kierkegaard og Pietismen* (Copenhagen: Munksgaard Forlag, 1967).

30. The principal aim of *Fermenta Cognitionis,* Baader wrote, was to "fix attention on the lesser known and even more highly misunderstood writings of our own Jacob Boehme, the true *Philosophus per Ignem* and reformer of the religious sciences." Cf. *Fermenta Cognitionis,* zweites Heft (Berlin: G. Reimer, 1822), p. iii.

31. The Danish title is *Mester Eckhart: et Bidrag til at Oplyse Middelalderens Mystik* (Copenhagen: Reitzels Forlag, 1840). For a translation of this important text in the Eckhart renaissance of the 19th century, cf. Hans Martensen, *Between Hegel and Kierkegaard: Hans L. Martensen's Philosophy of Religion,* trans. Curtis L. Thompsen and David J. Kangas (Atlanta: Scholar's Press, 1997), pp. 148–243.

32. The extraordinary, though still understudied, influence of this "Rhenish" mystical (or apophatic) tradition upon German idealism has been documented by people such as Werner Beierwalters and Cyril O'Regan. For an analysis of this influence, see in particular Werner Beierwalters' *Platonismus und Idealismus* (Frankfurt am Main: Vittoria Klostermann, 1972) and Cyril O'Regan's *The Heterodox Hegel* (Albany: SUNY Press, 1994).

33. Vincent McCarthy suggests either a reading or "at least a re-reading prompted by Rosenkrantz' works" at this date. See his article "Schelling and Kierkegaard on Freedom and Fall," in *International Kierkegaard Commentary, The Concept of Anxiety,* ed. Robert Perkins (Macon: Mercer University Press, 1985), pp. 89–109.

34. See especially Eckhart's German sermon 83, where he counsels that we "should eternally sink down, out of something into nothing." Cf. *Meister Eckhart: The Essential Sermons, Commentaries, Treatises and Defense,* trans. and intro. Edmund Colledge and Bernard McGinn (New York: Paulist Press, 1981), p. 208.

35. In his *Four Upbuilding Discourses* from 1844 Kierkegaard writes of a self "about to sink into his own nothingness." Cf. *Eighteen Upbuilding Discourses,* p. 305. Cf. also pp. 307, 310, and 399 for further instances. "Sinking into nothing" links also to the theme of "becoming nothing." In his *Two Upbuilding Discourses* from 1844 Kierkegaard writes: "If, however, a person knew how to make himself truly what he truly is—nothing—knew how to set the seal of patience on what he had understood—ah, then this life, whether he is the greatest or the lowliest, would even today be a joyful surprise." Cf. *Eighteen Upbuilding Discourses,* p. 226.

36. For a discussion of Boehme's proximity to and distance from Eckhart, see Cyril O'Regan's *Gnostic Apocalypse, Jacob Boehme's Haunted Narrative* (Albany: SUNY Press, 2002), pp. 69–80.

37. From sermon 52, *Beati pauperes spiritu.* See *Meister Eckhart, The Essential Sermons, Commentaries, Treatises and Defense,* p. 200.

1. THE INFINITE BEGINNING
(*THE CONCEPT OF IRONY*)

1. One could argue that part two of *The Concept of Irony,* which treats the romantic irony "after Fichte"—which is to say the irony that presupposes Fichtean subjectivity—looks at a third beginning in philosophy: the transcendental beginning. Insofar as I treat this beginning at length throughout this book, I can safely avoid discussing it here.

2. I do not mean to suggest that the study of romanticism and the concluding chapter, "Irony as a Controlled Element, the Truth of Irony," are not important. The importance they have, however, is largely redeemed in later writings—especially in the analysis of "Judge William's" ethical standpoint in *Either/Or* 2. In a second moment, however, deemed "religious," ethical control is itself problematized.

3. The entire book, of course, is also titled "The Concept of Irony," though with the subtitle "with continual reference to Socrates." There is an important distinction, however, between the logic of part one and of part two that prevents the book *as a whole* from being considered a concept in the *Hegelian* sense. According to its fundamental meaning as "infinite absolute negativity," irony cannot be thought as a concept in Hegel's sense. Part one seeks to vindicate "infinite absolute negativity," which signifies a kind of non-negatable negation. Part two, by contrast, argues for a *determinate negation,* for irony as a "mastered moment." How non-negatable negation becomes negatable negation is not explained by Kierkegaard. In fact, the two parts inscribe incompatible logics. Considering the repetition of the title, however, an explanation can be offered: part two begins all over again at an entirely different place and with entirely different presuppositions than part one—namely, with Hegelian presuppositions. This does not mean the book is a Hegelian book. On the contrary, the book articulates both a Hegelian logic and another kind of "logic" (irony) that prevents the appearance of anything like closure. The book as a whole is both Hegelian and non-Hegelian. For a discussion of the relation between the two parts, cf. my article "Conception and Concept: The Two Logics of *The Concept of Irony* and the Place of Socrates," in *Kierkegaard and the Word(s),* ed. Gordon Marino and Poul Houl (Copenhagen: Reitzels, 2003), pp. 180–91.

4. Kierkegaard famously comments in a journal entry from 1850, referring to a passage from *The Concept of Irony,* "What a Hegelian fool I was!" (*CI* 453; *Pap.* X3 A 477). The context of the comment, a reference to Socrates' ethical greatness, leads one to think the "Hegelianism" at issue was the prioritization of the ethical totality over the singular. Indeed, in the whole of part two of *The Concept of Irony,* which is where Kierkegaard pursues a critique of romanticism, the Hegelian priority on the social is evident.

5. As Hirsch notes, unless one reads Kierkegaard's presentation of Socrates side by side with Hegel's, one will get a false sense of his independence. See his *Kierkegaard-Studien,* p. 593. For a thorough discussion of the way Hegel's reading of Socrates has influenced Kierkegaard's, cf. Jon Stewart's *Kierkegaard's Relations to Hegel Reconsidered,* pp. 132–81.

6. See his translation of *The Concept of Irony, with Constant Reference to Socrates* (Bloomington: Indiana University Press, 1971), p. 403n31.

7. Hegel, *Lectures on the History of Philosophy,* vol. 1, p. 5 (*Hegel* 17:31).

8. Heidegger especially emphasizes the importance of Hegel's claim that philosophy constitutes a unified problematic rather than a disjointed series of world-views. Cf. Heidegger's essay "Hegel and the Greeks" in his *Pathmarks,* ed. William McNeil (Cambridge: Cambridge University Press, 1998), pp. 323–36.

9. *Lectures on the History of Philosophy,* vol. 1, p. 409 (*Hegel* 18:73).

10. Ibid., p. 384 (*Hegel* 18:42).

11. In fact Hegel's *Lectures on the History of Philosophy* of course begins much earlier than Socrates. Nevertheless, in Socrates the unique form of the philosophical concept itself appears in an overt, self-conscious way—for Socrates, but also for our retrospective gaze. The moment of founding is both historical and conceptual: it is open to a phenomenological analysis. For Hegel, this means it can be seen as one of the shapes of consciousness through which the concept must pass on its way toward fully explicit knowledge of itself as the concept.

12. *Lectures on the History of Philosophy*, vol. 1, p. 387 (*Hegel* 18:44–45). My translation.

13. *Lectures on the History of Philosophy*, vol. 1, p. 407 (*Hegel* 18:71).

14. Hegel's reading of Socrates here, it seems, essentially interprets him as a proto-Kant. That is to say, he interprets the Socratic standpoint in light of what for him is a real starting point: the spontaneous, apprensational function of transcendentally active consciousness. Being in its truth or reality is mediated by self-consciousness—that, for Hegel, is the common affirmation of Socrates and Kant. Along these lines, Hegel interprets interiority not simply as subjectivity, but more exactly as "unity of subjectivity and objectivity." Cf. *Lectures on the History of Philosophy*, vol. 1, p. 387 (*Hegel* 18:41).

15. Ibid., p. 407 (*Hegel* 18:71).

16. Ibid., pp. 396, 399 (*Hegel* 18:57, 60).

17. Ibid., p. 399 (*Hegel* 18:60).

18. Ibid., p. 398 (*Hegel* 18:60).

19. Kierkegaard's historical-phenomenological method for grasping the position of Socrates is to triangulate from the sources. Summarizing his results, he writes: "Consequently, with respect to Plato Aristophanes has subtracted, and with respect to Xenophon has added, but since in the latter case it is a matter only of negative quantities, this adding is in one sense a subtracting. If we now allow the lines . . . to emerge more clearly and set the limits of the unknown quantity, the position that simultaneously fits and fills the intervening space, it will look something like this: its relation to the idea is negative—that is, the idea is the boundary of the dialectic. Continually in the process of leading the phenomenon up to the idea (the dialectical activity), the individual is thrust back or flees back into actuality; but actuality itself has only the validity of continually being the occasion for wanting to go beyond actuality—yet without its taking place; whereas the individual takes the *molimina* [efforts] of this subjectivity back into himself, incloses them within himself in a personal satisfaction; but this position is precisely that of irony" (*CI* 154; *SKS* 1:204–205). Hegel, Kierkegaard argues, unduly privileges Plato's reading of Socrates—even though Hegel also admits that Aristophanes was "perfectly right" in his representation of Socrates as engaged primarily in "negative dialectic," and thus not as aiming at a positive conception. For a discussion of Hegel's approbation of Aristophanes in relation to Kierkegaard's position see Sylvia Agacinski's *Aparté: Conceptions and Deaths of Søren Kierkegaard*, trans. Kevin Newmark (Tallahassee: Florida State University Press, 1988), pp. 44–47.

20. There is a difference between Socratic recollection and both the Platonic and Hegelian version of it. According to its Platonic and Hegelian meanings (though they are by no means the same), to recollect is to move backward and inward to the point where the essence of things—lying always prior to concrete existence—is apprehended. Hegel in particular explicitly rewrites and translates Platonic recollection as the apprehension of the prior unity of thought and being, subject and object. To recollect would then coincide with an inward turn, a coiling up, so that an absolute beginning could be made in the Idea. It would be a momentary step back in order to take an absolute step forward. Yet for Kierkegaard's Socrates to recollect the Idea is to recollect only its non-recollectability.

21. There is a way in which the Socratic relation to the Idea (as Kierkegaard renders it) conforms to the double bind Kant later wrote of: "Human reason has a peculiar fate in one kind of its cognitions: it is troubled by questions that it cannot dismiss [i.e., questions con-

cerning the ground or unconditioned], because they are posed to it by the nature of reason itself, but that it also cannot answer, because they surpass human reason's every ability" (*CPR* A vii). Reason (*Vernunft*) is, by its very nature, a reference to what is "absolutely unconditioned" (*CPR* B 383); and yet the absolutely unconditioned cannot be thought as an object of possible experience—that is, it cannot be thought in any *determinate* way. Thus in Kant the Idea remains as an indeterminate ground (or horizon) of experience, meant to guide the understanding into its further use of grasping the plurality of experience always vis-à-vis more wholistically conceived conditions. The Idea is a ground that is never *given,* but always the telos of a movement of thought. This double bind is quite close to that of Kierkegaard's Socrates, except that for Kant the idea still functions as an explanatory ground—even if an ungiven one—for phenomena. It is a point of unification for phenomena. For Kierkegaard, by contrast, the idea positively interrupts and ungrounds phenomena.

22. John V. Smyth emphasizes the dimension of play within irony and is at the same time careful not to allow play to be interpreted as the mere opposite of work. See his *A Question of Eros: Irony in Sterne, Kierkegaard and Barthes* (Tallahassee: Florida State University Press, 1986), pp. 118–45.

23. *Hegel* 12:105–106; my translation. The term, as indicated, derives not from Hegel's interpretation of Socrates in his *Lectures on the History of Philosophy,* as does everything else in *The Concept of Irony,* but from his *Aesthetics.* To apply this term to the standpoint of Socrates is the unique gloss of Kierkegaard. However, from within a Hegelian conceptual field the gloss is coherent insofar as Hegelian manifestation presupposes the self-negation of the absolute.

24. This theme appears centrally in Hegel's philosophy of religion, where finite subjectivity is thought as the genuine "Other" to infinite or absolute subjectivity (i.e., God), the element in which it manifests and realizes itself. Thus Hegel, though grasping existing subjectivity in terms of an infinite negation, ultimately reduces its significance to the condition for the appearing of being, the locus in which absolute being manifests and realizes itself.

25. Thus total irony breaks with the basic structure of intelligibility that governs Hegel's phenomenology: the notion of an originary identity of essence and phenomenon that subsists within, and constitutes the ground of, their momentary difference. In fact, this is also the basic structure of intelligibility Plato presupposes, inasmuch as "in happy Greece essence and phenomenon were united as an immediate, natural qualification" (*CI* 212; *SKS* 1:256).

26. The actual picture to which Kierkegaard refers may be found in the Danish commentary volume to *SKS* 1, p. 169.

27. For a discussion of Kierkegaard's appropriation of Plato's *exaiphnes,* see chapter 6.

28. As a result, for Kierkegaard all poetry becomes in an essential sense "Platonic" and subsumable under the general operation of the Platonic beginning. All poetry is recollection in the Platonic rather than Socratic sense.

29. A contemporary example of this interpretation of the mythical in Plato can be found in Luc Brisson's *Plato the Myth Maker,* trans. Gerard Naddaf (Chicago: University of Chicago Press, 1998).

30. The language Kierkegaard uses here depends upon the Hegelian notions of estrangement and immediacy, along with the more general distinction between representation (*Vorstellung*) and concept (*Begriff*). Thus, even the reading of Plato is dominated by an essentially Hegelian philosophical apparatus. Nevertheless, Kierkegaard uses the terms only under the larger supervision of the critique of Hegel.

31. It must be noted, however, that Kierkegaard's understanding of the mythical leans heavily on Hegel. There are other understandings of the mythical in Plato that do not regard it as representative thinking. See for example John Sallis's reading of the *Timaeus* in his *Chorology* (Bloomington: Indiana University Press, 2000).

32. For a discussion of Hegel's critique of myth, see Jacques Derrida, *On the Name,* trans. David Wood, John P. Leavey, and Ian McLeod (Stanford: Stanford University Press, 1995), pp. 100–102.

33. Kierkegaard distinguishes the nothing of irony from both negative theology and dialectical thought in the following: "For irony, everything becomes nothing, but nothing can be taken in several ways. The speculative nothing is the nothing that disappears in each moment in the name of concretion, since it is itself the craving of the concrete, its *nisus formativus;* the mystic nothing is a nothing with regard to representation, a nothing that nevertheless is just as full of content as the silence of the night is full of sounds for someone who has ears to hear. Finally, the ironic nothing is the dead silence in which irony walks again and haunts (*spøger*) (the latter word taken altogether ambiguously)" (*CI* 258, altered; *SKS* 1:296). The ironic nothing, consequently, is neither dialectical nor mystical. The "mystical" nothing, as a nothing for representative thinking, is nothing as an excess of content, an excess of determination. Such a nothing, which bears close links to the sublime, probably refers just as much to Plato here as to negative theology.

34. The master metaphor that guides Hegel's reading of the history of philosophy as itself philosophy, i.e., as a unified problematic, is that of the plant producing itself through its various "moments." Hegel writes: "The principle of this projection into existence is that the germ cannot remain merely implicit, but is impelled towards development, since it presents the contradiction of being only implicit and yet not desiring so to be. But this coming without itself has an end in view; its completion fully reached, and its previously determined end is the fruit or produce of the germ, which causes a return to the first condition," *Lectures on the History of Philosophy,* vol. 1, p. 22 (*Hegel* 17:50–51).

2. ENDLESS TIME (*EITHER/OR* 1)

1. David Gouwens supplies a very useful survey of approaches to *Either/Or* 1 in his article "*Kierkegaard's* Either/Or, *Part One: Patterns of Interpretation,*" in *The International Kierkegaard Commentary,* Either/Or *Part I,* ed. Robert Perkins (Macon: Mercer University Press, 1995), pp. 5–50.

2. I refer to his *Broken Hegemonies,* trans. Reginald Lilly (Bloomington: Indiana University Press, 2003).

3. *Phenomenology of Spirit* 139 (*Hegel* 2:182).

4. *Phenomenology of Spirit* 140 (*Hegel* 2:183).

5. Alastair Hannay also finds the meaning of unhappy consciousness to be the central philosophical conflict between Kierkegaard and Hegel. See his *Kierkegaard* (London: Routledge, 1982), chapter 2.

6. See Ricoeur's article "Philosophy after Kierkegaard," in *Kierkegaard: A Critical Reader,* ed. Jonathan Rée and Jane Chamberlain, pp. 18–19.

7. See Hannay's *Kierkegaard,* p. 22.

8. *Phenomenology of Spirit* 140 (*Hegel* 2:183).

9. *Phenomenology of Spirit* 139 (*Hegel* 2:182).

10. *Phenomenology of Spirit* 126 (*Hegel* 2:166).

11. *Phenomenology of Spirit* 127 (*Hegel* 2:167).

12. Cf. Jean Hyppolite's discussion in *The Genesis and Structure of Hegel's Phenomenology of Spirit,* trans. Samuel Cherniak and John Heckman (Evanston: Northwestern University Press, 1974), pp. 190–215.

13. *Phenomenology of Spirit* 140 (*Hegel* 2:183).

14. See his *The Phenomenology of Moods in Kierkegaard* (The Hague: Martinus Nijhoff, 1978), p. 66.

15. "Ordinarily, he enjoys the honor of being regarded as being in his right mind, and yet he knows that if he were to explain to a single person how it really is with him, he would be declared insane. This is enough to drive one made, and yet this does not happen, and this is precisely his trouble" (*EOI* 225; *SKS* 2:218–19).

16. For a penetrating analysis of the category of madness in Kierkegaard, and its relation to German idealism, see John Llewelyn's article "On the Borderline of Madness," in *The New Kierkegaard*, ed. Elsebet Jegstrup (Bloomington: Indiana University Press, 2004), pp. 88–111.

17. Dorothea Glöckner makes this failure of language central to her analysis of unhappiness consciousness. She writes: "language never produces its subject, and always remains a speaking 'of' and 'about' something. However, this speaking 'of' and 'about' not only keeps a distance from its subject, but also makes it retreat into its singularity. Thus, language itself creates the absence of what it intends to express." See her article "The Unhappiest One— Merely an Inscription? On the Relationship between Immediacy and Language in the Work of Kierkegaard," in *Immediacy and Reflection in Kierkegaard's Thought*, ed. P. Cruysbergh (Leuven: Leuven University Press, 2003), pp. 41–53. See p. 52 for quotation.

18. Heidegger considers boredom in its revelatory power in his essay "What Is Metaphysics?" See *Martin Heidegger: Basic Writings,* ed. David Farrell Krell (San Francisco: Harper Collins, 1993), p. 99.

19. For an excellent discussion of the relation between Heidegger's analysis of boredom and that of A, see Pat Bigelow's *Kierkegaard and the Problem of Writing* (Tallahassee: Florida State University Press, 1987), pp. 114–32. Bigelow's analysis grasps the ontological or metaphysical horizon of "The Rotation of Crops" and so avoids merely reducing it to a statement of the "aesthetic point of view," and is one of the few analyses that does so.

20. A writes: "Guard against friendship" (*EOI* 295); "Never become involved in marriage" (*EOI* 296); "Never take any official post" (*EOI* 298).

21. In A 122, for example, Kant expresses the principle at stake in the transcendental deductions as follows: "all appearances must without exception enter the mind or be apprehended in such a way that they accord with the unity of apperception." Cf. *The Critique of Pure Reason,* p. 169. Kant does make an important distinction between the "ideal ground" of experience, the transcendental apperceptive unity of self-consciousness, and the "real ground" of experience, which is the "productive imagination." With regard to the latter, something that has a relation not only to romantic appropriations of Kant but to the "Crop Rotations" essay, Kant writes: "Hence the imagination is also a power of an a priori synthesis, and this is the reason why we give it the name of productive imagination. And insofar as the imagination's aim regarding everything manifold in appearance is nothing more than to provide necessary unity in the synthesis of appearance, this synthesis may be called the transcendental function of the imagination" (Ibid.). Kierkegaard's author, of course, transgresses Kant's distinction between the transcendental and the empirical by attempting to bring the productive imagination under the intentional supervision of consciousness.

22. The most extended analysis of the relation between the imagination and temporality in *The Critique of Pure Reason* is to be found in Heidegger's *Phenomenological Interpretation of Kant's* Critique of Pure Reason, trans. Parvis Emad and Kenneth Maly (Bloomington: Indiana University Press, 1997), pp. 227–73. Heidegger specifically privileges the first deduction, in which Kant relies upon the imagination as a transcendental power of synthesis.

23. *CPR* A 99; *Critique of Pure Reason,* p. 153.

24. *CPR* A 99; *Critique of Pure Reason,* p. 153.

25. *CPR* A 101; *Critique of Pure Reason,* p. 155.

26. *CPR* A 101; *Critique of Pure Reason,* p. 155.

27. *CPR* A 123; *Critique of Pure Reason,* p. 170.

28. I have abridged the story here. Kant goes on to argue that the unity brought about by the productive imagination is itself redeemable only vis-à-vis the categories of the under-

standing. He writes: "Hence the categories underlie all formal unity in the synthesis of the imagination, and, by means of this synthesis, underlie also the formal unity of all empirical use of the imagination down to the appearances." *CPR*, A 125, *Critique of Pure Reason*, p. 171.

29. Cf. his superb study analysis of Hegel's mediation in *In the Shadow of Hegel: Complementarity, History, and the Unconscious* (Gainesville: University Press of Florida, 1993), pp. 150–219.

30. Extending the metaphor of a rotation of crops, Elsebet Jegstrup interprets idleness as a kind of fallow period where all sorts of things spring from the empty ground with "no obvious purpose, no demands, no whys." She writes: "Only during an idle year can the field recover, regain its strength. Only during an idle year can thinking restore itself to its originary occupation: to think the in-between, think existence." See her essay "A rose by any other name. . ." in *The New Kierkegaard*, ed. Elsebet Jegstrup (Bloomington: Indiana University Press, 2004), p. 86.

3. ENTERING INTO PHILOSOPHY
(*DE OMNIBUS DUBITANDUM EST*)

1. According to an outline, the work, beginning with a discussion of Danish philosophy (Hans Martensen), was to have three subsequent chapters: on Hegel (chapter 2), Kant (chapter 3), and then Descartes and Spinoza (chapter 4) respectively. See *JC* 238 (*Pap.* IV B 2:18).

2. *Lectures on the History of Philosophy*, vol. 3, p. 224 (*Hegel* 19:335). As Jon Stewart suggests in his book *Kierkegaard's Relations to Hegel Reconsidered*, however, the title may also be an allusion to Hans Martensen's lectures on the history of philosophy, which Kierkegaard attended. Jon Stewart argues that, in fact, Kierkegaard's analysis only refers to Martensen, not to Hegel. However, this restriction seems unwarranted. Not only did Martensen himself lift the phrase from Hegel's *Lectures*, but in his notes Kierkegaard directly quotes Hegel's discussion of Descartes: "He [Johannes Climacus] regrets that he did not begin immediately with Descartes, all the more so because he recalls that Hegel praises Descartes for his 'childlike and simple exposition'" (*JC* 264–65; *Pap.* IV B, 13:17). Thus even if Kierkegaard's "narrative" constitutes a satire upon Martensen's lectures, as Stewart argues, this does not exclude its being a critical engagement with Hegel's reading of Descartes. The same goes for the issue of absolute knowledge. Stewart attempts to exonerate Hegel from the critique of absolute knowledge by suggesting that Kierkegaard intended to criticize only Martensen's caricature of Hegelian absolute knowing, not Hegel's "original doctrine itself." However, there are two problems with this: (1) Martensen himself actually criticizes, for theological reasons, Hegel's notion of absolute knowledge in his dissertation *The Autononomy of Self-Consciousness* (cf. "The Autonomy of Self-Consciousness in Modern Dogmatic Theology," trans. Curtis L. Thompson, in *Between Hegel and Kierkegaard: Hans L. Martensen's Philosophy of Religion*, p. 81). (2) Jon Stewart's understanding of absolute knowledge in Hegel treats it as a knowledge of the totality of transcendentals presupposed in any knowledge. This reading of Hegel, however legitimate, can surely not be simply stipulated as the "original doctrine itself." For a general critique of Stewart's book, see my article "Which Hegel? Reconsidering Hegel and Kierkegaard," in *Papers of the Nineteenth Century Theology Group*, ed. Andrew Burgess et al., vol. 35, pp. 15–34.

3. *Lectures on the History of Philosophy*, vol. 3, p. 217 (*Hegel* 19:328).

4. *Phenomenology of Spirit*, pp. 14–15 (*Hegel* 2:28).

5. In a notebook entry from 1839 Kierkegaard had already associated Hegel with the name Johannes Climacus: "Hegel is a Johannes Climacus who does not storm the heavens as do giants . . . but *climbs up* to them by means of syllogisms" (*JC* 231; *Pap.* II A, 335).

6. *Phenomenology of Spirit,* p. 15 (*Hegel* 19:328).

7. Ibid.

8. Ibid.

9. This is a point Heidegger emphasizes in his *Hegel's Concept of Experience,* trans. Kenley Royce Dove (New York: Octagon Books, 1983), pp. 43–48.

10. *Phenomenology of Spirit,* p. 10 (*Hegel* 2:23)

11. *Phenomenology of Spirit,* p. 11 (*Hegel* 2:24).

12. See John Sallis's essay "Hegel's Concept of Presentation, Its Determination in the Preface to the *Phenomenology of Spirit,*" in *The Phenomenology of Spirit Reader: Critical and Interpretive Essays,* ed. Jon Stewart (Albany: SUNY Press, 1998), p. 40.

13. Ibid.

14. *Lectures on the History of Philosophy,* vol. 3, p. 217 (*Hegel* 19:328).

15. Ibid., p. 224 (*Hegel* 19:335).

16. Ibid., p. 228 (*Hegel* 19:339).

17. Yet Hegel will also say that Descartes *only* begins, i.e., he does not redeem the promise of the beginning he himself inaugurates. In this sense there is a deep coherence between the way Hegel reads *Socrates* and the way he reads Descartes. Descartes, like Socrates, posits the identity of subject and object on the side of the subject, i.e., in terms of self-consciousness—and in that sense he begins. But what is necessary, according to Hegel, is to develop this beginning by showing the identity of subject and object *on the side of the subject* with the identity of subject and object *on the side of the object.* In other words, it is necessary to show how it is that the identity of subject and object within self-consciousness is itself dependent upon, and a result of, an objective process outside itself (a historical and material process); and, on the other hand, it is necessary to show how the identity of subject and object on the side of the object has come about through a teleological process, a purposive process, and is to that extent subjective.

18. In this sense, for Hegel modernity has Christianity—the Incarnation—as its guiding ontological presupposition.

19. *Lectures on the History of Philosophy,* vol. 1, p. 6 (*Hegel* 17:33).

20. Ibid., p. 30 (*Hegel* 17:59).

21. Ibid., p. 5 (*Hegel* 17:31–32).

22. Ibid., p. 27 (*Hegel* 17:56).

23. Ibid., p. 33 (*Hegel* 17:62).

24. *Phenomenology of Spirit,* p. 16 (*Hegel* 2:31).

25. Qualification is necessary, however, because this is not a transcendental problematic in the Kantian or Fichtean sense, according to which the step back from the phenomena to the conditions of their possibility is made with a view toward grounding the possibility of a *knowledge* of the phenomena. In idealism the transcendental, which is opposed to the empirical, is that which grounds. In Fichte's term, the transcendental ego is the *Erklärungsgrund* of the phenomenal order. Thus the transcendental question always concerns the possibility of objectivity. Here, by contrast, the problematic attempts to discover the essential possibility of doubt, an experience of a subject—not this or that particular subject, but any subject. It is a question concerning the subjectivity of the subject rather than the objectivity of the object.

26. In a footnote he refers to the movement of the first part of the *Phenomenology* from consciousness to self-consciousness, or reason, through the stages of "sense certainty" (*sinnliches Bewusstsein*), "perception" (*wahrnehmendes Bewusstsein*), and "understanding" (*Verstand*). Cf. *JC* 169; *Pap.* IV B, 147. It would appear from the notes that Kierkegaard had intended to think through all of these transitions "for himself" in the form of a narrative and thus follow the development of the *Phenomenology.* Of particular interest for him was the question as to how self-consciousness emerges out of consciousness: "It would be really in-

teresting to see how Hegel would formulate the transition from consciousness to self-consciousness, from self-consciousness to reason. When the transition consists merely of a heading, it is easy enough" (ibid.).

27. *Phenomenology of Spirit*, p. 60 (*Hegel* 2:83).

28. Ibid., pp. 63–64 (*Hegel* 2:88–89).

29. Ibid., p. 60 (*Hegel* 2:83).

30. This is not to say, of course, that on Hegel's terms every representation is true, only
that representation is the locus of whatever is true. The discovery that some representation
is false itself depends upon a more adequate representation, where "adequacy" is a function
of coherence rather than correspondence.

31. See his discussion of Hegel's "sense certainty" in his *Logic and Existence*, trans. Leonard Lawler and Amit Sen (Albany: SUNY Press, 1997), pp. 7–21.

32. Heinrich Schmidinger has analyzed the proximity and distance between Kierkegaard
and Fichte on this crucial point in his important article "Kierkegaard und Fichte" in *Gregorianum* 52 (1971): 499–542. Whereas both Fichte and Kierkegaard share, he argues, the essential practical and ethical understanding of actuality as emergence through the free deed
of the subject, the difference is this: for Fichte the act of radical self-positing establishes the
absolute and founding character of the ego, whereas Kierkegaard maintains a subject who is
"radically finite" (p. 531). The meaning of radical finitude comes out in the following:
"spirit is thus given when the human being relates to himself; but to relate to oneself is possible only once this 'self' is already given" (ibid.). It is not only the self that is given, but the
relation of the self to itself—which is to say its difference from itself—is also given. This results, Schmidinger notes, in a circular notion of self-constitution: "The entire act of the self-
constitution of spirit takes place circularly according to Kierkegaard. For in it the two sides
of the relation, which are to be synthesized, presuppose their opposition to one another,
even though this opposition is first produced only through the two terms" (p. 533). What
Schmidinger is getting at conforms with the analysis here: self-consciousness both presupposes and effects its difference from itself; it both presupposes and effects a "collision." What
Fichte erases is the original structure of presupposing, for that is what makes spirit radically
finite.

33. Cf. J. G. Fichte, *Introductions to the Wissenschaftslehre and Other Writings*, trans.
Daniel Breazeale (Indianapolis: Hackett, 1994), p. 42 (*Fichte* 1:459).

34. The "collision" that conditions consciousness resembles Fichte's "block" (*Anstoss*).
Fichte's *Wissenschaftslehre*, however, is an effort to explain experience in general. It thus involves a dialectic of three fundamental principles. The second of these is directly relevant to
Kierkegaard's text. In order to account for experience, which is always that of a subject over
against an object, and hence something twofold, and in order to make sense of moral striving, Fichte posits a "block" (*Anstoss*) that interrupts the pure thetic activity of the absolute
ego. The purely self-positing ego collides with something "other." By means of this collision,
something that is strictly transcendental, diremption is produced within the pure ego. Concrete consciousness emerges in the difference. Within experience, the concrete or empirical
ego can relate to its own pure thetic activity as something purely ideal. Fichtean dialectic
thus moves from identity through difference back to identity (though it will never have
achieved this—moral striving is infinite).

35. *Phenomenology of Spirit*, p. 53 (*Hegel* 2:76).

4. REPETITION (*REPETITION*)

1. *Radical Hermeneutics: Repetition, Deconstruction and the Hermeneutic Project*
(Bloomington: Indiana University Press, 1987), p. 34. See also Niels Nymann Eriksen's re-
cent work *Kierkegaard's Category of Repetition, A Reconstruction* (New York: Walter de

Gruyter, 2000), which poses the question in this way. He regards the question of repetition in a threefold way: as a question of historicality, a question of the Other, and a question of becoming. In addition he makes the highly interesting suggestion that Kierkegaard's category can be thematized only vis-à-vis the thematization of nihilism that takes place in Nietzsche's work. "The very meaning of repetition," he writes, "presupposes the breakdown of the dualisms of traditional metaphysics" (p. 8). The modern horizon of repetition thus signifies the moment in which the metaphysical impulses of Western thought have in some sense arrived at a moment of completion and, hence, overturning. My reading supports this basic line of interpretation.

2. Cf. *FTR* 302; *Pap.* IV B 117, 281.

3. On this point, see Gilles Deleuze in *Difference and Repetition,* trans. Paul Patton (New York: Columbia University Press, 1994), pp. 1–3.

4. Cf. his "Second Introduction" to the *Wissenschaftslehre* in *Introductions to the Wissenschaftslehre and Other Writings,* p. 47 (*Fichte* 1:463).

5. Fichte develops the contrast between idealism, which aims at the justification of freedom by showing reality to have its ground in the ego, and dogmatism, which seeks to justify the absoluteness of causal sequence by grounding experience in a transcendent "thing in itself," in paragraph five of his first introduction. See ibid., pp. 15–20 (*Fichte* 1:429–35).

6. Ibid., p. 18 (*Fichte* 1:433).

7. Ibid.

8. See especially book three of *Vocation of Man,* pp. 67–123 (*Fichte* 2:248–319).

9. This is where the problematic of *Repetition,* as one of freedom, departs from Fichte, and not only from Fichte, but from every effort to ground freedom in the generality of law—for example, in stoicism. In the notes Kierkegaard comments: "Consequently, what freedom fears here is not repetition but variation; what it wants is not variation but repetition. If this will to repetition is stoicism, then it contradicts itself and thereby ends in destroying itself in order to affirm repetition in that way, which is the same as throwing a thing away in order to hide it most securely" (*R* 302; *Pap.* IV B, 112). The will to repetition, as freedom's interest in retaining itself, will easily be confused with stoic apatheia. The stoic seeks a repetition of freedom through the conformity of will to the generality of law, the logos of being. Freedom preserves itself by passively submerging itself in being—which is the same as trying to hide something most securely, and so preserve it against all loss, by throwing it away.

10. This passage I refer to is this: "Many times it has happened: lifted out of the body into myself; becoming external to all other things and self-encentered; beholding a marvelous beauty; then, more than ever, assured of community with the loftiest order; enacting the noblest life, acquiring identity with the divine; stationing within It by having attained that activity; poised above whatsoever within the Intellectual is less than the Supreme: yet, there comes the moment of decent from intellection to reasoning, and after that sojourn in the divine, I ask myself how it happens that I can now be descending, and how did the Soul ever enter into my body, the Soul which, even within the body, is the high thing it has shown itself to be." Translation from Stephen MacKenna, *Plotinus: The Enneads* (Burdett, N.Y.: Larson Publications, 1992), p. 410.

11. See especially *Enneads* V 5, 8 for a critique of method. The radiant burst of the One is an event for which one can only wait. Plotinus writes: "But we ought not to question whence [it comes]; there is no whence, no coming or going in place; now it is seen and now not seen. We must not run after it, but fit ourselves for the vision and then wait tranquilly for its appearance, as the eye waits on the rising of the sun, which in its own time appears above the horizon." Ibid., p. 470.

12. Jean Wahl has pointed to the proximity and distance between Kierkegaard and Plotinus. He writes: "The tension of subjectivity is explained by the presence of transcendence.

The one who is more subjective, enclosed within himself, immediately discovers the transcendent. [The soul by itself before God alone], there is a retrieval here of the ideas of Plotinus. But [in Kierkegaard] the soul is more enclosed upon itself, and God is more enclosed upon God, than in Plotinus and the mystics who follow the Neoplatonists. There is not in Kierkegaard this same confluence of the soul with God and the same expansion, not the same overflowing of God into the soul. There is here a force of negation more powerful, an opposition of the individual more irreducible [than in Plotinus]." See Jean Wahl, Subjectivité et Transcendance, in *Kierkegaard: L'Un devant l'Autre* (Paris: Hachette Litérratures, 1998), p. 206.

13. In his *Lectures on the History of Philosophy* Hegel uses the term "the Eleatics" to refer to the position opposing Heraclitus. In addition, like Kierkegaard Hegel explicitly considers the Heraclitean dialectic in temporal, and not merely spatial, terms. Finally, Hegel thinks Heraclitus's great advance was to think being, not monistically like Parmenides, but precisely as mediation. Hegel writes: "Not this immediate being, but absolute mediation, Being as thought of, Thought itself, is the true Being," *Lectures on the History of Philosophy*, vol. 1, p. 293 (*Hegel* 17:364). Thus, Hegel interprets the relation between the Eleatics and Heraclitus as mediation—this is the framing that Kierkegaard's author contests.

14. Ibid., p. 283 (*Hegel* 17:349).

15. Ibid., p. 282 (*Hegel* 17:348). Although, according to Hegel, the Eleatic school also inaugurates an authentically speculative beginning, it is less secure than Heraclitus. The great speculative thought of Parmenides, in particular, Hegel records as follows: "it is necessary that saying and thinking should be Being; for Being is, but nothing is not at all" (252; *Hegel* 17:310). To this Hegel comments: "There the matter is stated in brief; and in this nothing, falls negation generally, or in more concrete form, limitation, the finite restriction. . . . Parmenides says that whatever form the negation may take, it does not exist at all" (ibid.). Hence, Being as Being is the absolute, simple One, the radical exclusion of any change, becoming, multiplicity, determination, finitude, etc. Absolute Being in this sense, however, only is in the thought of being—for sense experience, the absolute is not at all. Correlative with the idea that "only Being is, non-Being is not" is therefore the absolute identity of thought and Being—a genuinely speculative affirmation. On Hegel's narrative it is Zeno, another Eleatic, who develops the Parmenidean dialectic in the explicit denial of the reality of movement. Zeno does not deny the appearance of movement, but rather, on the basis of the speculative interpretation of being as alone what is, he denies the truth or reality of movement. Hegel writes: "the fact that there is movement is as sensuously certain as that there are elephants; it is not in this sense that Zeno meant to deny movement. The point in question concerns its truth. Movement, however, is held to be untrue, because the conception of it involves a contradiction; by that he meant to say that no true Being can be predicated of it" (266; *Hegel* 17:324).

16. Ibid., p. 283 (*Hegel* 17:349).

17. Ibid., p. 284 (*Hegel* 17:350).

18. Ibid., p. 283 (*Hegel* 17:349).

19. Ibid., p. 287 (*Hegel* 17:355).

20. Ibid.

21. Ibid., p. 286 (*Hegel* 17:355).

22. Ibid., p. 293 (*Hegel* 17:364).

23. *Hegel's Science of Logic*, p. 824.

24. Niels Eriksen suggests an absolutely decisive quality of repetition by saying that "repetition never takes place when elements within a totality recur, but only when the totality itself recurs." He continues: "Repetition in the proper sense, therefore, does not allow for a spectator, for it only happens to the whole, to a totality, a world, consciousness." See his *Kierkegaard's Category of Repetition*, p. 10.

25. This phrase would be to say, in a precise way, that repetition constitutes not an event in or of the world, but the event whereby there is a world. Mooney writes of this: "What is 'repeated,' restored, is a world infused with objects of sustaining value, an enigmatic, value-saturated world whose power, allure, and potential for support far exceeds whatever muffled thoughts or passing theory might arise about the ground or source of that world bequeathed." Thus, as I also will argue, the problematic of repetition leads to the groundlessness of what appears. See his essay "Repetition: Getting the World Back," in *The Cambridge Companion to Kierkegaard,* ed. Gordon Marino and Alastair Hannay (Cambridge: Cambridge University Press, 1998), pp. 282–307. Citation from pp. 301–302.

26. See for example *FTR* 310; *Pap.* IV 117, 290.

27. *Philosophical Investigations into the Essence of Human Freedom and Related Matters,* p. 222 (*Schelling* 4:231).

28. Ibid., p. 238 (*Schelling* 4:251).

29. Ibid.

30. Ibid.

31. Ibid., p. 228 (*Schelling* 4:239).

32. Ibid.

33. From this point of view one can see how, from Kierkegaard's point of view, it would be a monstrosity to confuse repetition with the regularities of the world such as the rotations of the stars. This would be to confuse repetition with immanent continuity, or duration.

34. Kierkegaard owned Jacob Boehme's collected works and it can be established, at a minimum, that he read at least Boehme's *The Way to Christ.* Cf. *Pap.* III A 125. In addition, Kierkegaard was well acquainted with the texts of Franz von Baader—both his *Vorlesungen uber die Speculative Dogmatik* and *Fermenta Cognitionis*—in which both Eckhart and Boehme figure prominently.

35. Yet, it must be said, both Boehme and Schelling remain ambiguous on the role of otherness in relation to divine self-constitution. In his *The Way to Christ,* for example, Boehme writes: "No thing may be revealed to itself without contrariety. If it has no thing that resists it, it always goes out from itself and does not go into itself again. If it does not go into itself again, as into that out of which it originally came, it knows nothing of its cause." See his treatise "The Seventh Treatise on the Precious Gate of Divine Contemplation," in *The Way to Christ,* trans. Peter Erb (New York: Paulist Press, 1978), p. 196. For Boehme this dialectic operates at the most general level as the dynamic through which the hidden God manifests himself as God, i.e., as ground, only through the production of a "counter-stroke" (*Gegenwurf*)—i.e., through the act of creation. This would seem to suggest that, not unlike Hegel, God needs otherness in order to constitute Godself as God. It is no surprise, perhaps, that Hegel too could claim Boehme as a speculative thinker in his sense. Hegel's appropriation of Boehme is explicitly flagged in paragraph 248 of the *Encyclopedia of the Philosophical Sciences* as well as in his discussion of Boehme in his *Lectures on the History of Philosophy* (vol. 3). Hegel's appropriation of Boehme, in which he retrieves the central idea that divine self-manifestation occurs through a dialectical struggle of contraries, nevertheless emphasizes its possibilities for a radically immanent, totalizing thinking. The links between Boehme and Hegel have been articulated most clearly and forcefully by Cyril O'Regan and David Walsh. See O'Regan's *Gnostic Apocalypse,* pp. 216–19; and especially his *The Heterodox Hegel,* pp. 152–53, 180–87, 223–31. See also David Walsh, *The Mysticism of Inner-worldly Fulfillment: A Study of Jacob Boehme* (Gainesville: University Presses of Florida, 1983). I would suggest, however, that Hegel's appropriation of Boehme is problematic. Even if there is an "erotic" dimension to God in Boehme (as O'Regan argues), i.e., a self-seeking, this coexists with a just as radical "agapaic" dimension of letting otherness be.

36. Alexander Koyré writes: "in relation to God [Boehme] posits a creature who is just as free as God himself and who ought to collaborate with God in the very work of creation—

a creature free to the point that its freedom comes to limit the divine omnipotence, free in an inalienable way and thus in all of its acts purely and entirely responsible for its action." Cf. *La Philosophie de Jacob Boehme* (Paris: J. Vrin, 1979), p. 478.

37. Dorothea Glöckner argues that repetition and recollection must be thought, not simply as particular acts, but as the acts through which consciousness first constitutes itself. See her book *Kierkegaards Begriff der Wiederholung* (Berlin, New York: Walter de Gruyter, 1998).

38. *Lectures on the History of Philosophy*, vol. 2, p. 34 (*Hegel* 18:204).

39. *Symposium*, 211.

40. Repetition thus refers to the ontological conditions of life rather than knowledge. In this regard Kierkegaard refers explicitly to Schelling's "philosophy of nature (in the stricter sense)" (*FTR* 322; *Pap.* IV B 117, 7), which is presumably a reference to Schelling's *Ideas for a Philosophy of Nature.* This supposition is strengthened by noticing that, in the introduction to that text, Schelling engages in a very explicit retrieval of the thought of Leibniz. Schelling writes that "the time has come when [Leibniz'] philosophy can be re-established." See his "Introduction" to the second edition (1803) of *Ideas for a Philosophy of Nature*, trans. by Errol Harris and Peter Heath (New York: Cambridge University Press, 1988), p. 16 and pp. 27-29. Though, it must be added, Schelling's retrieval of Leibniz, though basic, always operates within a more foundational retrieval of Spinoza.

41. John Caputo is certainly right to link repetition, as a task, to the act of *interpretation* rather than the act of knowledge. In this regard, this is a deep link between repetition and the renewal of any decision that has a primarily future orientation—for example, a promise. A promise must be recollected forward, i.e. interpreted ever anew. One could not keep a promise without recollecting the promise, and yet to keep one's promise in the midst of life is to have to recollect it in always different ways, i.e. in always new, unanticipated circumstances and in relation to unanticipated consequences. What it means to give one's word continually demands renewal, a new beginning in each moment. Of course there is continuity between moments, but continuity only follows from repetition, it does not precede it. At a limit, one could even imagine a scenario where, in order to keep one's word, it would be necessary to break one's word. See Caputo's *Radical Hermeneutics*, pp. 30f.

42. Sylviane Agacinski understands the section on farce to be central to the book as well: "If *Repetition* operates a mise en abyme on itself and on the concept of the book . . . then the farce at the heart of *Repetition* does not occur as a digression or hole in the text." See her *Aparté: Conceptions and Deaths of Søren Kierkegaard*, p. 166.

43. Kant lists four "modalities" of judgments about beauty: they are disinterested, universal, they relate to a purposiveness without a purpose, and they presume a *sensus communis.* See *The Critique of Judgment,* trans. Werner Pluhar (Indianapolis: Hackett, 1987), sections 1–23.

44. Ibid., p. 99.

45. Ibid.

46. Ibid., p. 116.

47. As John Sallis observes, to this extent the dialectic of the sublime articulates the fundamental metaphysical move: the separation of the phenomena and what lies beyond the phenomena and the orientation of human beings within the phenomenal world basically toward what lies beyond. See his *Spacings—of Reason and Imagination in the Texts of Kant, Fichte, Hegel* (Chicago: University of Chicago Press, 1987), pp. 85–90.

48. George Pattison points to the fundamentally ontological horizon of recollection in this sense: "So, in Constantin Kierkegaard brings out the inner equation of Platonic idealism: that to journey beyond the image bearing surface of life and art (upward?) to the realm of the ideal, which is beyond all images, is to undertake a training for death and to escape from the flux of time in which alone a repetition might be possible." See his article "The

Magic of Theatre: The Drama of Existence in Kierkegaard's *Repetition* and Hesse's *Steppen-wolf*," in *International Kierkegaard Commentary: Fear and Trembling and Repetition,* ed. Robert Perkins (Macon: Mercer University Press, 1994), p. 368.

49. I refer, of course, to his fateful engagement with Regina Olsen.

50. Eriksen adds: "This procedure of projecting oneself into a distant future and then back again to the present moment is 'the second power of the dream.'" See his *Kierkegaard's Category of Repetition,* p. 31.

51. Cf. *Being and Time,* trans. Joan Stambaugh (Albany: SUNY Press, 1996), p. 127.

52. The position of Job, we can see, presupposes the Schellingian-Boehmean account of creation as repetition, creation as divine *Gelassenheit.* God may be a radical condition of self-consciousness, but cannot be its ground—not, at least, as long as self-consciousness is grasped in its radicality as self-positing.

53. "The young man I have brought into being as a poet" (*FTR* 228; *SKS* 4:94).

54. On this point see also Louis Mackey, *Points of View, Readings of Kierkegaard* (Tallahassee: Florida State University Press, 1986), p. 95; and John Caputo, *Radical Hermeneutics,* p. 27.

55. *Difference and Repetition,* p. 8.

56. Cf. Elrod, *Being and Existence in Kierkegaard's Pseudonymous Works,* p. 229.

5. ABSOLUTE RELATION TO THE AB-SOLUTE
(*FEAR AND TREMBLING*)

1. What I am referring to especially is a "divine command" theory of ethics according to which God's command would constitute the unique and authoritative origin of any imperative. On this reading of *Fear and Trembling* the conflict at issue is between God's commands and commands traceable to autonomous consciousness. The point would be to say that, in case of such conflict, God's command ought to "trump" the principles of practical reason. For a divine command reading see C. Steven Evans's "Is the Concept of an Absolute Duty to God Morally Unintelligible?" in *Kierkegaard's* Fear and Trembling, *Critical Appraisals,* ed. Robert Perkins (University: University of Alabama Press, 1981), pp. 140–51. For an important rebuttal of this reading, see Ronald Green's article "Enough Is Enough! *Fear and Trembling* Is *Not* about Ethics," *Journal of Religious Ethics* 21, no. 2 (Fall 1993): 191–209. Green argues that the book constitutes, albeit obliquely, a "modern discussion of the classical Pauline-Lutheran theme of the justification by faith" (192)—particularly, whether God can suspend ethics in the name of forgiveness.

2. One should also note that the text opens as a fairy tale: "Once upon a time there was a man who as a child had heard that beautiful story of how God tempted Abraham and of how Abraham withstood the temptation, kept the faith, and, contrary to expectation, got a son a second time" (*FTR* 9; *SKS* 4:105). One thus has to know how to keep aesthetic distance, how *not* to take the binding of Isaac seriously. The binding of Isaac is not *in itself* important; it is important only as a figure for something else.

3. See his article "The View from Pisgah, A Reading of *Fear and Trembling,*" in *Kierkegaard: A Collection of Critical Appraisals,* ed. Josiah Thompson (New York: Anchor Books, 1972), pp. 422–23.

4. Edward Mooney's *Knights of Faith and Resignation: Reading Kierkegaard's Fear and Trembling* (Albany: SUNY Press, 1992) organizes the entire book around the category of the ordeal. He articulates various forms of the ordeal in play in *Fear and Trembling:* ordeals of meaning, of love, of reason, of reconciliation, and of silence. Crucially involved in his conception of the ordeal are "terrible deadlocks," or double binds, that render an encounter with what ungrounds impossible to avoid. My approach dovetails quite strongly with Mooney's.

5. Cf. *Elements of the Philosophy of Right,* trans. H. B. Nisbet (New York: Cambridge University Press, 1991), p. 157.

6. Cf. *Introduction to the Philosophy of History,* trans. Leo Rauch (Indianapolis: Hackett, 1988), p. 42.

7. Yet Johannes could also refer to Pythagoras: "the single individual as the single individual is higher than the universal, something I can also express symbolically in a statement by Pythagoras to the effect that the odd number is more perfect than the even number" (*FTR* 62; *SKS* 4:155).

8. This is the reason, as Edward Mooney argues, that Abraham cannot be assimilated to fanaticism. He writes: "The knight of faith does not seek out dilemma [i.e., the suspension of the ethical], but is unhappily saddled with it. . . . If the knight of faith can be Abraham or a serving maid or a shopman, then we are forced away from reading the story as advocating sacrifice on demand," *Knights of Faith and Resignation,* p. 84.

9. Kant expresses this idea in the opening sentences of his *Religion* book as follows: "So far as morality is based upon the conception of [the human being] as a free agent who, just because he is free, binds himself through his reason to unconditional laws, it stands in need neither of the idea of another Being over him, for him to apprehend his duty, nor of an incentive other than the law itself, for him to do his duty." Cf. *Religion within the Limits of Reason Alone,* trans. Theodore Green and Hoyt Hudson (New York: Harper, 1960), p. 3.

10. Kant writes: "But there is something so strange in this idea of the absolute value of a mere will, in which no account is taken of any useful results, that in spite of all the agreement received even from ordinary reason, yet there must arise the suspicion that such an idea may perhaps have as its hidden basis merely some high-flown fancy, and that we may have misunderstood the purpose of nature in assigning to reason the governing of our will." Cf. *Grounding for the Metaphysics of Morals,* trans. James W. Ellington (Indianapolis: Hackett, 1981), p. 8.

11. For Nietzsche, these questions were not obvious. Nietzsche's well-known "genealogy" finds moral interest to be a modality or manifestation of a fundamental life-drive, a will to power. Apart from his particular narrative of the "transvaluation of values," at least Nietzsche raises the question of the interest that stands underneath the moral interest.

12. *Grounding for the Metaphysics of Morals,* p. 52.

13. Ibid., p. 53.

14. My translation. Cf. *Hegel's Philosophy of Mind,* trans. A. V. Miller (Oxford: Oxford University Press, 1983), p. 276.

15. See Levinas's essay "Existence and Ethics," p. 32.

16. Ibid.

17. Ibid., p. 31.

18. Ibid., p. 28. It is evident here that Levinas interprets the "anxiety and distress"—which indeed are fundamental to Johannes's account of Abraham—along the lines of Heideggarian concern (*Sorge*).

19. Ibid., p. 33. From another side Levinas's objection against the priority of the "religious" over the "ethical" could be reinforced. According to Feuerbach, too, faith is always and essentially a sacrifice of the other person to God. By rendering thanks to God for a meal, for example, I cover over and exclude the concrete mediations without which there would be no meal. In other words, I take from the mediated sphere of the human, of labor, and give to God. I render the other invisible in the very act of thanking and responding to God.

20. Set side by side with Levinas, John Llewelyn suspects Kierkegaard's egology as well. He writes: "With Kierkegaard, however, the self chooses itself. It remains egological, if not egoistic. With Kierkegaard selfhood is affect or passion. With Levinas it is the affect of affect, the passion of passion before the face of another. In the first place this is the face of another human being." See his article "On the Borderline of Madness," p. 106.

21. These are the terms of *Otherwise than Being or Beyond Essence,* trans. Alphonso Lingis (Pittsburgh: Duquesne University Press, 1981).

22. Ibid., p. 52.

23. Ibid., p. 53.

24. Ibid., p. 52.

25. Ibid.

26. *The Gift of Death,* trans. David Wills (Chicago: University of Chicago Press, 1995), p. 66.

27. Ibid., pp. 68–69.

28. Derrida sketches the relations between Kierkegaard and Levinas in the following way: "One of them [Kierkegaard] keeps in reserve the possibility of reserving the quality of the wholly other, in other words of the *infinite other,* for God alone. . . . The other [Levinas] attributes to or recognizes in this infinite alterity of the wholly other, every other, in other words each, each one, for example each man and woman. Even in its critique of Kierkegaard concerning ethics and generality Levinas' thinking stays within the game—the play of difference and analogy—between the face of God and the face of my neighbor, between the infinitely other as God and the infinitely other as another human. . . . Kierkegaard would have to admit, as Levinas reminds him, that ethics is also the order of and respect for absolute singularity, and not only that of the generality or of the repetition of the same. He cannot therefore distinguish so easily between the ethical and the religious. But for his part, in taking into account absolute singularity, that is, the absolute alterity obtaining in relations between one human and another, Levinas is no longer able to distinguish between the infinite alterity of God and that of every human. His ethics is a religious one." Ibid., pp. 83–84.

29. For a discussion of the relations between Levinas and Derrida in the interpretation of *Fear and Trembling,* cf. John Caputo's essay "Instants, Secrets and Singularities: Dealing Death in Kierkegaard and Derrida," in *Kierkegaard in Post/Modernity,* ed. Martin J. Matuštík and Merold Westphal (Bloomington: Indiana University Press, 1995), pp. 224–28. For a critique of Derrida's reading, cf. David Wood's essay "Thinking God in the Wake of Kierkegaard," in *Kierkegaard: A Critical Reader,* ed. Jonathan Rée and Jane Chamberlain (Massachusetts: Blackwell, 1998), pp. 62–68.

30. Ibid., p. 67.

31. Ibid., p. 79.

32. Derrida, no doubt, would want to transform insight into the aporia of responsibility into the possibility of a permanent *critique* of ethical purity. The point would be to show the incompleteness of every ethical program, of all "clean hands," in the name of a justice that remains always *to come.* This would be to convert tragic wisdom into something like messianic affirmation; and in this sense, the "religious," or at least its trace, arises again at the heart of the ethical (or *as* the ethical?). This double gesture of inscribing possibility within some aporia, i.e., impossibility, is one Derrida repeats across a number of thematics: gift, hospitality, forgiveness. This reading of Derrida forms the horizon of Mark Dooley's effort to link *Fear and Trembling* to the Derridean problematic of justice. See Dooley's *The Politics of Exodus* (New York: Fordham University Press, 2001).

33. Ibid., p. 45.

34. In comedy the concealed factor is a bit of nonsense, in tragedy something more serious. Johannes's strategy is thus to consider various kinds of concealment in their tension with the ethical demand for disclosure in order to throw light on the possibility of some essential concealment that cannot become disclosed either comically or tragically.

35. Could it be because Sarah is a woman? For in the midst of his discussion of Sarah, Johannes suddenly changes tack and imagines Sarah to be a man. In that case, he says, "the demonic is immediately present" (*FTR* 104; *SKS* 4:193). Imagined as a man, Sarah becomes similar to Gloucester from Shakespeare's *Richard III*—a character become demonically self-

enclosed as a result of physical deformity. The demonic exaggerates self-positing to the point of defiance of any givens. Yet it gains its energy for this exaggeration by way of a single point of givenness: itself, its suffering, as exceptional. A man could not, apparently, avoid the demonic, and so any analogy between a man in Sarah's position and Abraham would collapse. It may also be that Kierkegaard is imagining himself as Sarah.

36. Another reason for saying that Abraham tolerates no analogies may also be in play: as the *unique* figure of pure releasement, capable of letting go his own absolutely, Abraham fulfills the role the Eckhartian tradition, at least, assigned to Christ. In the *German Theology*, a text Kierkegaard refers to in 1843, we find the following: "[Christ] was the freest, most unfettered, least I-bound will that ever appeared, ever was, ever will be in human form," *The Theological Germanica of Martin Luther*, trans. Bengt Hoffman (New York: Paulist Press, 1980), p. 141. Perhaps Kierkegaard's author is thinking Abraham as Christ—at least, that is, Christ insofar as he would fulfill the purely human (im)possibility of existence at the limit. Perhaps, then, the insistence upon the uniqueness of Abraham discloses Christ's palimpsestic presence in this text. That would explain why the problematic of sin is alluded to but explicitly bracketed from *Fear and Trembling*. "Sin," Johannes writes, "is not the first immediacy; sin is a later immediacy. In sin the single individual is already higher than (in the direction of the demonic paradox) the universal." (*FTR* 98; *SKS* 4:188). Sin is a later immediacy, qualified as demonic, in the sense that it comes about vis-à-vis an instant no longer recallable: an event not within presence, but one that qualifies the present as something *posited* through the self. Sin interprets positing not as the truth of consciousness, but as its untruth. Though a "later immediacy," sin cannot explain Abraham's position: "If there is any question of an analogy, it must be the paradox of sin, but this again is in another sphere and cannot explain Abraham [i.e., Christ?] and is itself far easier to explain than Abraham" (*FTR* 112; *SKS* 4:200).

37. In his *Knights of Faith and Resignation* Ed Mooney puzzles over the phrase, suggesting its "vaguely blasphemous ring," p. 40. He suggests the following: "is the idea that, through faith, my self is given new birth, through the engendering power of a new father? On this view, the father whose faithful work provides the condition for his son's return, a new son, also provides the condition, it seems, for newly being himself a son," pp. 40–41. Mooney's intuitions are sound. The only thing to be added is to recognize that to give birth to one's own father is a trope within Eckhartian apophaticism.

38. Derrida uses this phrase in several places, first of all in his short book *Speech and Phenomena*, trans. David B. Allison (Evanston: Northwestern University Press, 1973), pp. 88–104.

39. Cf. *Meister Eckhart, The Essential Sermons*, p. 194. The theme of *Gottesgeburt*, or the birth of the Son in the soul, also appears centrally in sermons 2 and 6. For an analysis of the theme of the birth of God in the soul in Eckhart, see Reiner Schürmann's *Wandering Joy*, pp. 72–78, 165–67. Schürmann shows that what characterizes the Eckhartian event of birth is not a movement of ecstasies beyond temporality, as in other forms of Neoplatonism, but precisely a penetration into time. In explicit contrast with Plotinus, Schürmann writes: "In Eckhart there is no appeal to a privileged experience, no regret of falling back into the body after a repose in the divine, and above all no opposition between a higher world and a lower world into which the soul is resigned to redescend. If in his comprehension of time Eckhart is indebted to Neoplatonic mysticism, he modifies its meaning throughout, moving away from an 'ecstatic' comprehension to a 'worldly' comprehension of the instant: flight from the present situation turns into a way of being with it," *Wandering Joy*, p. 15.

40. The theme of *Gelassenheit* is omnipresent in Eckhart's German sermons as well as in pietists such as Arndt, Boehme, Teersteegen, etc. Cf. for example sermon 52. For an analysis of Eckhart's *Gelassenheit*, cf. John Caputo's *The Mystical Element in Heidegger's Thought* (New York: Fordham University Press, 1978), pp. 118–27 and Reiner Schürmann's *Wan-*

dering Joy: Meister Eckhart's Mystical Philosophy (Great Barrington, Mass.: Lindisfarne Books, 2001), pp. 81–96.

41. Without developing the point, Agacinski explicitly links Eckhart's "dialectic of detachment" to that of repetition and faith. See her *Aparté,* p. 143.

42. *Introduction to the Philosophy of History,* p. 82.

43. The reference to Fichte becomes all the more forceful as soon as one recalls the problematic of his texts: they seek to establish the priority of faith to knowledge, the inner to the outer, a "divine world order" (*eine göttliche Weltregierung*) to the order of history. In his essay "On the Basis of Our Belief in a Divine Governance of the World" Fichte clarifies his notion of faith: "This is the true faith. This moral order is what we take to be *divine.* It is constituted by right action. This is the only possible confession of faith: joyfully and innocently to accomplish whatever duty demands in every circumstance, without doubting and without pettifogging over the consequences. In this way, what is divine becomes living and actual for us. Every one of our actions is accomplished under this presupposition, and all of the consequences of our acts are preserved only within the divine." Cf. *Introductions to the Wissenschaftslehre and Other Writings,* p. 150. Faith is the resolution toward moral duty under the presupposition that a good act *necessarily* bears fruit—not, perhaps, within the "external" or phenomenal order, where there is no necessary coincidence between act and effect, but within the "living and efficaciously acting moral order"—the inner, spiritual world—that for Fichte "is itself God" (p. 151). True atheism, for Fichte, lies in "refusing to hearken to the voice of one's conscience until one believes one has first seen the success of the same" (p. 150). Concern for the result is atheism; faith is resolution in the absence of any exterior attestation. Faith therefore has nothing to do with consolation, nor is it in any way a reduced, imperfect form of knowledge; rather, it coincides with the originary *resolution* of the subject to act in obedience to the moral law without calculating consequences. Fichte returns to these themes even more powerfully in his 1800 *Die Bestimmung des Menschen* (*The Vocation of Man*), which Kierkegaard read in 1838. In that text he inaugurates also the powerful problematic of the voice and the call: faith issues forth from the interiority of subjectivity, the site of its auto-affection, the place in the soul where the call resonates in each moment and imposes the absolute task of responding to one's being. Playing on the relation between vocation (*Bestimmung*) and voice (*Stimme*), Fichte writes: "Your vocation is not merely to know, but to act according to your knowledge. This is what I clearly hear in my inmost soul as soon as I collect myself for a moment and pay attention to myself. You do not exist for idle self-observation or to brood over devout sensations. No, you exist for activity. Your activity, and your activity alone, determines your worth. This voice leads me out of mental representations, out of mere knowledge, to something that lies outside of it and is its complete opposite." Cf. *Vocation of Man,* p. 68.

44. Ibid., p. 81.

45. Ibid., p. 100.

6. THE INSTANT (*THE CONCEPT OF ANXIETY*)

1. The critical task of *The Philosophical Fragments* is to separate, against speculative theology, the event of divine self-manifestation from what can be recollectively reorganized as systematic knowledge. It accomplishes this by pointing to an event—the appearance of "the god in time"—an event that, nevertheless, lacks proper phenomenality. The god can appear in time only as "incognito." The incarnation thus would be a beginning without a principle; a matter not of knowledge, but of "contemporaneity."

2. See Hegel's reading of the fall and evil in his *Lectures on the Philosophy of Religion, The Lectures of 1827*, ed. Peter Hodgson, trans. R. F. Brown, P. C. Hodgson, and J. M. Stewart (Berkeley: University of California Press, 1988), pp. 442–50.

3. Vincent McCarthy is certainly correct to see in the phenomenon of anxiety the self accessing its own spiritual potentiality. What remains unclear in his account, however, is the status of potentiality. McCarthy, in sync with the general trend of commentary, understands potentiality within the larger archeo-teleological dynamic of the "stages of existence." See his *The Phenomenology of Moods in Kierkegaard,* pp. 127–33.

4. Cf. Vincent McCarthy's essay "Schelling and Kierkegaard on Freedom and Fall," pp. 89–109; Louis Dupré's essay "Of Time and Eternity," in *International Kierkegaard Commentary: The Concept of Anxiety,* ed. Robert Perkins (Macon: Mercer University Press, 1985), pp. 111–131; Jochem Hennigfeld's essay "Angst—Freiheit-System: Schellings Freiheitsschrift und Kierkegaards Der Begriff Angst" as well as Axel Hutter's "Das Unvordenkliche der menschlichen Freiheit: Zur Deutung der Angst bei Schelling und Kierkegaard," both of which appear in *Kierkegaard und Schelling: Freiheit, Angst und Wirklichkeit,* ed. Jochem Hennigfeld and Jon Stewart (Berlin: Walter de Gruyter, 2003).

5. See his "Das Unvordenkliche der menschlichen Freiheit."

6. Axel Hutter links *das Unvordenkliche* explicitly to the chora of Plato. See "Das Unvordenkliche der menschlichen Freiheit," p. 119.

7. On how Schelling reconfigures onto-theology, see Heidegger's *Schelling's Treatise on the Essence of Human Freedom,* trans. Joan Stambaugh (Athens: Ohio University Press, 1985), p. 97.

8. It is Boehme who, depending upon but departing from Eckhart, inaugurates the theme of the ground (though Boehme says, perhaps more accurately, *Ungrund*). Boehme's *Ungrund* is the abyss of divine freedom, the divine will prior to any ends or determination—not merely from a finite point of view, but in itself. The *Ungrund* is the dark, contractive will toward "ownhood" (*Eigenheit*) that God definitively suppresses in favor of the will to self-communication. Yet, for Boehme as for Schelling, personality cannot be revealed to itself, cannot therefore be as personality, outside the tensions in these drives and outside overcoming the dark, wrathful will of the *Ungrund*. Most important, though, is that through the notion of the *Ungrund* Boehme achieves a conception of the divine creative act that allows a radical and positive conception of evil. Boehme's transformation of Eckhart's thought, which at the same time is deeply invested in it, is decisive for the development of idealism—especially, though in very different ways, for the later Schelling and Hegel. What Boehme adds to the apophatic tradition is, first of all, a fundamental emphasis upon the divine will and divine freedom. O'Regan summarizes: "In Boehme the basic mechanism of transvaluation-devaluation of Eckhartian ontotheology is will. Will executes this devaluation, first, by undoing the would-be complacency and stillness or repose of the Unground as the divine nothing—features promoted by Eckhart and sponsored by Pseudo-Dionysius and Plotinus before him—and, second, by launching the process of manifestation in and through which a determinate, self-reflexive divine comes to be." Cf. *Gnostic Apocalypse,* p. 73.

9. See Miklos Vetö's *De Kant à Schelling, Les deux voies de l'Idéalismus allemande* (Grenoble: Éditions Jerome Millon, 2000), pp. 255–72.

10. See especially Robert F. Brown's *The Later Philosophy of Schelling: The Influence of Boehme on the Works of 1809–1815* (Lewisburg: Bucknell University Press, 1977), pp. 114–150.

11. *Philosophical Investigations into the Essence of Human Freedom and Related Matters,* p. 241 (*Schelling* 4:255).

12. Ibid., p. 242 (*Schelling* 4:256).

13. Schelling does utilize the Boehmean term *Un-Grund* toward the end of his essay *Of Human Freedom,* though he does so idiosyncratically. Boehme's *Un-Grund* is Schelling's Grund. For Schelling, the *Un-Grund* constitutes a non-dialectical point of indifference that simultaneously holds together and holds apart the "will of the ground" and the "will of love."

14. *Philosophical Investigations into the Essence of Human Freedom,* pp. 238–39 (*Schelling* 4:252).

15. Ibid., p. 256 (*Schelling* 4:273).

16. See Hennigfeld's essay "Angst—Freiheit—System," p. 107.

17. McCarthy writes: "What most immediately distinguishes Kierkegaard's treatment from Schelling's is that Kierkegaard does not carry the analysis of human freedom back to God and divine freedom. But the workings of human freedom are essentially the same for both. How human freedom relates structurally to God's being is simply not a theme of Kierkegaard's work. And yet it cannot be radically different from Schelling's conception either, even if Kierkegaard would never seriously entertain the details of Schelling's theogony." See his article "Schelling and Kierkegaard on Freedom and Fall," p. 103.

18. Hegel too follows Boehme in this regard. Cf. O'Regan, *The Heterodox Hegel,* pp. 180–87, 223–31; Walsh, *The Mysticism of Innerwordly Fulfillment.*

19. *Philosophical Investigations into the Essence of Human Freedom,* pp. 249–50 (*Schelling* 4:265).

20. O'Regan is especially clear on this point. See *The Heterodox Hegel,* pp. 151–68.

21. *Philosophical Investigations into the Essence of Human Freedom,* p. 238 (*Schelling* 4:252).

22. Jochem Hennigfeld increases the ambiguity by pointing out that Schelling's divine ground nevertheless decisively "comes to itself" only in human consciousness. Schelling knots together human existence and divine existence via his notion of the ground—hence, "anthropological" and "theological" discourses cannot decisively be separated. See his "Angst—System—Freiheit," p. 107.

23. In the end it is the Boehmean background to both Schelling's text and *The Concept of Anxiety* that accounts for their commonality. Recall from chapter four how creation as repetition reprises Boehme's understanding of creation as letting-be. From the present standpoint, one can see how this act conditions the full dynamic of *The Concept of Anxiety.* Creation as *Gelassenheit* constitutes the very basis of anxiety and the very condition of sin, for the creature who is *let-be,* to the point of having to define himself without the support of any principle, is anxious. God's withdrawal from the creature, whereby the creature is exposed to the *Afgrund* of possibility, constitutes simultaneously the perfection of the creature (since it is thereby given autonomy), the condition of anxiety (since it is abandoned), and the radical possibility of sin (since it can determine itself unconditionally). Innocence is always already anxiety. This, I maintain, is the deep Boehmean configuration underlying both Schelling's *Philosophical Investigations into the Essence of Human Freedom* and *The Concept of Anxiety.* Only in terms of this background, I maintain, will it be possible to understand the way in which anxiety can become "saving" at the end of *The Concept of Anxiety.*

24. In later journal entries, however, it does become an explicit problem. See for example my article "Absolute Subjectivity: Kierkegaard and the Question of Onto-theo-egology," in *Philosophy Today,* Winter 2003, pp. 378–91.

25. One might usefully think of Derrida's arche-writing or différance, i.e., of language as a differential system without pure presences, but as that which conditions presence.

26. The Danish word, *Øieblikket,* which the Hongs and Thomte translate as "the moment," is better translated "instant." As Vigilius specifically points out, the word *Øieblikket* relates to the *glance* of the eye (not the blink of the eye as Thomte suggests). Kierkegaard's author places some importance on the metaphysical implications of the glance in order to mark its epochal difference from "Greek thought." He writes: "It is remarkable that Greek art culminates in the plastic, which precisely lacks the glance. This, however, has its deep source in the fact that the Greeks did not in the profoundest sense grasp the concept of spirit and therefore did not in the deepest sense comprehend sensuousness and temporality. What a striking contrast to Christianity, in which God is pictorially represented as an eye" (*CA* 87; *SKS* 4:391).

27. See his essay "Of Time and Eternity," p. 127.

28. Eckhart's analysis of the relation of time and eternity has a privileged place in this genealogy, however. Eckhart moves beyond Neoplatonism, Plotinus in particular, by rejecting any ecstatic understanding of the instant: the instant is not the moment of a departure from time, but rather the condition for a radical penetration into time. On this point cf. Schürmann, *Wandering Joy,* pp. 15–16.

29. Perhaps this is why Kierkegaard's author writes: "[The human being], then, is a synthesis of psyche and body, but he is also a synthesis of the temporal and the eternal. That this has often been stated, I do not object to at all, for it is not my wish to discover something new, but rather it is my joy and dearest occupation to ponder over that which is quite simple" (*CA* 85; *SKS* 4:388).

30. See also Niels Eriksen's discussion of the meaning of "the blink of the eye" in relation to *Frithiof's Saga* in his *Kierkegaard's Category of Repetition*, pp. 69-74.

31. Mark Taylor interprets the instant as a *coincidentia oppositorum* in his *Journeys to Selfhood,* pp. 176f.

32. Plotinus appeals to the sudden nature of the breakthrough to the One beyond being in, for example, *Ennead* V.3.17. For a discussion of the sudden in Neoplatonic mysticism, see Deidre Carabine, *The Unknown God, Negative Theology in the Platonic Tradition: Plato to Eriiugena* (Louvain: Peter's Press, n.d.), pp. 142, 296.

33. See, for example, Eckhart's extraordinary meditation on the verse (Acts 9:8) "Paul rose from the ground and with eyes open saw nothing." Eckhart uses this verse to develop an account of vision that ultimately subverts the metaphorical link, central for Plato, between vision and knowledge, for Paul saw *nothing*. The eye is ultimately blind. See sermon 71 in *Meister Eckhart, Teacher and Preacher*, pp. 320-325.

34. See Eckhart's sermon 10 in *Meister Eckhart, Teacher and Preacher*, p. 263. This idea is repeated also in the *Theologia Germanica*, chapter 7: "Now, the created soul of man also has two eyes. One represents the power to peer into the eternal. The other gazes into time and the created world…" Cf. *The Theologia Germanica of Martin Luther*, p. 68.

35. That the vision into the eternal is nothing other than the soul's reception of its own being "immediately" from God stands behind Eckhart's famous line, "the eye in which I see God is the same eye in which God sees me. My eye and God's eye are one eye and one seeing, one knowing and one loving." See *Meister Eckhart, Teacher and Preacher*, p. 270. Hegel is reputed to have heard of Eckhart's comment from Franz von Baader and to have endorsed it as the essence of his own thought. On this point see O'Regan's *The Heterodox Hegel*, p. 250. Nevertheless, any appropriation of Eckhart by Hegel would be conditioned by a speculative reinterpretation of the glance: that is, from the non-knowing of Eckhart to Hegel's own absolute knowing.

36. The passage he principally refers to from the *Parmenides* dialogue is the following: "But when, being in motion, it [the one, being] comes to a stand, or, being at rest, it changes to being in motion, it cannot itself occupy any time at all for this reason. Suppose it is first at rest and later in motion, or first in motion and later at rest; that cannot happen to it without its changing. But there is no time during which a thing can be at once neither in motion nor at rest. On the other hand it does not change without making a transition. When does it make the transition, then? Not while it is at rest or while it is in motion, or while it is occupying time. Consequently, the time at which it will be when it makes the transition must be that queer thing, the instant. The word 'instant' appears to mean something such that from it a thing passes to one or other of the two conditions. There is no transition from a state of rest so long as the thing is still at rest, nor from motion so long as it is still in motion, but this queer thing, the instant, is situated between the motion and the rest; it occupies no time at all, and the transition of the moving thing to the state of rest, or of the stationary thing to being in motion, takes place to and from the instant" (*Parmenides.* 156, c-d).

37. The criticism works against both the Parmenidean thesis that "only being is, non-being is not" and the Hegelian beginning of thought with pure being. In each case, there is a moment at least in which thought grasps—in perhaps a non-conceiving but positive conception—absolute being, or being absolved of non-being. This would be a moment of identity, beyond all representation, between the absolute and the thought of the absolute. For Parmenides this would be a radically aporetic moment, whereas for Hegel it would signify the inclusiveness of absolute knowledge; yet in each case non-being would attest its non-being and being would attest its being. Pure identity would be achieved.

38. Louis Dupre especially emphasizes the eternality of the past as its immutability and the distinction between this "Greek" view and that of Vigilius. He writes: "Whatever comes into existence may be immutable once it exists, but it does not thereby become eternal. The immutability of the past annihilates the merely possible by becoming irreversible and thus excluding possible alternatives, but it never attains the intrinsic necessity of the eternal." Cf. "Of Time and Eternity," p. 125.

39. See, for example, Eckhart's German sermon 83. Also, see Boehme's third treatise in his *The Way to Christ*, entitled "*Von der Wahren Gelassenheit;*" he interpretes *Gelassenheit* as the will of the soul to "sink itself into nothing" and to "press into the nothing" (pp. 120–21). In the treatise "The Precious Gate of Divine Contemplation" he appeals again to the metaphor: "[The soul must] sink with the resigned life-will into the supra-sensual, unconditioned Eternal One, as into the first ground of life's beginning. It again must give itself into the ground out of which life sprang. Thus is it again in its eternal place, as in the *termperamentum,* in (true) rest," p. 208. Tersteegen, whom Kierkegaard describes as "incomparable" (*Pap.* X 3 A 202), utilizes the image of sinking very often in his poems. For example his poem *Der göttliche Augenblick* (The Divine Instant) begins with the injunction: "Sink yourself into the still Now, the divine instant (*Senk dich ins stille Nun, den göttliche Augenblick*)." Cf. Gerhard Tersteegen, *Eine Auswahl aus seinen Schriften,* ed. Walter Nigg (Wuppertal: R. Brockhaus Verlag, 1968), p. 37. See also his poem *Ersenkung in Gott,* p. 40.

40. *Meister Eckhart, the Essential Sermons,* p. 259.

CONCLUSION

1. *Phenomenology of Spirit,* p. 56 (*Hegel* 2:79).
2. Ibid., pp. 5–6 (*Hegel* 2:17).
3. He writes: "Thus there is more to be learned philosophically from his 'edifying' writings rather than from his philosophical work." See *Being and Time,* p. 407n6. What is quite strange is that Heidegger gave no further account of what could be learned philosophically from the edifying writings; nor did he attempt to reconcile this judgment with his conviction that, philosophically, Kierkegaard's thought is wholly derivative upon German idealism as well as ancient thought. From what perspective, we may ask, does Kierkegaard's philosophical insight flow in the edifying writings? Some account must be given of this. From this perspective Michel Henry "categorically rejects" Heidegger's estimation of Kierkegaard. Kierkegaard's thought, he suggests, "actually presupposes a conception of ontology radically different from that of the Greeks and Hegel and even from that of Heidegger himself." See *The Essence of Manifestation,* trans. Girard Etzkorn (The Hague: Martinus Nijhoff, 1973), p. 676. I have attempted to articulate precisely what this "ontology" is, regarding it as a rearticulation of Eckhartian metaphysics.
4. A notable exception to this is George Pattison's book *Kierkegaard's Upbuilding Discourses* (London: Taylor and Francis, 2002).

BIBLIOGRAPHY

Adorno, Theodore. *Kierkegaard: The Construction of the Aesthetic.* Trans. Robert Hullot-Kentor. Minneapolis: University of Minnesota Press, 1989.

Agacinski, Sylviane. *Aparté: Conceptions and Deaths of Søren Kierkegaard.* Trans. Kevin Newmark. Tallahassee: Florida State University Press, 1988.

Anz, Wilhelm. *Kierkegaard und der deutsche Idealismus.* Tübingen: Mohr-Siebeck, 1956.

Baader, Franz. *Fermenta Cognitionis,* zweites Heft. Berlin: G. Reimer, 1822.

Beierwalters, Werner. *Platonismus und Idealismus.* Frankfurt am Main: Vittoria Klostermann, 1972.

Benz, Ernst. *The Mystical Sources of German Romantic Philosophy.* Pittsburg: Pickwick Press, 1983.

Bigelow, Pat. *Kierkegaard and the Problem of Writing.* Tallahassee: Florida State University Press, 1987.

Boehme, Jacob. *The Way to Christ.* Trans. Peter Erb. New York: Paulist Press, 1978.

Brisson, Luc. *Plato the Myth Maker.* Trans. Gerard Naddaf. Chicago: University of Chicago Press, 1998.

Brown, Robert. *The Later Philosophy of Schelling: The Influence of Boehme on the Works of 1809–1815.* Lewisburg: Bucknell University Press, 1977.

Caputo, John. "Instants, Secrets and Singularities: Dealing Death in Kierkegaard and Derrida." In *Kierkegaard in Post/Modernity,* ed. Martin J. Matuštík and Merold Westphal. Bloomington: Indiana University Press, 1995.

———. *The Mystical Element in Heidegger's Thought.* New York: Fordham University Press, 1978.

———. *Radical Hermeneutics: Repetition, Deconstruction and the Hermeneutic Project.* Bloomington: University of Indiana Press, 1987.

Collins, James. *The Mind of Kierkegaard.* Princeton: Princeton University Press, 1983.

Deleuze, Gilles. *Difference and Repetition.* Trans. Paul Patton. New York: Columbia University Press, 1994.

Derrida, Jacques. *The Gift of Death.* Trans. David Wills. Chicago: University of Chicago Press, 1995.

———. *Margins of Philosophy.* Trans. Alan Bass. Chicago: University of Chicago Press, 1982.

———. *On the Name.* Trans. David Wood, John P. Leavey, and Ian McLeod. Stanford: Stanford University Press, 1995.

———. *Speech and Phenomena.* Trans. David B. Allison. Evanston: Northwestern University Press, 1973.

———. *Writing and Difference.* Trans. Alan Bass. London: Routledge Press, 1978.

Dooley, Mark. *The Politics of Exodus.* New York: Fordham University Press, 2001.

Dunning, Stephen. *Kierkegaard's Dialectic of Inwardness: A Structural Analysis of the Theory of the Stages.* Princeton: Princeton University Press, 1985.

Dupré, Louis. "Of Time and Eternity." In *International Kierkegaard Commentary: The Concept of Anxiety,* ed. Robert Perkins. Macon: Mercer University Press, 1985.

Eckhart, Johannes. *Die Deutschen und lateinishen Werke. Herausgegaben im Auftrage der Deutschen Forshungsgemeinschaft.* Stuttgart and Berlin: W. Kolhammer, 1936–.

―――. *Meister Eckhart: The Essential Sermons, Commentaries, Treatises, and Defense.* Trans. and intro. Edmund Colledge and Bernard McGinn. New York: Paulist Press, 1981.

―――. *Meister Eckhart, Teacher and Preacher.* Ed. Bernard McGinn, Frank Tobin, and Elvira Borgstadt. New York: Paulist Press, 1986.

Elrod, John. *Being and Existence in Kierkegaard's Pseudonymous Works.* Princeton: Princeton University Press, 1975.

Eriksen, Niels Nyman. *Kierkegaard's Category of Repetition, A Reconstruction.* New York: Walter de Gruyter, 2000.

Evans, C. Steven. "Is the Concept of an Absolute Duty to God Morally Unintelligible?" In *Kierkegaard's* Fear and Trembling, *Critical Appraisals,* ed. Robert Perkins. University: University of Alabama Press, 1981.

Fahrenbach, Helmut. *Kierkegaards existenzdialektische Ethik.* Frankfurt am Main: Vittorio Klostermann, 1968.

Fichte, Johann. *Introductions to the Wissenschaftslehre and Other Writings.* Trans. Daniel Breazeale. Indianapolis: Hackett, 1994.

―――. *J. G. Fichte Science of Knowledge.* Trans. Peter Heath and John Lachs. Cambridge: Cambridge University Press, 1982.

―――. *The Vocation of Man.* Trans. Peter Preuss. Indianapolis: Hackett, 1986.

Glöckner, Dorothea. "The Unhappiest One—Merely an Inscription? On the Relationship between Immediacy and Language in the Work of Kierkegaard." In *Immediacy and Reflection in Kierkegaard's Thought,* ed. P. Cruysbergh. Leuven: Leuven University Press, 2003.

Gonzalez, Dario. *Essai sur l'Ontologie Kierkegaardienne, Idéalité et determination.* Paris: L'Harmattan, 1998.

Gouwens, David. "*Kierkegaard's* Either/Or, *Part One: Patterns of Interpretation.*" In *The International Kierkegaard Commentary,* Either/Or *Part I,* ed. Robert Perkins. Macon: Mercer University Press, 1995.

Green, Ronald. "Enough Is Enough! *Fear and Trembling* Is *Not* about Ethics." *Journal of Religious Ethics* 21, no. 2 (Fall 1993): 191–209.

―――. *Kierkegaard and Kant: The Hidden Debt.* Albany: SUNY Press, 1992.

Hannay, Alastair. *Kierkegaard.* London: Routledge, 1982.

Hegel, G. W. F. *Elements of the Philosophy of Right.* Trans. H. B. Nisbet. New York: Cambridge University Press, 1991.

―――. *Encyclopedia of the Philosophical Sciences.* Vols. 1–3. Trans. William Wallace. Oxford: Oxford University Press, 1973.

―――. *Hegel's Philosophy of Mind.* Trans. A. V. Miller. Oxford: Oxford University Press, 1983.

―――. *Hegel's Science of Logic.* Trans. A. V. Miller. Amherst, N.Y.: Humanity Books, 1999.

―――. *Introduction to the Philosophy of History.* Trans. Leo Rauch. Indianapolis: Hackett, 1988.

―――. *Lectures on the History of Philosophy.* Vols. 1–3. Trans. E. S. Haldane and Frances Simson. Lincoln: University of Nebraska Press, 1995.

―――. *Lectures on the Philosophy of Religion.* Ed. Peter Hodgson. Trans. R. F. Brown, P. C. Hodgson, and J. M. Stewart. Berkeley: University of California Press, 1988.

―――. *Phenomenology of Spirit.* Trans. A. V. Miller. Oxford: Oxford University Press, 1952.

Heidegger, Martin. *Being and Time.* Trans. Joan Stambaugh. Albany: SUNY Press, 1996.

―――. *Hegel's Concept of Experience.* Trans. Kenley Royce Dove. New York: Octagon Books, 1983.

———. *Hegel's Phenomenology of Spirit.* Trans. Parvis Emad and Kenneth Maly. Bloomington: Indiana University Press, 1988.

———. *Identity and Difference.* Trans. Joan Stambaugh. Chicago: University of Chicago Press, 2002.

———. *Introduction to Metaphysics.* Trans. Ralph Manheim. New Haven: Yale University Press, 1959.

———. *Martin Heidegger: Basic Writings.* Ed. David Farrell Krell. San Francisco: Harper Collins, 1993.

———. *Pathmarks.* Ed. William McNeil. Cambridge: Cambridge University Press, 1998.

———. *Phenomenological Interpretation of Kant's* Critique of Pure Reason. Trans. Parvis Emad and Kenneth Maly. Bloomington: Indiana University Press, 1997.

———. *Schelling's Treatise on the Essence of Human Freedom.* Trans. Joan Stambaugh. Athens: Ohio University Press, 1985.

———. *What Is Called Thinking?* Trans. Glenn Gray. New York: Harper, 1968.

Hennigfeld, Jochem. "Angst—Freiheit-System: Schellings Freiheitsschrift und Kierkegaards Der Begriff Angst." In *Schelling: Freiheit, Angst und Wirklichkeit,* ed. Jochem Hennigfeld and Jon Stewart. Berlin: Walter de Gruyter, 2003.

Henry, Michel. *The Essence of Manifestation.* Trans. Girard Etzkorn. The Hague: Martinus Nijhoff, 1973.

Hirsch, Emmanuel. *Kierkegaard-Studien.* Gutersloh: C. Bertelsmann, 1933.

Hutter, Axel. "Das Unvordenkliche der menschlichen Freiheit: Zur Deutung der Angst bei Schelling und Kierkegaard." In *Schelling: Freiheit, Angst und Wirklichkeit,* ed. Jochem Hennigfeld and Jon Stewart. Berlin: Walter de Gruyter, 2003.

Hyppolite, Jean. *The Genesis and Structure of Hegel's Phenomenology of Spirit.* Trans. Samuel Cherniak and John Heckman. Evanston: Northwestern University Press, 1974.

———. *Logic and Existence.* Trans. Leonard Lawlor and Amit Sen. Albany: SUNY Press, 1997.

Jegstrup, Elsebet, ed. *The New Kierkegaard.* Bloomington: Indiana University Press, 2004.

Kant, Immanuel. *The Critique of Judgment.* Trans. Werner S. Pluhar. Indianapolis: Hackett Publishing Company, 1987.

———. *The Critique of Pure Reason.* Trans. Werner S. Pluhar. Indianapolis: Hackett, 1996.

———. *Grounding for the Metaphysics of Morals.* Trans. James W. Ellington. Indianapolis: Hackett, 1981.

———. *Religion within the Limits of Reason Alone.* Trans. Theodore Green and Hoyt Hudson. New York: Harper, 1960.

Koyré, Alexander. *La Philosophie de Jacob Boehme.* Paris: J. Vrin, 1979.

Levinas, Emmanuel. "Existence and Ethics." In *Kierkegaard: A Critical Reader,* ed. Jonathan Rée and Jane Chamberlain. Massachusetts: Blackwell, 1998.

———. *Otherwise than Being or Beyond Essence.* Trans. Alphonso Lingis. The Hague: Martinus Nijhoff, 1981.

———. *Totality and Infinity.* Trans. Alphonso Lingis. Pittsburgh: Duquense University Press, 1969.

Llewelyn, John. "On the Borderline of Madness." In *The New Kierkegaard,* ed. Elsebet Jegstrup. Bloomington: Indiana University Press, 2004.

Luther, Martin, ed. *Theologia Germanica.* Trans. Bengt Hoffman. New York: Paulist Press, 1980.

MacKenna, Stephen. *Plotinus: The Enneads.* Burdett, N.Y.: Larson Publications, 1992.

Mackey, Louis. *Kierkegaard: A Kind of Poet.* Philadelphia: University of Pennsylvania, 1971.

———. *Points of View.* Tallahassee: Florida State University Press, 1986.

———. "The View from Pisgah, A Reading of *Fear and Trembling.*" In *Kierkegaard: A Collection of Critical Appraisals,* ed. Josiah Thompson. New York: Anchor Books, 1972.

Malantschuk, Gregor. *Kierkegaard's Thought.* Trans. Howard Hong and Edna Hong. Princeton: Princeton University Press, 1971.

Martensen, Hans. *Between Hegel and Kierkegaard: Hans L. Martensen's Philosophy of Religion.* Trans. Curtis L. Thompson and David J. Kangas. Atlanta: Scholars Press, 1997.

Matustik, Martin, and Merold Westphal, eds. *Kierkegaard in Post/Modernity.* Bloomington: University of Indiana Press, 1995.

McCarthy, Vincent. *The Phenomenology of Moods in Kierkegaard.* The Hague: Martinus Nijhoff, 1978.

———. "Schelling and Kierkegaard on Freedom and Fall." In *International Kierkegaard Commentary, The Concept of Anxiety,* ed. Robert Perkins. Macon: Mercer University Press, 1985.

Mooney, Edward. *Knights of Faith and Resignation: Reading Kierkegaard's Fear and Trembling.* Albany: SUNY Press, 1992.

———. "Repetition: Getting the World Back." In *The Cambridge Companion to Kierkegaard,* ed. Gordon Marino and Alastair Hannay. Cambridge: Cambridge University Press, 1998.

Nancy, Jean-Luc. *Hegel, The Restlessness of the Negative.* Trans. Jason Smith and Steven Miller. Minneapolis: University of Minnesota Press, 2002.

Neuhouser, Frederick. *Fichte's Theory of Subjectivity.* Cambridge: Cambridge University Press, 1994.

O'Regan, Cyril. *Gnostic Apocalypse, Jacob Boehme's Haunted Narrative.* Albany: SUNY Press, 2002.

———. *The Heterodox Hegel.* Albany: SUNY Press, 1994.

Pattison, George. *Kierkegaard's Upbuilding Discourses: Philosophy, Theology and Literature.* New York: Routledge, 2002.

Plotnitsky, Arkady. *In the Shadow of Hegel: Complementarity, History, and the Unconscious.* Gainesville: University of Florida Press, 1993.

Ricoeur, Paul. "Philosophy after Kierkegaard." In *Kierkegaard: A Critical Reader,* ed. Jonathon Reé and Jane Chamberlain. Oxford: Blackwell, 1998.

Sallis, John. *Chorology.* Bloomington: Indiana University Press, 2000.

———. "Hegel's Concept of Presentation, Its Determination in the Preface to the *Phenomenology of Spirit.*" In *The Phenomenology of Spirit Reader: Critical and Interpretive Essays,* ed. Jon Stewart. Albany: SUNY Press, 1998.

———. *Spacings—of Reason and Imagination in the Texts of Kant, Fichte, Hegel.* Chicago: University of Chicago Press, 1987.

Schelling, Friedrich. *Ideas for a Philosophy of Nature.* Trans. Errol Harris and Peter Heath. New York: Cambridge University Press, 1988.

———. *Philosophical Investigations into the Essence of Human Freedom and Related Matters.* Trans. Priscilla Hayden-Roy. In *Philosophy of German Idealism,* ed. Ernst Behler. New York: Continuum, 1987.

———. *System of Transcendental Idealism.* Trans. Peter Heath. Charlottesville: University of Virginia Press, 1997.

Schmidinger, Heinrich. "Kierkegaard und Fichte," in *Gregorianum* 52 (1971): 499–542.

Schürmann, Reiner. *Broken Hegemonies.* Trans. Reginald Lilly. Bloomington: Indiana University Press, 2003.

———. *Wandering Joy: Meister Eckhart's Mystical Philosophy.* Great Barrington, Mass.: Lindisfarne Books, 2001.

Sells, Michael. *Mystical Languages of Unsaying.* Chicago: University of Chicago Press, 1994.

Shestov, Lev. *Kierkegaard and the Existential Philosophy.* Trans. Elinor Hewitt. Athens: Ohio University Press, 1969.

Smyth, John Vignaux. *A Question of Eros: Irony in Sterne, Kierkegaard and Barthes.* Tallahassee: Florida State University Press, 1986.

Stewart, Jon. *Kierkegaard's Relations to Hegel Reconsidered.* Cambridge: Cambridge University Press, 2003.

Tauler, Johannes. *Predigten.* Vols. 1–2. Ed. George Hofman. Einsiedeln-Trier: Johannes Verlag, 1987.

Taylor, Mark C. *Altarity.* Chicago: University of Chicago Press, 1987.

———. *Journeys to Selfhood: Hegel and Kierkegaard.* Berkeley: University of California Press, 1980.

———. *Kierkegaard's Pseudonymous Authorship: A Study of Time and the Self* (Princeton: Princeton University Press, 1975.

Tersteegen, Gerhard. *Eine Auswahl aus seinen Schriften.* Ed. Walter Nigg. Wuppertal: R. Brockhaus Verlag, 1968.

Theunissen, Michael. *Der Begriff Ernst bei Søren Kierkegaard.* Freiberg-Breisgau: Verlag Karl Alber, 1972.

Thulstrup, Marie. *Kierkegaard og Pietismen.* Copenhagen: Munksgaards Forlag, 1967.

Thulstrup, Niels. *Kierkegaard's Relation to Hegel.* Trans. George L. Stengren. Princeton: Princeton University Press, 1980.

Vetö, Miklos. *De Kant à Schelling, Les deux voies de l'Idéalismus allemande.* Grenoble: Éditions Jerome Millon, 2000.

Wahl, Jean. *Etudes Kierkegaardienne.* Paris: J. Vrin, 1949.

———. *Kierkegaard: L'Un devant l'Autre.* Paris: Hachette Litérratures, 1998.

Walsh, David. *The Mysticism of Innerworldly Fulfillment: A Study of Jacob Boehme.* Gainesville: University Presses of Florida, 1983.

Wood, David. "Thinking God in the Wake of Kierkegaard." In *Kierkegaard: A Critical Reader,* ed. Jonathan Rée and Jane Chamberlain. Massachusetts: Blackwell, 1998.

INDEX

duration: 83, 84,
duty: 126, 131, 132–143, 149

earnestness: 26, 106, 171
Eckhart, Meister/Eckhartian tradition: 9–11,
    138, 155, 161–162, 182, 187, 191–192,
    194, 197, 201n26, 202nn27, 31, 36, 37,
    213n34, 218n39, 222nn28, 34, 35
edifying, the: 197–198
egology: 2, 4, 41, 57, 63, 73–74, 84, 137,
    160, 162, 195, 197
Eigenwille: 10, 162, 167–168, 176, 191
Eleatics: 97–99, 212nn13, 15
Elrod, John: 123, 200n19, 215n56
Eriksen, Niels: 112, 210n1, 212n24,
    215n50, 222n30
eros/erotic: 33, 111, 113
eternity/the eternal: 154, 180, 196; time
    and, 180–189
ethical: 126, 127–128, 134
Evans, C. Stephen: 215n1
event: 38–39, 120, 122–123, 147, 150,
    172–173, 187, 189, 196, 197
evil: 62, 169–170, 179
exception/exceptionality: 119–121; 127,
    137, 141, 144, 147–149
existence: ix-x, 8–9, 43
exteriority: 195–198

faith: 8, 10, 126, 131, 134, 149, 163, 193,
    197; as double movement, 151–155; as
    releasement, 150–155, 158, 197
fall: 164, 170
farce: 106–111
fate: 146–147, 192–193
Fichte, J. G.: 1–2, 80, 84, 87, 94–95, 103,
    116, 131, 161–162, 176, 181; faith in,
    94–95, 158, 219n43; *Vocation of Man,*
    2, 94, 133, 158
finitude: 126, 140, 152
first philosophy: 171–172
forgiveness: 124, 192
freedom: 63–64, 93–94, 103, 155, 166,
    180; *Afgrund* of, 167–170, 175, 178
Frithiof's Saga: 185–186
future: 70–71

Gelassenheit (*see also* releasement and let-
    ting-go): 9–10, 126, 140, 151, 155,
    191–194

gift: 4, 55–56, 126, 148, 155; of death,
    142–143, 148; of presence, 198
glance of the eye: 185–187
Glöckner, Dorothea: 207n17, 214n37
God: 6, 117, 126
Godhead: 10
Good, the: 180
Gouwens, David: 206n1
Green, Ronald: 215n1
ground: 3, 6, 13, 22–24, 25, 31; of exis-
    tence, 100; as eternal beginning, 101;
    Schelling on, 168–169
guilt: 114, 116–118, 121, 122, 124, 141,
    179

Hannay, Alastair: 48, 206n5
Hegel: *Aesthetics,* 27; and beginning, 1–6;
    Encyclopedia, 133; *Lectures on the His-
    tory of Philosophy,* 1, 12, 15, 19, 27, 72,
    74, 97–99, 104; on modernity, 72–74;
    Phenomenology of Spirit, 1, 47–50, 65,
    66–68, 77, 78, 87; *Philosophy of History,*
    156; *Science of Logic,* 3, 98, 164; and
    stages, 7; on the tragic, 129
Heiberg, J. L.: 92–93
Heidegger, Martin: 4–5, 115, 172, 185,
    198, 200n17, 200n18, 203n8, 207n18,
    209n9, 220n7, 223n3
Hennigfeld, Jochem: 169, 220n4,
    221nn16, 22
Henry, Michel: 223n3
Heraclitus: 97–99, 212n13
Hirsch, Emmanuel: 200n17, 203n5
history of thought finding itself: 16,
    37–40
historicity: 156–157
hope: 51–53, 100, 105
Hutter, Axel: 167, 220n4, 220n6
Hyppolite, Jean: 82, 206n12

Idea: 24, 27, 33–34, 36, 37, 38–39, 41,
    73, 111, 156–157
idealism: 1–6,
idleness: 63–64
ignorance: 18, 20, 165
imagination: 60–61
immanence: 113, 128, 129, 136
immediacy: 3, 7, 80–83, 90, 144, 163–164
impossible/impossibility: 8, 153, 193
incarnation: 50–51
inclosedness: 178

tragedy/the tragic: 129–130, 146–147, 193
transcendence; 115, 172; movement as, 99; time as, 99, 124
transparency: 179
trauma: 53

Unground (*Un-Grund*): 10, 162, 220n13
unhappy consciousness/Unhappiest One: 47–56, 149, 151, 155

Vetö, Miklos: 168, 220n9

Wahl, Jean: 10, 200n17, 211n12
Walsh, David: 221n18
Weigel, Valentin: 202n26
whylessness: 166–167
wish-fulfillment: 193
withdrawal: of ground, 32; of essence, 29–30; of presence, 185
Wood, David: 217n29
world: 100, 115

DAVID J. KANGAS is Associate Professor of Religion at Florida State University. He teaches religion and continental philosophy, and serves as translator and member of the editorial board for the forthcoming eleven-volume critical edition of *Kierkegaard's Journals and Notebooks.*

www.ingramcontent.com/pod-product-compliance
Lightning Source LLC
Chambersburg PA
CBHW070447100426
42812CB00004B/1228